THIRTY-FIVE
LETTERS OF CICERO

Selected and edited
with introductions and notes

BY

DAVID STOCKTON

FELLOW AND TUTOR
BRASENOSE COLLEGE, OXFORD

OXFORD UNIVERSITY PRESS

1969

Oxford University Press, Ely House, London W. 1

GLASGOW NEW YORK TORONTO MELBOURNE WELLINGTON
CAPE TOWN SALISBURY IBADAN NAIROBI LUSAKA ADDIS ABABA
BOMBAY CALCUTTA MADRAS KARACHI LAHORE DACCA
KUALA LUMPUR SINGAPORE HONG KONG TOKYO

PREFACE

THIS edition is intended for use in sixth forms and for certain undergraduate courses. Although I have included a vocabulary, the use of a good Latin dictionary is strongly recommended.

I am particularly indebted to the Revd. L. M. Styler, Vice-Principal of Brasenose College, for his generous help and advice, which have resulted in the correction of many slips and inelegancies and obscurities. My discussions with him have never failed to be enlightening.

I should like to dedicate this little book to the memory of the late James Gabriel Worth, for many years sixth-form classics master at Emanuel School, London. His stimulating teaching, wide humanity, and gentle scholarship can never be forgotten by those who were lucky enough to become his pupils and remain his friends.

DAVID STOCKTON

Brasenose College, Oxford
May 1969

CONTENTS

Cover photograph. Bust of Cicero from the Uffizi Gallery, Florence. *Mansell Collection*

Introduction

   Cicero's Life   vii

   The Political Scene   xxi

   The Letters   xxvi

   The Survival of the Letters   xxx

   The Text   xxxi

   Acknowledgements   xxxii

Letters 1 to 35: *Text and Introductions*   1

Letters 1 to 35: *Notes*   72

Appendix 1: *The Roman Calendar*   204

Appendix 2: *Roman Money*   207

Concordance of Letters   210

Vocabulary   211

Index of Proper Names   233

Index of Subjects   238

INTRODUCTION

CICERO'S LIFE

MARCUS TULLIUS CICERO was born on 3 January 106[1] at Arpinum, a town in the Volscian highlands some seventy miles south east of Rome. His family was of considerable local consequence, and he was related to the family of the great general Gaius Marius (also a native of Arpinum), and hence indirectly to Julius Caesar, whose aunt Marius had married. Already in his early schooldays Cicero was remarked as a boy of extraordinary talent; and, although he could count no senators among his ancestors, his early promise and his father's ambitions suggested a career at the bar and in politics. Accordingly, in his mid teens he was taken under the wing of the two great lawyer-politicians, Scaevola the Augur and Scaevola the Pontiff (who were related by marriage to Marius). He also sat at the feet of the two leading orators of their generation, Lucius Crassus and Marcus Antonius.

The Social War between Rome and her Italian allies found Cicero at the age of seventeen serving under Pompeius Strabo, the father of Pompey the Great, whose acquaintance he must have made at this time. Pompey, born in the same year as Cicero, was to shoot far ahead of him—an army commander at twenty-five, consul at thirty-six—but throughout his life, with rare and brief interludes of pique or disappointment, Cicero remained an admirer of Pompey's, casting himself for the role of Laelius to Pompey's Scipio (Letter 3). Also serving with Strabo at this time was a young man named Lucius Sergius Catilina, with whom Cicero's relations were to be less constant (Letter 2). Later in the war, Cicero also served for a brief period under Sulla.

---

[1] All dates in this book are B.C. unless otherwise indicated.

During the disturbed years of the eighties, when the Social War merged into the Civil War between Cinna and Sulla, Cicero completed his training and took his first steps in his chosen profession as an advocate. The earliest surviving speech we have is the *pro Quinctio*, a complicated partnership case dating from the year 81, when Cicero was twenty-five. Next year came the *pro Roscio Amerino*. In this speech, a remarkably courageous onslaught on the tawdry and racketeering background to the Sullan victory and 'restoration', Cicero really made his reputation as a pleader: henceforth, he tells us (*Brutus* 312) his services were eagerly sought.

In 79 Cicero left Rome to spend two years abroad for further study, mainly under the great Greek masters of rhetoric. Part of this time he was at Athens pursuing philosophy in the company of a friend whose importance in Cicero's life cannot be exaggerated. Titus Pomponius Atticus came of an old and well-to-do family of the Roman equestrian class. He had left Rome for Athens in the early eighties, and he made his home there more or less permanently for the next twenty years (whence his *cognomen*, Atticus, by which he is best known). Three years older than Cicero, he was throughout their long friendship a steadying influence and an unfailing resource—not least in money matters. His sister in due course married Cicero's younger brother, Quintus, an alliance which while proving less than ideally happy for Quintus and Pomponia served to cement the ties between the two friends. For us the richest fruits of their long amity are the sixteen surviving volumes of letters which Cicero addressed to Atticus on a wide range of subjects both public and private. Beginning in 68 and continuing down to 44, they are a treasure beyond price. To Atticus above all others Cicero unburdened himself of his hopes and fears with a delightful frankness: and Atticus' long absences from Rome meant that there was much occasion for correspondence between the two.

All his life Atticus remained studiedly uncommitted to one side or the other in politics, beginning in the eighties when he managed to keep in with both the Marians and Sulla. He maintained amicable relations with one and all, lending his money and expertise to anyone who might be useful—or dangerous. There is no cause to reproach him. He could look back at the end of a long life and a violent epoch and declare: 'J'ai survécu.' In fact he did better than merely survive, for he lived to see his daughter married to the future right-hand-man of the Emperor Augustus, the great marshal Agrippa; and their child, his grand-daughter, became the first wife of the future Emperor Tiberius. It was perhaps only typical of Atticus that his daughter's marriage was arranged by Mark Antony, and that in this one episode were united the great enemies, Octavian and Antony, themselves the men who had signed the warrant for the execution of Atticus' old friend Cicero. Predictably, Atticus died in his bed in 32 at the age of seventy-seven.[1]

Only to his own brother Quintus did Cicero reveal as much of himself as he did to Atticus. Quintus was by four years the younger, and like his brother followed a political career. He was aedile in 65 and praetor in 62, then he went on to be governor of the province of Asia. He later served successively as legate under Pompey and Caesar, and in 51 transferred from Gaul to accompany his brother when the latter went out to be governor of Cilicia. Quintus was a far less able man than his elder brother, quick-tempered and given to histrionics; though undoubtedly competent, without his brother's help and influence he would probably not of himself have risen even as high as the praetorship. In 43 he was put on the proscription list along with his brother, and killed only a few days earlier.

In 76 Marcus Cicero became quaestor at the minimum age of thirty. He thus entered the senate, of which he was to remain a member till his death. As quaestor he served at

[1] A 'Life' of Atticus by Cornelius Nepos survives.

Lilybaeum (Marsala) as virtually lieutenant-governor of western Sicily; but after his return in 74 he never of his own choice left Italy again (after his consulship, as after his praetorship, he declined to accept a provincial governorship, though such waivers were very unusual)—on this decision, see the light-hearted passage, sections 64–6, of the *pro Plancio*.

Much of Cicero's time and energy in these years was given to his legal work in the courts, very frequently in unsensational cases on behalf of Roman business interests (the *equites* or 'knights' as this class of men was broadly termed). This activity produced very tangible returns in the shape of the political support of this class, and also in terms of hard cash, for though Roman advocates were strictly forbidden to accept fees there were many ways of getting round this formal restriction. But what really made Cicero's public reputation was his amazing prosecution of Verres, the corrupt governor of Sicily. The sheer scale of this prosecution is breathtaking. The *Verrines* occupy nearly all the fat third volume of the Oxford Text of Cicero's speeches. The industry, versatility, organizational brilliance, mastery of detail, variation of pace and interest, and simple oratorical power which Cicero now displayed were of an order never before dreamed of, and they made him the unquestioned leader of the Roman bar.[1] He made a deep mark in politics too. The year 70, the year of Verres' trial, saw the dismantling of the main scaffolding of the Sullan constitution, with the restoration to the tribunes of their full political power and the abolition of the senatorial monopoly of the courts. The Verres trial was part of this movement, and in his speeches Cicero made it clear that he was to be counted among the supporters of the cause of reform.

It is not easy for us, who live in a world dominated by print

---

[1] Only the first part of the *Verrines* (*actio prima*) was actually delivered to the court. But Cicero published the remainder despite the fact that the abandonment of the defence prevented him from delivering the *actio secunda*.

and electrical communications, to savour and appreciate the power and elation of great oratory. We have to try to imagine ourselves in a world ignorant of newspapers and weekly magazines, of radio and television, even of books for the most part. We have to picture a world where orators were critically evaluated by their audiences much as football stars are today by the crowds in the stands, or opera singers at La Scala. The citizens of ancient states gathered together in squares and amphitheatres to listen to the arguments for and against particular proposals, and then vote for one or the other. The august senators of Rome sat in the Curia and listened too, and then voted for or against the resolution. The jurymen sat in their seats and heard what counsel had to say, and they could not turn back the pages of the speeches, as we can, and ask whether what was said in section 22 is entirely harmonious with the argument presented in section 87. The orators were the purveyors of facts, of interpretation; often of half-truths and misrepresentation. A quick wit (and no other Roman of his generation could match the speed of Cicero's wit) and a knack for the killing repartee could reduce an opponent's serious arguments to ridicule.

Cicero possessed every art of the public speaker. In addition, as the schoolboy stumbles through the Latin of his speeches, wrestling with the syntax, missing the jokes (or bored by the long lines of print offered by the commentator in elucidation), often largely ignorant of the allusions and nuances and the political background so essential to understanding, he needs also to imagine a man with the presence and acting ability of an Olivier. But before giving up in despair he should recall the judgement of the wild young poet who seldom fails to spark sympathy and approval from the young of any age:

> Disertissime Romuli nepotum
> Quot sunt quotque fuere, Marce Tulli,
> Quotque post aliis erunt in annis (Catullus, *Carmen* 49).

Thus he will not have to rely on the questionable judgement of 'old, bald-headed scholars' who labour so innocently over the lines of young poets. He can take Catullus' word for Cicero's oratorical genius, or measure it by the actions of tough and practical men like Julius Caesar and Crassus and Mark Antony and Octavian. The man who composed the *First Verrine* and the *Second Philippic*, the *pro Caelio* and the *pro Cluentio*, could be a frightful adversary or a priceless ally.

The great Roman literary critic Quintilian has something to say about Cicero's (no longer extant) speech *pro Cornelio* which gives some idea of the effect his oratory had on the Roman audiences of his day (*Inst. Or.* 8. 3. 3):

Had Cicero in his defence of Cornelius been content simply to put the facts before the court in clear unvarnished Latin, would he ever have succeeded in getting the Roman people to show their admiration not merely by their cries of acclamation, but by actually bursting into applause? Of course not. It was the sublimity and magnificence of his eloquence, the brilliance and the authority, that wrung that thunderous reception from his listeners. No more would his speech have won such unprecedented acclaim if it had been of the ordinary everyday kind of utterance. It is my belief that the audience were unaware of what they were doing; that their applause was not a matter of deliberate decision or judgement, but that they were spellbound and quite unconscious of where they were and broke into a spontaneous transport of sheer delight.

Not at all a bad effect to achieve when you are defending a brilliant popular tribune on a charge of high treason!

In 69 Cicero became aedile, and in 66 (the year before the *pro Cornelio*) he was praetor. During these years he was generally one of those who favoured what we might term 'moderate' or 'constitutionalist' reform. But it was not until the year 66 that, a forty-year-old praetor, he delivered his first purely political speech. This was the *pro lege Manilia*, in which he argued strongly for the appointment of Pompey to the supreme command in the east against Mithridates. Cicero was now lining up his sights for a shot at the consulship, which he could hold in 63 if all went well (Letter 1). The political backing of Pompey, who in these years bestrode the Roman world like a colossus, was invaluable. Further, Pompey's appointment was favoured by the business interests, whose support Cicero had long nursed and knew to be indispensable to his political ambition.

The years from 66 to 63 saw a powerful bid made, during Pompey's absence, by Publius Crassus to win political advantage and vast patronage by supporting wide-ranging programmes of radical social reform. Crassus was aided and abetted by men like Catiline and Antonius (Cicero's rivals for the consulship of 63) and by Julius Caesar, who was six years Cicero's junior and, though not a praetor until 62, a fast-rising politician of immense promise (or danger, depending on your point of view). Partly in defence of Pompey's interests, partly following his own political nose, and partly through personal inclination (for Cicero, for all that he favoured social and economic reform in theory, was never somehow very much attracted by concrete proposals to do something about it), Cicero gradually edged away from his earlier popularist–reformist position and moved closer to the conservative nobility. And conservative opinion, if a little belatedly, swung into line behind a man who more and more openly promised unflinching and unswerving opposition to any serious attack on the *status quo*. At the elections in summer 64 Antonius edged Catiline out of a consulship and into third place, thereby depriving contemporary Rome and posterity of what would surely have been one of the liveliest years in the history of the Republic, a joint consulship of Cicero and Catiline. But the 'new man' Cicero, with no hereditary patent of nobility (the proud patrician noble Catiline called him 'a naturalized immigrant'—'inquilinus civis urbis Romae'), the brilliant son of a solid country-town family, was triumphantly declared elected at the head of the poll, and at the earliest permissible legal age: *consul prior* and *suo anno*. When every allowance is made for luck and circumstance, it was a truly remarkable achievement to be the first 'new man' to break through into the consulship since Sulla had restored the nobility to power nearly twenty years earlier, and one which was due above all else to Cicero's own natural gifts, and to the political sense and doggedness with which he applied them.

In a speech in 66 Cicero had listed the glittering prizes that lay at the summit of a successful senatorial career: 'position, authority, magnificence at home, reputation and influence abroad, the bordered toga, the curule chair of office, the outward pageant of power, the rods, armies, commands, provinces': 'locus, auctoritas, domi splendor, apud exteras nationes nomen et gratia, toga praetexta, sella curulis, insignia, fasces, exercitus, imperia, provinciae' (*pro Cluentio* 154). The knight's son from Arpinum had come a very long way. Though he did not know it, he had reached the summit. On the other side lay only bitterness and disappointment.

As consul in 63 Cicero stood firm as a rock, and on him broke and were flung back the violent waves of social reform. Then, in the latter part of the year, Catiline broke loose. Baulked yet again in his bid for the consulship (that of 62), abandoned by his backer Crassus who saw no point in throwing good money after bad by continuing to support so consistent a loser, without much hope but with enough pride for a whole regiment, Catiline embarked on a course of open revolution. Much of Italy stood in desperate need of remedies for its unhappy condition: of land reform and new schemes of colonization, of alleviation of the harsh laws of debt, of some relaxation of the tight grip in which a few 'haves' held fast and throttled a multitude of 'have-nots'. Hopes had been raised of remedy, only to be dashed. While longer-headed and luckier men like Crassus and Caesar drew off to bide their time and live to fight another and better day, the gambler Catiline put himself at the head of these 'legions of the lost'. But once again Cicero was too strong, too clever, too tough for him. While we may deplore the consul's callousness and insensitivity to the sorry condition of much of Italy, we cannot withhold a cool respect for the energy and skill of his administration. Catiline was isolated and forced into the open. Public opinion was alienated from him, even amongst the poor. Efficient measures of defence were set in hand, and a highly effective information service organized. Threatened *coups de main* were averted, the conspiracy at Rome unmasked, and its leading members led off to execution at the consul's orders. Early in 62 the last desperate venture of the revolution was cut to pieces in a desperate but hopeless battle. Catiline's body was recovered surrounded by the government dead: his men were a little way behind, lying where they had fallen and died without yielding an inch of ground.

Cicero's success was brilliant, and brought a unique reward. For the first time in the history of the Republic of Rome a solemn thanksgiving was vowed to the gods in honour not of military feats in the field but of a civilian consul in pursuit of the duties of his office at Rome. But the success turned Cicero's head. He could never forget the glory of 63, the 'immortal glory of the Nones': and he never let anyone else forget it either. As Seneca later remarked wryly of that consulship, it was 'non sine causa, sed sine fine laudatus' (*de brev. vitae* 5). And it left Cicero with three legacies which were to prove disastrous. It led him, by nature a man of considerable vanity and ebullient optimism (as he himself acknowledged), grossly to overestimate his own importance and influence. It left him with the Micawberish belief that he could head a third force in politics, a *concordia bonorum omnium*, a union, that is, of all sound and respectable men of property of both the senatorial and equestrian classes throughout Italy. Both these beliefs were delusions. The nobility had backed Cicero in 63 out of self-interest, but many of them disliked and mistrusted this bumptious upstart and secretly (and not always secretly) relished his subsequent discomfitures. The *concordia ordinum* did not long survive the crisis of 63 and the particular conditions that had given it birth by drawing the 'haves' together in common defence against the threat then presented to property and social and economic stability (as they saw it). The third legacy was the Achilles' heel by which Cicero was brought low. By ordering the execution of the arrested conspirators without trial he had exposed himself to attack for having committed a capital offence; and that attack was vigorously and joyfully pursued by Publius Clodius, whom Cicero bitterly estranged in 61, and who emerged thereafter as the most powerful, most energetic, and most brilliantly gifted popular leader at Rome (Letters 4–8).

The rest of Cicero's life is discussed in the introductions to the separate letters in this selection. Here we need only note the highlights.

When in December 60 Julius Caesar, about to enter on his consulship of 59, offered to include Cicero in the new political partnership he was just arranging with Pompey (and subsequently Crassus was brought into it as well), Cicero bravely but unwisely declined. Blinded by the brilliance of past glories to the realities of the situation, and deeply distrustful of Caesar's long-term plans, he chose instead a course of opposition (Letters 5–7). Despite repeated warnings, he persisted. Finally, early in 58, Clodius unleashed his attack. Cicero found himself almost isolated: Pompey looked the other way, Caesar stood close at hand and watched, the 'old army of loyalists of 63' was conspicuous only by its absence, the nobility ran for cover or laughed up their sleeves. Cicero departed for his lonely exile, a bitter experience the scars of which never fully healed (Letter 8). It lasted for eighteen months, until Pompey effected his return, with Caesar acquiescing on the understanding that Cicero would in future behave himself (Letter 9). But Cicero was soon at it again. He saw what he took to be sure signs that the 'First Triumvirate' of Pompey, Caesar, and Crassus was in ruins, and early in 56 he flung himself gleefully into the attack on Caesar, confident that Pompey was behind him (Letter 11). But that wily politician gave Cicero rope only to hang himself while helping Pompey. The 'Triumvirate' was re-cemented at Lucca in the late spring of 56, and Cicero brought sharply to heel. At last the scales dropped from his eyes and he saw the world in all its harsh reality. Active support for the 'Triumvirate' he could not and would not give, for they stood for all that was abhorrent to his political principles, and Cicero for all his trimming in political tactics was always honest to his basic principles. But he abandoned his over-great hopes, and bowed his neck to the yoke of necessity (Letter 12). He conformed.

From now on Cicero was virtually in retirement from politics, though he continued a close observer and reporter of them (Letter 13). He engaged in court cases, often at the behest of Pompey or Caesar, for his mastery in this field remained unchallenged and unchallengeable. But from these years of political retirement flowed in staggering volume his works on philosophy and rhetoric. It is impossible to exaggerate the influence these works were to have. In these treatises, more even than in his speeches, Cicero took firm hold of the Latin language and from it fashioned a magnificently lucid and supple instrument. By careful experiment and constant discussion with his friends he wrestled to adapt Latin to the expression of abstract ideas and by so doing he forged the basic vocabulary of abstract thought which is the common legacy of the languages of Western Europe. His philosophical work is neither original nor profound; but it is distinguished by an unfailing and massive common sense and practicality, and was often the vehicle by which Greek thinking was transmitted at second hand to later centuries which knew little or no Greek. Many of its qualities are those which we think of as truly and best Roman; and its shortcomings in theory and soundness in experience (not to mention the charm and brilliance of the language in which it was expressed) gave to this work a greater appeal and a wider range of readers and a more pervading influence than many subtler and more original but more abstract writings have commanded. Not that Cicero's work had appeal only for the middlebrows of the world. Men like St. Augustine and Jerome acknowledged an immense debt to Cicero, whose theoretical works could elicit pious respect from Erasmus and the genuine flattery of a real and lively interest from the educated élite of the eighteenth century, the great age of reason.

The outbreak of Civil War in 49 posed a cruel dilemma for Cicero. In the end he joined Pompey, old loyalty prevailing over dark doubts (Letters 29–30). But he was quite rightly convinced that, whichever side won, the Republic he had known and loved must lose. After Pharsalus and the death of Pompey, he returned to Italy, but still lived largely in retirement, a retirement made all the more gloomy by the death early in 45 of the one person he loved more than anything else in the world, his daughter Tullia (Letter 31). Any brief flicker of hope he had had that Caesar might after all restore normal government or be amenable to advice had quickly proved to be only a fool's lantern (Letter 32).

It is not surprising then that the murder of Caesar in March 44 found Cicero, for all that he had always been fond of Caesar personally, ecstatic at the death of a 'tyrant'. At first he went on as before, but early misgivings about the way in which the 'liberators' (as he termed Caesar's murderers) were muffing their chances and leaving the field clear for the dangerous and hated Mark Antony (Letter 33) were gradually dispelled. By the autumn Cicero was bracing himself for a return to the arena, and at the end of the year he emerged from his long sojourn in the shadows to lead with all his seniority and prestige and experience and oratorical power the fight to save the Republic (Letter 35). The old fires flashed again, and never more brilliantly than in the devastating *Second Philippic*, the first really free political speech Cicero had been at liberty to publish for a dozen years. The old energy and organizing skill were still there at call. Along with Brutus and Cassius, but far their senior in *auctoritas* and public reputation, he stood once again as in 63 at the control centre of affairs.

It was a fine close to the long public career of a basically upright and immensely able man that he should at the end have come out of doubt and out of darkness to the day's rising, that having whimpered for so long he should have gone with a bang. The Roman world at large did not share Cicero's enthusiasm for the old Republic. Even if the clock could have been turned back for a little while, it would not have kept good time. The luck was against him, and the big battalions were too big. Octavian proved an eerily supple and long-headed nineteen-year-old, who was allowed (as he had to be allowed) to grow too strong to be held on Cicero's leash. When Octavian made his peace with Antony, the game was up, and Cicero had lost. He tried half-heartedly to escape from Italy and to join Brutus and Cassius with their army in Macedonia, but he was too old and tired to 'go again to his travels'. The man who had writhed in torment ten years earlier when his enemy Gabinius had slapped the single brutal word 'exsul' in his face could not bring himself to go through that all over again. His old hysterics forgotten, he calmly quieted his servants and turned to face the party of soldiers that had overtaken him. He was just a month short of his sixty-fourth birthday.

* * * * * *

Plutarch included a 'Life' of Cicero in his *Parallel Lives*; and his 'Lives' of Pompey, Crassus, and Caesar are also relevant. Cornelius Nepos' 'Life' of Atticus has already been mentioned. Of modern books in English on Cicero, two old ones still seem to me the best: Strachan-Davidson's *Cicero and the Fall of the Roman Republic*; and Gaston Boissier's *Cicero and his Friends*, a book which combines warmth and charm and scholarship in a rare amalgam. More recently there appeared H. J. Haskell's *This Was Cicero*: Haskell is no professional scholar, but an American newspaper man, an editor and a political correspondent, and this shows in his work, which is not always reliable; but the book is very fresh and very readable and has much merit. Somewhat tangentially, one ought perhaps also to draw particular attention to M. Gelzer's *Caesar* and Sir Ronald Syme's *Sallust*, though here we have the work not of amateurs but of the two greatest Roman historians of modern times.

Jerome Carcopino's *Cicero: the Secrets of his Correspondence*, (English trans. 1957) deserves a separate comment. This book is immensely readable, packed with information, lively, imaginative, and fascinating: it is, also, erratic, careless, spiteful, and consistently ungenerous and biased. It is, in a nutshell, well worth reading, but with vigilant wariness.

Histories of the Roman world in Cicero's lifetime are well known. Here I will simply mention, as the most detailed and fully documented and utterly reliable, Rice Holmes's *The Roman Republic* (in three volumes); volume IX of the *Cambridge Ancient History*; and, for a concise history, the admirable *From the Gracchi to Nero* of H. H. Scullard. Warde Fowler's *Social Life at Rome in the Age of Cicero* remains very good value; and for the background of the political machinery and practices of this period there is Lily Ross Taylor's *Party Politics in the Age of Caesar*. And there are two recent articles by P. A. Brunt which are important and stimulating: in *JRS* 1962 ('The

Army and the Land in the Roman Revolution'), and *Past and Present*, Number 35, December 1966 ('The Roman Mob').

THE POLITICAL SCENE

The student of history remains the prisoner of his own times. His outlook, his attitudes, are formed by the society in which he has been brought up. The fault of anachronism is the most insidious of all in a historian. It is enormously difficult for us, when studying Roman politics, wholly to disabuse ourselves of false or half-true analogies with modern politics. We must make the effort all the same.

We are accustomed to a fairly tight party organization for electoral and legislative purposes. We take it for granted that each party has a durable and acknowledged leadership and hierarchy; that normally it will vote as one unit in Parliament; that it will never seek to influence the verdicts of an independent judiciary. None of these assumptions holds good for the Rome of Cicero's lifetime. There were something like organized political groups, but in a far less rigid and disciplined form. Politics tended to be much more personal, and family groupings and dynastic marriages had a large part to play. So too had patronage and influence, the fruits of office for which men strove eagerly. Broadly speaking, there was a group of conservative minded men, the *boni* or *optimates*, interested in keeping things as they were and preserving their material advantages. There were also the reformers, whose motives might range over the whole spectrum from a desire to exploit popular grievances for narrow personal advantages to an honest hatred of corruption and oppression and inefficiency. They were often called *populares*, not so much from the nature of their programmes (though these needed to be popular to win popular support) as from their methods, which were in general to bypass the senate and its machinery and appeal directly to the assemblies of the people. But we must be careful not to identify *popularis* with 'democratic'. There were no democrats, as we understand the term, among the politicians of Cicero's day.

Between the powerful families of the ruling oligarchy and the mass of the people we must also take note of a large and rather inchoate middle group, which centred around the financial interests of the *equites* or 'knights', but contained also a good many of the well-to-do in the country towns of Italy. Cicero himself had been born into this class, and he usually identified himself publicly with its interests and hoped to direct its voting power at elections and trials. It might attach itself either to the optimate or to the *popularis* side in furtherance of its own material advantage. Its support was of the first importance, since generally it lay with the knights to tilt the balance this way or that—in politics, that is: open war was another matter.

Gaius Gracchus was the man most responsible for welding the knights into a coherent political group, needing their support in 123 and 122 to carry a radical programme in the teeth of optimate opposition. Secure in their gains, they had abandoned him to defeat. Again from about 110 onwards they had aligned themselves with reforming politicians, helping to carry Marius to the consulship in 108 and later backing the tribune Saturninus, once again to sheer off when the pace got too hot. They had opposed Livius Drusus in 91, and had been badly mauled by Sulla. But Rome was a capitalist society, and the capitalists could not be eliminated from it even by Sulla's violence and confiscations.

Cicero's pet scheme of a *concordia ordinum* aimed at a durable alignment of the two orders of senate and knights, a union of all sound men of property and substance. The central feature of such an alliance was political co-operation in defence of stability and the rights of property, co-operation above all in elections and in the lawcourts.

Roughly from 70 onwards the knights were in opposition to the optimates in support of Pompey and reform. By 63 they had been frightened off and could be welded into a union with the senate. As we saw, the alliance was short-lived: it ran aground on the twin reefs of the trial of Clodius and the revision of the Asian tax-contract. The split did a great deal to let Caesar into the consulship of 59.

The relation between legislation and the courts is indissoluble. Laws need teeth if they are to bite, and the teeth can be provided only by courts which are prepared to enforce punishment on transgressors. All the criminal and constitutional statutes in the world are so much waste paper if the courts cannot be trusted to return a true verdict. The Roman courts could not be trusted. Bribery on a large scale, and political bias, saw to that. Not the least important feature of the power of the knights was the fact that, in Cicero's day, they formed the majority of the juries who sat in these courts.

As remarked earlier, the political groups or 'parties' of Cicero's Rome had no permanent and responsible leaders—this being itself in large measure a consequence of the system of annually changing magistrates. Normally there was no such position as 'party leader'. There were a number of *principes viri* or *principes civitatis* of varying power and authority. Everything depended on the wealth, patronage, influence, and not least personal magnetism and authority of each leader, on his capacity for winning and organizing supporters and effecting those compromises which are an irremovable feature of the political game in any country in any age. Such men were not necessarily consuls or ex-consuls: the usually rigid ladder of office, the *cursus honorum*, meant that no man, however able, could move on to higher offices until he had attained the minimum legal age. Julius Caesar, for example, could not legally be consul until the year 59, however much more important he was than some of the second-raters who held the consulship in the late sixties. Similarly, the Clodius of the early fifties should not be dismissed simply as an instrument in the hands of more senior men just because he had climbed only the lower rungs of office: he was a political power in his own right, at least from 58 onwards. Crassus, apart from his brief tenure of a censorship in 65, held no office or commission of formal consequence between his first consulship in 70 and his second in 55: his great importance as a political leader cannot, however, be questioned. His power lay in his enormous wealth and patronage, and in his mastery of the Roman political machine.

So long as Catulus was alive, the conservative nobles had something approaching a leader, but when he died in the critical year of 60 ('Motum ex Metello consule civicum . . .') no other man came forward to fill his shoes and command a similar influence and confidence. Cato, for all his comparative youth and sometimes insufferable stuffiness, had the courage and strength of character to stampede the *optimates* on occasion (usually, so Cicero thought, in quite the wrong direction), but that was all: his true power began when his life ended and a legend was born. It is clear that the *optimates*, riven by internal jealousies and suspicions, were seriously handicapped as a group in the fifties by this lack of central control and cohesion.

Rome's career had begun as a city state, but her very success had sown the seeds that blossomed into future troubles. As she extended her power, the *populus Romanus* spread further and further afield, moving out to people the new colonies which were sited along the strategic trunk roads that were driven through Italy or to settle on individual plots of conquered Italian land. With the great overseas expansion of the second century came an influx into Rome of unemployed or under-employed proletarians driven from the land in the economic upheaval of these years—and also of large numbers of foreign slaves, the profits of conquest. Many of these slaves gained their freedom and with it (under the Roman system) Roman citizenship. By the end of the first century A.D. the satirist Juvenal was to complain that the Syrian Orontes had long mingled its flood with the Tiber: 'Iam pridem Syrus in Tiberim defluxit Orontes' (*Sat.* iii. 62). But already before the Republic was dead Cicero could refer to the citizenry of the imperial capital as a wretched, half-starved apology for a *plebs* (*misera et ieiuna plebicula*) or as the dregs of Romulus (*faex Romuli*).

This diaspora of the citizens of Rome, together with the increasing deracination and pauperization of the city population, combined to throw the old political machine out of gear. More and more Rome's citizens were prevented by sheer distance from attending in their own persons and on their own feet the central assemblies in the city. More and more were the actual city dwellers manipulable by the bribery and intimidation and seigneurial influence of the rich aristocratic houses, who constituted a mixed plebeio-patrician nobility of office. The basis on which the old city state of Rome had rested had quite crumbled away, and nothing had been put in its place to bear the weight of the structure. The result had been the growth of a ruling oligarchy of birth and wealth, inheriting wide resources of influence and patronage, which manipulated the urban populace and became increasingly less responsible and responsive to the sovereign people by whom they were nominally elected and to whom they were nominally answerable.

The people of Rome—or as many of them as could physically attend the assemblies in the capital city—could meet only under the presidency of a proper officer. They could do no more than vote yes or no to the proposals laid before them by these officers. Normally, legislation was dealt with by the tribal assemblies, either of the *populus Romanus* or of the *plebs*

Romana. The *plebs* was simply the *populus* minus its patrician members; and in Cicero's time there was only a handful of patricians left, so that for all practical purposes the people who attended the tribal assembly of the *populus* (*comitia tributa*) were exactly the same as those who attended the tribal assembly of the *plebs* (*concilium plebis*). The important difference between the two assemblies was that the officers who introduced legislation to the former were the consuls and praetors, while the latter was presided over by the tribunes of the *plebs*. Thus the plebeian assembly tended on the whole to be the assembly where reform legislation was introduced and carried, since it was far commoner to find aspiring politicians at the tribunician stage of the *cursus honorum* who were ready to act in this way than to find such people among the more settled and established and noble-dominated consuls and praetors. The tribunes were also very important in that they had the power to veto (*intercedere, intercessio*) all legislative and many administrative and executive decisions, so that their blocking and obstructive power was of great use to more powerful and senior politicians. The consuls and praetors were elected by the centuriate assembly (*comitia centuriata*): unlike the tribal assemblies, this assembly was heavily weighted in favour of the richest citizens, so that here again the sort of man who might find favour with the *concilium plebis* and be there elected to a tribunate was not necessarily the sort of man who would win the suffrage of the wealthier, more conservative, less dissatisfied voters who largely dominated the centuriate assembly.

THE LETTERS

Altogether, we have not far short of a thousand letters written by or to Cicero. They are not, however, evenly distributed over the period from 68 to 43. Down to 60 there are thirty letters; from 59 to 55 another hundred; from 54 to 50 about one hundred and seventy; from 49 to 44 nearly four hundred; while the 18 months from the beginning of 44 to July 43 provide over two hundred. And even within apparently rich periods some years are surprisingly thin in surviving letters: thus we have only eight letters from 57, and only three from 52.

The letters fall into four groups. There are the sixteen volumes of the *Epistulae ad Atticum*, and the sixteen volumes of the *Epistulae ad familiares*. Far smaller in size are the three short volumes of the *Epistulae ad Quintum fratrem* and the single volume of the *Epistulae ad Marcum Brutum* (all of the latter dating from the last year of Cicero's life).

Taken together, these letters constitute a priceless mine of information about Cicero's life and times, ranging from bread-and-butter letters of recommendation to formal dispatches to the senate, from brief invitations to dinner to discussions of high policy and secret plans, from domestic details about house-decoration and family tiffs to justifications of past politics and analyses of future prospects. As Cornelius Nepos wrote of the Atticus letters, to read them is virtually to have a detailed history of the period (*vita Attici* 16). One cannot improve on the assessment of Jerome Carcopino (*Les Secrets de la correspondance de Cicéron*: introd., pp. 9–10):

Now as vivid and clear as Voltaire's, now as lively and picturesque as Mme de Sévigné's, now as enigmatic and tantalising as Mérimée's, as bitter and corrosive as Saint-Simon's . . . a masterpiece which is a perfect blend of every quality and every style: narrative and portrait, argument and anecdote, maxim and metaphor, invective and irony, seductive coquetry and stinging sarcasm.

Quite unlike the later letters of Seneca and Pliny the Younger, the Ciceronian letters are genuine everyday correspondence. They were written as we write our own letters, without thought for publication or literary immortality or careful attention to the rules of a literary genre (see Letter 14, introduction), often without too much regard for the rules of grammar and syntax. It is in this that lie both their charm and their great historical and human importance. They are a valuable corrective to the public utterances of Cicero (who like every other politician was not always completely honest and frank when addressing the world at large), and to the narrative accounts of the historians of this period. Far more important, they are a rich supplement to our other sources of information, giving to the last years of the Republic a richness of texture and depth of pile lacking in any other period of ancient history.

'Te totum in tuis litteris vidi.' In his letters Cicero comes alive to us as a real person, a creature of flesh and blood, with human hopes and fears, strengths and weaknesses, moments of greatness and of pettiness, of worry and elation, so that we come to know him as we can know no other person in ancient history, and to feel that we could walk into a room and sit down next to him at table and talk to him with utter naturalness and understanding and no sense of remoteness or mystery. And not only Cicero. Other men's ghosts come back to life, and take on flesh and bones in these pages: the gay, shrewd, irrepressible, rakish, and infinitely likeable Caelius Rufus (Letters 21 and 26); the stiff, pompous, contortedly upright Cato (Letter 24); the gentle, rather boring Servius Sulpicius Rufus (Letter 31); the obscure, awkward, utterly admirable Gaius Matius (Letter 34). Pompey writes coldly to an ebullient Cicero (Letter 3), or with testy restraint to a bungling Ahenobarbus (Letter 28); Caesar in his letters demonstrates the charm and blarney which is so often attested at second hand (Letters 15 and 29); Quintus Cicero explodes in petulance (Letters 20 and 30); a young lawyer is packed off to Gaul and Britain to make his fortune (Letters 15–17); a difficult consular is placated (Letter 10); a pair of consuls-designate, experienced in war but not in debate, badger Cicero into giving them lessons in public speaking at the seaside (Letter 33); villas are rented and bought and sold, rooms decorated, books published, holidays arranged, jokes repeated, heads shaken over tiresome wives, trusted servants written to in terms that throw a flood of light on the social conditions of the age (Letter 27).

To attempt in thirty-five letters to give a cross-section of what can be found in more than nine hundred would be madness. The correspondence of Cicero calls for a great deal of help by way of commentary simply because it is so rich and uninhibited, and the language less disciplined and closer to the language of everyday speech than that of the literary works to which the ordinary reader is accustomed. Space and retail prices impose limits on what can be included, and the exigencies of school and college timetables on what can be studied. I have thought it better to produce a selection of reasonable compass and some homogeneity (even if the homogeneity be only that of my own arbitrary choice) than a larger number of letters more sketchily annotated—and probably doomed to further pruning by the teachers and examining boards who might use it.

In making this selection I have set out first to please myself in the hope that others may thereby be satisfied. Some letters I should have liked to include were ruled out because their length or their difficulty would have curtailed the selection still further. I have deliberately set my face against choosing letters to illustrate this or that detail of social life. These letters are about the man, Cicero. I have tried to show him, and to produce a selection that will provide a series of links between the main phases of Cicero's mature years from 65 to 44. I have carefully avoided getting enmeshed in the exciting but over-full details of the last eighteen months of Cicero's life—the three letters included from this period (Letters 33–5) being essentially by way of a postscript to what has gone before and a farewell in view of what is soon to come. In the introduction to, and commentary on, each letter I have set out to supply, not merely assistance with the translation of the Latin and the understanding of the syntax, but above all what seems to me the indispensable background of social and historical information without which the study of these letters would be largely wasted labour.

THE SURVIVAL OF THE LETTERS

For a long time the fashionable view was that the Atticus letters were published about A.D. 60, the *ad familiares* a little earlier. This view was attacked with great gusto by the French scholar Carcopino in the first part of his book *Cicero: the Secrets of his Correspondence*. Whatever doubts one may have about some of Carcopino's positive arguments, he effectively demolished the old position, and there is every reason to accept that Cicero's letters (whose immense intrinsic importance and interest were not hard to recognize) were published within a decade or so of his death. Certainly, Cornelius Nepos, who composed his life of Atticus about 35 to 30 B.C., knew of a number of 'volumes of letters addressed to Atticus between Cicero's consulship and the end of his life, which would give the reader very nearly a detailed history of those times' (*vita Attici* 16). As to the *epistulae ad familiares* we are less well informed, but the elder Seneca (*circa* 55 B.C. to A.D. 40) was able to quote from the letter we know as *ad famm.* xv. 19 (*Suas.* 1. 5. 5). We certainly know that *a* collection of Cicero's letters was thought of by Cicero himself shortly before his death, for in a letter he wrote to Atticus in July 44 (and Cornelius Nepos' name occurs in the same passage) he says: 'There is no "collected edition" of my letters. But Tiro has about seventy, and there are some that can be got from you. These I must look over thoroughly and correct before they can be published' (*ad Att.* xvi. 5. 5).

After the long night of the Dark Ages the letters to Atticus were rediscovered by Petrarch in the Cathedral Library at Verona on 16 June 1345. We know the exact date because that very same day Petrarch sat down and wrote a letter to none other than Cicero himself to say how affected he was.[1] Petrarch made a copy of the manuscript in his own hand—it must have been quite bulky, for later it fell from its place and did a serious injury to his leg.

The story now moves to Florence, whose Chancellor from 1375 to 1406 was Coluccio Salutati. Coluccio knew of the Petrarch find, and he also knew that Verona had been sacked in 1390 by Giangaleazzo Visconti, the ruler of Milan, and that a number of the Verona manuscripts had found their way into the hands of this family. So Coluccio wrote to his friend Pasquino Cappelli, Chancellor of Milan, asking him for a copy of the Atticus manuscript. Pasquino found a manuscript of Cicero's letters in the Cathedral Library at Vercelli, had a copy made, and sent it off. Coluccio was beside himself with joy—'tanto etenim me munere felicitasti, quod vix prae gaudio apud me sim'—for the manuscript which had been copied for him was not the Atticus manuscript but a manuscript of the hitherto unknown *ad familiares*.[2]

(The Quintus and Brutus letters derive from the same manuscript source as the Atticus letters.)

THE TEXT

The text of the letters printed in this selection is substantially that of the current Oxford editions by Purser, Shackleton Bailey, and Watt. In order to present the reader with a clean text, I have omitted brackets (both pointed and square)

---

[1] This letter is printed on pp. 119–20 of F. E. Harrison, *Millennium: A Latin Reader, A.D. 374–1374* (Oxford University Press, 1968).

[2] See Reynolds and Wilson, *Scribes and Scholars*, pp. 108–13 (Oxford University Press, 1968).

denoting additions and deletions. I have not hesitated to print a clear text incorporating a conjectural reading in places where the Oxford editors have contented themselves with marking the text as corrupt (though, when I have done so, I have owned up to it in the notes). Although I do not always agree with the Oxford Text readings, I have refrained from tampering with them save in three or four instances where either later knowledge has produced agreed corrections (and Purser's text of the *ad familiares* is now getting on for seventy years old) or my own conviction has proved too strong to ignore.

ACKNOWLEDGEMENTS

I should have been stupid not to plunder the work of earlier commentators. I owe them much, and I am grateful. Most notable is the complete edition with notes and commentary in six volumes by Tyrrell and Purser (*The Correspondence of Cicero*: Dublin, 1885–1933). Otherwise I have made most use (where relevant) of the editions of How (*Cicero: Select Letters*, Oxford, 1925) and Shackleton Bailey (*Cicero's Letters to Atticus*, Cambridge, 1965 onwards), the latter of which also provides a translation of the Atticus letters.

LETTERS 1–35

TEXT AND INTRODUCTIONS

LETTER 1

Cicero to Atticus. June 65

Writing to Atticus very shortly before the consular elections of July 65, Cicero outlines the position about his own proposed candidature for one of the two consulships of 63 (the elections for which would be held twelve months hence, in July 64). Cicero tells Atticus that he plans to begin canvassing in a few days time, makes some comments on his likely competitors, and sums up the chances for the current elections. He excuses himself for having got on the wrong side of Atticus' uncle.

On Atticus, see Introduction, pp. viii–ix; on Cicero's life and career down to 65, Introduction, pp. vii–xiv.

Scr. Romae paulo ante xvi Kal. Sext. an. 65.

CICERO ATTICO SALVTEM.

Petitionis nostrae, quam tibi summae curae esse scio, 1
huius modi ratio est, quod adhuc coniectura provideri possit.
5 Prensat unus P. Galba; sine fuco ac fallaciis more maio-
rum negatur. Vt opinio est hominum, non aliena rationi
nostrae fuit illius haec praepropera prensatio; nam illi ita
negant vulgo ut mihi se debere dicant; ita quiddam spero
nobis profici, cum hoc percrebrescit, plurimos nostros
10 amicos inveniri. Nos autem initium prensandi facere cogitabamus eo ipso tempore quo tuum puerum cum his litteris
proficisci Cincius dicebat, in campo comitiis tribuniciis a. d.
xvi Kal. Sext. Competitores qui certi esse videbantur Galba

et Antonius et Q. Cornificius. Puto te in hoc aut risisse aut ingemuisse; ut frontem ferias, sunt qui etiam Caesonium 15 putent. Aquilium non arbitrabamur, qui denegavit et iuravit morbum et illud suum regnum iudiciale opposuit. Catilina, si iudicatum erit meridie non lucere, certus erit competitor. De Aufidio et de Palicano non puto te exspectare 2 dum scribam. De iis qui nunc petunt Caesar certus putatur. 20 Thermus cum Silano contendere existimatur; qui sic inopes et ab amicis et existimatione sunt ut mihi videatur non esse ἀδύνατον Turium obducere; sed hoc praeter me nemini videtur. Nostris rationibus maxime conducere videtur Thermum fieri cum Caesare; nemo est enim ex iis qui nunc petunt 25 qui, si in nostrum annum reciderit, firmior candidatus fore videatur, propterea quod curator est viae Flaminiae, quae tum erit absoluta sane facile; eum libenter nunc Caesari consuli accuderim. Petitorum haec est informata adhuc cogitatio. Nos in omni munere candidatorio fungendo summam 30 adhibebimus diligentiam; et fortasse, quoniam videtur in suffragiis multum posse Gallia, cum Romae a iudiciis forum refrixerit, excurremus mense Septembri legati ad Pisonem, ut Ianuario revertamur. Cum perspexero voluntates nobilium, scribam ad te. Cetera spero prolixa esse his dumtaxat urbanis 35 competitoribus. Illam manum tu mihi cura ut praestes, quoniam propius abes, Pompei, nostri amici; nega me ei iratum fore si ad mea comitia non venerit. Atque haec huius modi sunt.

3   Sed est quod abs te mihi ignosci pervelim. Caecilius, avun- 40 culus tuus, a P. Vario cum magna pecunia fraudaretur, agere coepit cum eius fratre Caninio Satyro de iis rebus quas eum dolo malo mancipio accepisse de Vario diceret. Vna agebant ceteri creditores, in quibus erat L. Lucullus et P. Scipio et is quem putabant magistrum fore si bona veni- 45 rent, L. Pontius; verum hoc ridiculum est, de magistro. Nunc cognosce rem. Rogavit me Caecilius ut adessem contra

Satyrum. Dies fere nullus est quin hic Satyrus domum
meam ventitet; observat L. Domitium maxime, me habet
50 proximum; fuit et mihi et Quinto fratri magno usui in
nostris petitionibus. Sane sum perturbatus cum ipsius Satyri 4
familiaritate tum Domiti, in quo uno maxime ambitio nostra
nititur. Demonstravi haec Caecilio; simul et illud ostendi,
si ipse unus cum illo uno contenderet, me ei satis facturum
55 fuisse; nunc in causa universorum creditorum, hominum
praesertim amplissimorum, qui sine eo quem Caecilius suo
nomine perhiberet facile causam communem sustinerent,
aequum esse eum et officio meo consulere et tempori. Durius
accipere hoc mihi visus est quam vellem et quam homines
60 belli solent, et postea prorsus ab instituta nostra paucorum
dierum consuetudine longe refugit. Abs te peto ut mihi hoc
ignoscas et me existimes humanitate esse prohibitum ne
contra amici summam existimationem miserrimo eius tempore
venirem, cum is omnia sua studia et officia in me contulisset.
65 Quod si voles in me esse durior, ambitionem putabis mihi
obstitisse; ego autem arbitror, etiam si id sit, mihi ignoscen-
dum esse, 'ἐπεὶ οὐχ ἱερήιον οὐδὲ βοείην . . .'; vides enim in quo
cursu simus et quam omnis gratias non modo retinendas
verum etiam adquirendas putemus. Spero tibi me causam
70 probasse, cupio quidem certe.

Hermathena tua valde me delectat et posita ita belle est 5
ut totum gymnasium eius ἀνάθημα esse videatur; multum
te amamus.

LETTER 2

Cicero to Atticus. Mid-July 65

This letter was written very soon after Letter 1, to tell Atticus of the
birth of a son to Cicero, who is thinking of defending Catiline at his
forthcoming trial for extortion. Atticus is entreated to come to Rome

to help enlist support for Cicero in his campaign to be elected consul for 63.

Scr. Romae paulo post ep. 1 an. 65.

⟨CICERO ATTICO SALVTEM.⟩

1 L. Iulio Caesare C. Marcio Figulo coss., filiolo me auctum scito, salva Terentia.

Abs te iam diu nihil litterarum. Ego de meis ad te rationi- 5 bus scripsi antea diligenter. Hoc tempore Catilinam, competitorem nostrum, defendere cogitamus. Iudices habemus quos voluimus, summa accusatoris voluntate. Spero, si absolutus erit, coniunctiorem illum nobis fore in ratione petitionis; sin aliter acciderit, humaniter feremus. 10

2 Tuo adventu nobis opus est maturo; nam prorsus summa hominum est opinio tuos familiaris nobilis homines adversarios honori nostro fore; ad eorum voluntatem mihi conciliandam maximo te mihi usui fore video. Qua re Ianuario ineunte, ut constituisti, cura ut Romae sis. 15

LETTER 3

Cicero to Pompey. Spring or early summer 62

As consul in 63, Cicero had broken the back of the popular reform programme advanced in that year, and driven the extremist *popularis* wing into open revolt and destruction. Now an ex-consul, he writes to congratulate Pompey on the successful completion of his mission in Asia Minor, where Pompey had been sent as supreme commander against Mithridates in 66. Although Cicero expresses his disappointment at Pompey's lack of enthusiasm for his own achievements as consul, he looks forward confidently to a fruitful co-operation between the two of them in political life: a hope doomed to frustration.

Scr. Romae circa m. Apr. an. 62

M. TVLLIVS M. F. CICERO S. D. CN. POMPEIO CN. F.
MAGNO IMPERATORI.

S. T. E. Q. V. B. E. Ex litteris tuis, quas publice misisti, **1**
5 cepi una cum omnibus incredibilem voluptatem; tantam
enim spem oti ostendisti, quantam ego semper omnibus
te uno fretus pollicebar. Sed hoc scito, tuos veteres hostis,
novos amicos, vehementer litteris perculsos atque ex magna
spe deturbatos iacere. Ad me autem litteras quas misisti, **2**
10 quamquam exiguam significationem tuae erga me voluntatis
habebant, tamen mihi scito iucundas fuisse; nulla enim re
tam laetari soleo quam meorum officiorum conscientia;
quibus si quando non mutue respondetur, apud me plus
offici residere facillime patior. Illud non dubito quin, si
15 te mea summa erga te studia parum mihi adiunxerint, res
publica nos inter nos conciliatura coniuncturaque sit. Ac **3**
ne ignores quid ego in tuis litteris desiderarim, scribam
aperte, sicut et mea natura et nostra amicitia postulat. Res
eas gessi, quarum aliquam in tuis litteris et nostrae neces-
20 situdinis et rei p. causa gratulationem exspectavi; quam
ego abs te praetermissam esse arbitror, quod vererere ne
cuius animum offenderes. Sed scito ea, quae nos pro salute
patriae gessimus, orbis terrae iudicio ac testimonio com-
probari; quae, cum veneris, tanto consilio tantaque animi
25 magnitudine a me gesta esse cognosces, ut tibi multo
maiori, quam Africanus fuit, me non multo minorem quam
Laelium facile et in re p. et in amicitia adiunctum esse
patiare.

LETTER 4

Cicero to Atticus. 13 February 61

The main talking-point at Rome is the threatened trial of Publius
Clodius for alleged profanation of the rites of the *Bona Dea*. These
were being celebrated one evening early in December 62 at the house
of the *Pontifex Maximus*, Julius Caesar, by a distinguished company of
ladies (including the Vestal Virgins). All males were rigorously ex-
cluded, but Clodius was said to have been discovered in the house, up
to no good. The whole affair is very much clouded by exaggerations
and inconsistencies in the ancient accounts: for a full discussion, see
Balsdon, *Historia* 15 (1966) 65–73.

In this letter, Pompey's first public appearances after his return to
Rome are reported in scathing terms. Cicero also tells Atticus about
the riotous proceedings which marked the attempt to pass a special
bill of impeachment against Clodius, and concludes with some brief
private business.

Scr. Romae Id. Febr. an. 61.

CICERO ATTICO SALVTEM.

1 Vereor ne putidum sit scribere ad te quam sim occupatus,
sed tamen ita distinebar ut vix huic tantulae epistulae
tempus habuerim, atque id ereptum e summis occupationi- 5
bus.

Prima contio Pompei qualis fuisset scripsi ad te antea:
non iucunda miseris, inanis improbis, beatis non grata, bonis
non gravis; itaque frigebat. Tum Pisonis consulis impulsu
levissimus tribunus pl. Fufius in contionem producit Pom- 10
peium; res agebatur in circo Flaminio et erat in eo ipso loco
illo die nundinarum πανήγυρις. Quaesivit ex eo placeretne ei
iudices a praetore legi, quo consilio idem praetor uteretur;
id autem erat de Clodiana religione ab senatu constitutum.
2 Tum Pompeius μάλ' ἀριστοκρατικῶς locutus est senatusque 15
auctoritatem sibi omnibus in rebus maximi videri semperque

visam esse respondit, et id multis verbis. Postea Messalla
consul in senatu de Pompeio quaesivit quid de religione et
de promulgata rogatione sentiret. Locutus ita est in senatu ut
20 omnia illius ordinis consulta γενικῶς laudaret, mihique ut
adsedit dixit se putare satis ab se etiam de istis rebus esse
responsum. Crassus, postea quam vidit illum excepisse 3
laudem ex eo quod suspicarentur homines ei consulatum
meum placere, surrexit ornatissimeque de meo consulatu
25 locutus est, cum ita diceret, se, quod esset senator, quod
civis, quod liber, quod viveret, mihi acceptum referre; quotiens coniugem, quotiens domum, quotiens patriam videret,
totiens se beneficium meum videre. Quid multa? totum
hunc locum quem ego varie meis orationibus, quarum tu Ari-
30 starchus es, soleo pingere, de flamma, de ferro (nosti illas
ληκύθους), valde graviter pertexuit. Proxime Pompeium
sedebam; intellexi hominem moveri Crassum inire eam
gratiam quam ipse praetermisisset, an esse tantas res nostras
quae tam libenti senatu laudarentur, ab eo praesertim qui
35 mihi laudem illam eo minus deberet quod meis omnibus
litteris in Pompeiana laude perstrictus esset. Hic dies me 4
valde Crasso adiunxit, et tamen ab illo aperte tecte quicquid
est datum libenter accepi. Ego autem ipse, di boni! quo modo
ἐνεπερπερευσάμην novo auditori Pompeio! si umquam mihi
40 περίοδοι, si καμπαί, si ἐνθυμήματα, si κατασκευαὶ suppedita-
verunt, illo tempore. Quid multa? clamores. Etenim haec erat
ὑπόθεσις: de gravitate ordinis, de equestri concordia, de con-
sensione Italiae, de intermortuis reliquiis coniurationis, de
vilitate, de otio. Nosti iam in hac materia sonitus nostros;
45 tanti fuerunt ut ego eo brevior sim quod eos usque istinc
exauditos putem.

Romanae autem se res sic habent. Senatus Ἄρειος πάγος: 5
nihil constantius, nihil severius, nihil fortius. Nam cum dies
venisset rogationi ex senatus consulto ferendae, concursabant
50 barbatuli iuvenes, totus ille grex Catilinae, duce filiola

Curionis, et populum ut antiquaret rogabant. Piso autem consul lator rogationis idem erat dissuasor. Operae Clodianae pontis occuparant; tabellae ministrabantur ita ut nulla daretur 'VTI ROGAS'. Hic tibi in rostra Cato advolat, commulcium Pisoni consuli mirificum facit, si id est commul- 55 cium, vox plena gravitatis, plena auctoritatis, plena denique salutis. Accedit eodem etiam noster Hortensius, multi praeterea boni; insignis vero opera Favoni fuit. Hoc concursu optimatium comitia dimittuntur; senatus vocatur. Cum decerneretur frequenti senatu, contra pugnante Pisone, ad 60 pedes omnium singillatim accidente Clodio, ut consules populum cohortarentur ad rogationem accipiendam, homines ad quindecim Curioni nullum senatus consultum facienti adsenserunt; facile ex altera parte CCCC fuerunt. Acta res est; Fufius tribunus tum concessit. Clodius contiones miseras 65 habebat, in quibus Lucullum Hortensium C. Pisonem Messallam consulem contumeliose laedebat; me tantum 'comperisse' omnia criminabatur. Senatus et de provinciis praetorum et de legationibus et de ceteris rebus decernebat ut ante quam rogatio lata esset ne quid ageretur. 70

6 Habes res Romanas. Sed tamen etiam illud quod non speraram audi: Messalla consul est egregius, fortis constans diligens, nostri laudator amator imitator. Ille alter uno vitio minus vitiosus quod iners, quod somni plenus, quod imperitus, quod ἀπρακτότατος, sed voluntate ita καχέκτης ut Pom- 75 peium post illam contionem in qua ab eo senatus laudatus est odisse coeperit; itaque mirum in modum omnis a se bonos alienavit; neque id magis amicitia Clodi adductus fecit quam studio perditarum rerum atque partium. Sed habet sui similem in magistratibus praeter Fufium neminem; bonis 80 utimur tribunis pl., Cornuto vero Pseudocatone; quid quaeris?

7 Nunc ut ad privata redeam, Τεῦκρις promissa patravit; tu mandata effice quae recepisti. Quintus frater, qui Argi-

85 letani aedifici reliquum dodrantem emit HS $\overline{\text{DCCXXV}}$, Tusculanum venditat, ut, si possit, emat Pacilianam domum.
Cum Lucceio in gratiam redii; video hominem valde
petiturire; navabo operam. Tu quid agas, ubi sis, cuius
modi istae res sint, fac me quam diligentissime certiorem.
90 Id. Febr.

LETTER 5

Cicero to Atticus. Late April 59

Cicero writes from his villa at Formiae to Atticus, who is in Rome and
is keeping him informed of what is going on in the capital. Caesar is
now consul, and with the help of Pompey and Crassus is pushing
through a reform programme in the teeth of the opposition of his
fellow consul, Marcus Calpurnius Bibulus. Cicero himself is tem-
porarily on good terms with Publius Clodius.

Scr. in Formiano inter vii et prid. Kal. Mai. an. 59.

CICERO ATTICO SALVTEM.

Vt scribis, ita video non minus incerta in re publica quam 1
in epistula tua, sed tamen ista ipsa me varietas sermonum
5 opinionumque delectat; Romae enim videor esse cum tuas
litteras lego et, ut fit in tantis rebus, modo hoc modo illud
audire. Illud tamen explicare non possum, quidnam inveniri
possit nullo recusante ad facultatem agrariam. Bibuli autem 2
ista magnitudo animi in comitiorum dilatione quid habet
10 nisi ipsius iudicium sine ulla correctione rei publicae?
Nimirum in Publio spes est; fiat, fiat tribunus pl., si nihil
aliud ut eo citius tu ex Epiro revertare; nam ut illo tu careas
non video posse fieri, praesertim si mecum aliquid volet disputare. Sed id quidem non dubium est quin, si quid erit
15 eius modi, sis advolaturus. Verum ut hoc non sit, tamen, sive
ruet sive eriget rem publicam, praeclarum spectaculum mihi
propono, modo te consessore spectare liceat.

3 Cum haec maxime scriberem, ecce tibi Sebosus! Nondum plane ingemueram, 'salve' inquit Arrius. Hoc est Roma decedere! quos ego homines effugi cum in hos incidi? Ego vero 'in montis patrios et ad incunabula nostra' pergam. Denique si solus non potuero, ero cum rusticis potius quam cum his perurbanis, ita tamen ut, quoniam tu nihil certi scribis, in Formiano tibi praestoler usque ad III Non. Mai.

4 Terentiae pergrata est adsiduitas tua et diligentia in controversia Mulviana. Nescit omnino te communem causam defendere eorum qui agros publicos possideant; sed tamen tu aliquid publicanis pendis, haec etiam id recusat. Ea tibi igitur et Κικέρων, ἀριστοκρατικώτατος παῖς, salutem dicunt.

LETTER 6

Cicero to Atticus. About August 59

Cicero is in Rome, and Atticus in Epirus. The Caesar–Pompey–Crassus coalition (the 'First Triumvirate') has run into a trough of widespread unpopularity, and Cicero fears serious violence. He comments on the unhappy plight of Pompey, and on the threat to his own security from Clodius.

Scr. Romae paulo post viii Kal. Sext. an. 59.

CICERO ATTICO SALVTEM.

1 De re publica quid ego tibi subtiliter? Tota periit atque hoc est miserior quam reliquisti, quod tum videbatur eius modi dominatio civitatem oppressisse quae iucunda esset multitudini, bonis autem ita molesta ut tamen sine pernicie, nunc repente tanto in odio est omnibus ut quorsus eruptura sit horreamus. Nam iracundiam atque intemperantiam illorum sumus experti qui Catoni irati omnia perdiderunt, sed

10 ita lenibus uti videbantur venenis ut posse videremur sine
dolore interire; nunc vero sibilis vulgi, sermonibus hone-
storum, fremitu Italiae vereor ne exarserint. Equidem sperabam, ut saepe etiam loqui tecum solebam, sic orbem rei **2**
publicae esse conversum ut vix sonitum audire, vix im-
15 pressam orbitam videre possemus; et fuisset ita, si homines
transitum tempestatis exspectare potuissent; sed cum diu
occulte suspirassent, postea iam gemere, ad extremum vero
loqui omnes et clamare coeperunt.

Itaque ille noster amicus insolens infamiae, semper in **3**
20 laude versatus, circumfluens gloria, deformatus corpore,
fractus animo, quo se conferat nescit; progressum prae-
cipitem, inconstantem reditum videt; bonos inimicos habet,
improbos ipsos non amicos. Ac vide mollitiem animi: non
tenui lacrimas cum illum a. d. vIII Kal. Sext. vidi de edictis
25 Bibuli contionantem; qui antea solitus esset iactare se magnificentissime illo in loco summo cum amore populi, cunctis
faventibus, ut ille tum humilis, ut demissus erat, ut ipse etiam
sibi, non iis solum qui aderant, displicebat! O spectaculum **4**
uni Crasso iucundum, ceteris non item! nam quia deciderat
30 ex astris, lapsus potius quam progressus videbatur, et, ut
Apelles si Venerem, aut Protogenes si Ialysum illum suum
caeno oblitum videret, magnum, credo, acciperet dolorem,
sic ego hunc omnibus a me pictum et politum artis coloribus
subito deformatum non sine magno dolore vidi. Quamquam
35 nemo putabat propter Clodianum negotium me illi amicum
esse debere, tamen tantus fuit amor ut exhauriri nulla posset
iniuria. Itaque Archilochia in illum edicta Bibuli populo ita
sunt iucunda ut eum locum ubi proponuntur prae multitudine eorum qui legunt transire nequeamus, ipsi ita acerba
40 ut tabescat dolore, mihi me hercule molesta, quod et eum
quem semper dilexi nimis excruciant et timeo tam vehemens
vir tamque acer in ferro et tam insuetus contumeliae ne
omni animi impetu dolori et iracundiae pareat.

5　　Bibuli qui sit exitus futurus nescio; ut nunc res se habet,
admirabili gloria est. Qui cum comitia in mensem Octobrem 45
distulisset, quod solet ea res populi voluntatem offendere,
putarat Caesar oratione sua posse impelli contionem ut iret
ad Bibulum; multa cum seditiosissime diceret, vocem exprimere non potuit. Quid quaeris? sentiunt se nullam ullius
partis voluntatem tenere; eo magis vis nobis est timenda.　　50
6　　Clodius inimicus est nobis. Pompeius confirmat eum nihil
esse facturum contra me; mihi periculosum est credere, ad
resistendum me paro; studia spero me summa habiturum
omnium ordinum. Te cum ego desidero, tum vero res ad
tempus illud vocat; plurimum consili animi praesidi denique 55
mihi, si te ad tempus videro, accesserit. Varro mihi satis facit.
Pompeius loquitur divinitus. Spero nos aut certe cum summa
gloria aut etiam sine molestia discessuros.

　　Tu quid agas, quem ad modum te oblectes, quid cum Sicyoniis egeris ut sciam cura.　　　　　　　　　　　　　　　　60

LETTER 7

Cicero to his brother Quintus. About November 59

This is the tail-end of a very long letter to Quintus, who is nearing the
end of his governorship of the province of Asia (roughly, western
Asia Minor). The cheerful confidence of Marcus that massive support
will enable him to beat off Clodius was doomed to disappointment
within a very few months, and contrasts poignantly with the following letter in this selection (Letter 8).

15　　Nunc ea cognosce quae maxime exoptas. Rem publicam
funditus amisimus, adeo ut Cato, adulescens nullius consili
sed tamen civis Romanus et Cato, vix vivus effugerit quod,
cum Gabinium de ambitu vellet postulare neque praetores
diebus aliquot adiri possent vel potestatem sui facerent, in 5

contionem ascendit et Pompeium 'privatum dictatorem' ap-
pellavit; propius nihil est factum quam ut occideretur. Ex
hoc qui sit status totius rei publicae videre potes. Nostrae **16**
tamen causae non videntur homines defuturi; mirandum in
10 modum profitentur, offerunt se, pollicentur. Equidem cum
spe sum maxima tum maiore etiam animo: spe, ut superiores
fore nos confidam; animo, ut in hac re publica ne casum
quidem ullum pertimescam. Sed tamen se res sic habet: si
diem nobis dixerit, tota Italia concurret, ut multiplicata gloria
15 discedamus; sin autem vi agere conabitur, spero fore studiis
non solum amicorum sed etiam alienorum ut vi resistamus.
Omnes et se et suos amicos, clientis, libertos, servos, pecunias
denique suas pollicentur. Nostra antiqua manus bonorum
ardet studio nostri atque amore. Si qui antea aut alie-
20 niores fuerant aut languidiores, nunc horum regum odio se
cum bonis coniungunt. Pompeius omnia pollicetur et Caesar;
quibus ego ita credo ut nihil de mea comparatione deminuam.
Tribuni pl. designati sunt nobis amici; consules se optime
ostendunt; praetores habemus amicissimos et acerrimos civis,
25 Domitium, Nigidium, Memmium, Lentulum; bonos etiam
alios, sed hos singularis. Qua re magnum animum fac habeas
et spem bonam. De singulis tamen rebus quae cottidie
gerantur faciam te crebro certiorem.

LETTER 8

Cicero to his brother Quintus. Early August 58

In the latter part of March 58, Cicero's nerve broke under Clodius'
threats and he left Rome to go into self-imposed exile. He travelled
south to Brundisium, which he reached about a month later. Thence
he crossed the Adriatic and finally reached Thessalonica in Macedonia
on 23 May. There he stayed till late November, owing much to the
kindness of his friend Gnaeus Plancius, who was serving as quaestor in

Macedonia in 58 and whom Cicero was later to defend brilliantly in
the courts (*pro Plancio*). At the end of November he moved back west
to Dyrrachium on the Adriatic, partly to be nearer Italy and news
from Rome, partly to avoid Piso (consul 58) who had been appointed
governor of Macedonia.

This letter was written during the stay at Thessalonica, and shows
Cicero in very low spirits. Cicero was an extremely volatile character,
and could as easily plummet to the depths of abject and even hysterical
gloom as soar to ebullient optimism. For the moment he has virtually
given up any hope of restoration, and (as is usual in his letters from exile) puts the blame for his sorry plight partly on his own irresolution,
partly on the failure of his friends to strengthen his resolve to stay and
fight Clodius, and partly on the jealousy (*invidia*) of his personal
enemies. For once he had left Rome he found it easy to convince himself that had he not panicked he could have beaten Clodius off.

Scr. Thessalonicae c. Non. Sext. an. 58.

MARCVS QVINTO FRATRI SALVTEM.

1   Amabo te, mi frater, ne, si uno meo facto et tu et omnes mei corruistis, improbitati et sceleri meo potius quam
imprudentiae miseriaeque adsignes. Nullum est meum pec- 5
catum nisi quod iis credidi a quibus nefas putaram esse me
decipi aut etiam quibus ne id expedire quidem arbitrabar.
Intimus, proximus, familiarissimus quisque aut sibi per-
timuit aut mihi invidit. Ita mihi nihil misero praeter fidem
2 amicorum, cautum meum consilium, defuit. Quod si te 10
satis innocentia tua et misericordia hominum vindicat hoc
tempore a molestia, perspicis profecto ecquaenam nobis spes
salutis relinquatur. Nam me Pomponius et Sestius et Piso
noster adhuc Thessalonicae retinuerunt, cum longius discedere propter nescio quos motus vetarent; verum ego magis 15
exitum illorum litteris quam spe certa exspectabam; nam
quid sperem potentissimo inimico, dominatione obtrecta-
3 torum, infidelibus amicis, plurimis invidis? De novis autem

tribunis pl. est ille quidem in me officiosissimus Sestius et
20 (spero) Curtius, Milo, Fadius, Fabricius, sed valde adversante
Clodio, qui etiam privatus eadem manu poterit contiones
concitare; deinde etiam intercessor parabitur. Haec mihi 4
proficiscenti non proponebantur, sed saepe triduo summa
cum gloria dicebar esse rediturus. 'Quid tu igitur?' inquies.
25 Quid? multa convenerunt quae mentem exturbarent meam,
subita defectio Pompei, alienatio consulum, etiam praetorum,
timor publicanorum, arma. Lacrimae meorum me ad mortem
ire prohibuerunt; quod certe et ad honestatem et ad effugien-
dos intolerabilis dolores fuit aptissimum. Sed de hoc scripsi
30 ad te in ea epistula quam Phaethonti dedi. Nunc tu, quoniam
in tantum luctum et laborem detrusus es quantum nemo umquam, si levare potest communem casum misericordia
hominum, scilicet incredibile quiddam adsequeris; sin plane
occidimus, me miserum! ego omnibus meis exitio fuero, qui-
35 bus ante dedecori non eram. Sed tu, ut ante ad te scripsi, 5
perspice rem et pertempta et ad me, ut tempora nostra non
ut amor tuus fert, vere perscribe. Ego vitam, quoad aut
putabo tua interesse aut spem servandam esse, retinebo. Tu
nobis amicissimum Sestium cognosces; credo tua causa
40 velle Lentulum, qui erit consul; quamquam sunt facta verbis
difficiliora. Tu et quid opus sit et quid sit videbis. Omnino
si tuam solitudinem communemque calamitatem nemo de-
spexerit, aut per te aliquid confici aut nullo modo poterit;
sin te quoque inimici vexare coeperint, ne cessaris; non enim
45 gladiis tecum sed litibus agetur. Verum haec absint velim.
Te oro ut ad me de omnibus rebus rescribas et in me
animi aut potius consili minus putes esse quam antea, amoris
vero et offici non minus.

Cicero to Atticus. About mid-September 57

On 4 August 57 a bill recalling Cicero from exile was at last carried in the centuriate assembly. Anticipating this decision, Cicero had that same day sailed from Dyrrachium, landing at Brundisium on 5 August. He made a triumphant progress through Italy, and entered Rome on 4 September, at once resuming an active role in politics by moving that Pompey be appointed to a special commission in charge of corn supplies. In this letter he writes to tell Atticus the story of his return and of his activities at Rome since his return.

Scr. Romae medio fere mense Sept. an. 57.

CICERO ATTICO SALVTEM.

1   Cum primum Romam veni fuitque cui recte ad te litteras darem, nihil prius faciendum mihi putavi quam ut tibi absenti de reditu nostro gratularer. Cognoram enim, ut vere scribam, 5 te in consiliis mihi dandis nec fortiorem nec prudentiorem quam me ipsum nec etiam pro perpetua mea in te observantia nimium in custodia salutis meae diligentem, eundemque te, qui primis temporibus erroris nostri aut potius furoris particeps et falsi timoris socius fuisses, acerbissime discidium 10 nostrum tulisse plurimumque operae studi diligentiae laboris **2** ad conficiendum reditum meum contulisse. Itaque hoc tibi vere adfirmo, in maxima laetitia et exoptatissima gratulatione unum ad cumulandum gaudium conspectum aut potius complexum mihi tuum defuisse; quem semel nactus 15 nisi numquam dimisero, ac nisi etiam praetermissos fructus tuae suavitatis praeteriti temporis omnis exegero, profecto hac restitutione fortunae me ipse non satis dignum iudicabo.

3   Nos adhuc, in nostro statu quod difficillime reciperari 20 posse arbitrati sumus, splendorem nostrum illum forensem

et in senatu auctoritatem et apud viros bonos gratiam magis
quam optaramus consecuti sumus; in re autem familiari,
quae quem ad modum fracta dissipata direpta sit non ignoras,
25 valde laboramus, tuarumque non tam facultatum, quas ego
nostras esse iudico, quam consiliorum ad conligendas et con-
stituendas reliquias nostras indigemus.

Nunc etsi omnia aut scripta esse a tuis arbitror aut etiam 4
nuntiis ac rumore perlata, tamen ea scribam brevi quae te
30 puto potissimum ex meis litteris velle cognoscere.

Prid. Non. Sext. Dyrrachio sum profectus, ipso illo die quo
lex est lata de nobis. Brundisium veni Non. Sext. Ibi mihi
Tulliola mea fuit praesto natali suo ipso die, qui casu idem
natalis erat et Brundisinae coloniae et tuae vicinae Salutis;
35 quae res animadversa a multitudine summa Brundisinorum
gratulatione celebrata est. A. d. III Id. Sext. cognovi, cum
Brundisi essem, litteris Quinti fratris mirifico studio omnium
aetatum atque ordinum, incredibili concursu Italiae, legem
comitiis centuriatis esse perlatam. Inde a Brundisinis hone-
40 stissime ornatus iter ita feci ut undique ad me cum gratulatione legati convenerint. Ad urbem ita veni ut nemo ullius 5
ordinis homo nomenclatori notus fuerit qui mihi obviam non
venerit, praeter eos inimicos quibus id ipsum, se inimicos
esse, non liceret aut dissimulare aut negare. Cum venissem ad
45 portam Capenam, gradus templorum ab infima plebe com-
pleti erant; a qua plausu maximo cum esset mihi gratulatio
significata, similis et frequentia et plausus me usque ad
Capitolium celebravit in foroque et in ipso Capitolio miranda
multitudo fuit.

50 Postridie in senatu, qui fuit dies Non. Sept., senatui 6
gratias egimus. Eo biduo, cum esset annonae summa caritas
et homines ad theatrum primo, deinde ad senatum con-
currissent, impulsu Clodi mea opera frumenti inopiam esse
clamarent, cum per eos dies senatus de annona haberetur et
55 ad eius procurationem sermone non solum plebis verum

etiam bonorum Pompeius vocaretur idque ipse cuperet mul-
titudoque a me nominatim ut id decernerem postularet, feci
et accurate sententiam dixi. Cum abessent consulares, quod
tuto se negarent posse sententiam dicere, praeter Messallam
et Afranium, factum est senatus consultum in meam sen- 60
tentiam ut cum Pompeio ageretur ut eam rem susciperet
lexque ferretur. Quo senatus consulto recitato continuo
cum multitudo more hoc insulso et novo plausum meo
nomine recitando dedisset, habui contionem; omnes magi-
stratus praesentes praeter unum praetorem et duos tribunos 65
pl. dederunt.

7   Postridie senatus frequens et omnes consulares; nihil
Pompeio postulanti negarunt; ille legatos quindecim cum
postularet, me principem nominavit et ad omnia me alterum
se fore dixit. Legem consules conscripserunt qua Pompeio 70
per quinquennium omnis potestas rei frumentariae toto orbe
terrarum daretur; alteram Messius, qui omnis pecuniae dat
potestatem et adiungit classem et exercitum et maius imperium in provinciis quam sit eorum qui eas obtineant. Illa
nostra lex consularis nunc modesta videtur, haec Messi non 75
ferenda; Pompeius illam velle se dicit, familiares hanc.
Consulares duce Favonio fremunt; nos tacemus, et eo magis
quod de domo nostra nihil adhuc pontifices responderunt.
Qui si sustulerint religionem, aream praeclaram habebimus,
superficiem consules ex senatus consulto aestimabunt; sin 80
aliter, demolientur, suo nomine locabunt, rem totam
aestimabunt.

8   Ita sunt res nostrae, 'ut ín secundis flúxae, ut in adversís
bonae'. In re familiari valde sumus, ut scis, perturbati.
Praeterea sunt quaedam domestica quae litteris non com- 85
mitto. Quintum fratrem insigni pietate virtute fide prae-
ditum sic amo ut debeo. Te exspecto et oro ut matures venire
eoque animo venias ut me tuo consilio egere non sinas.
Alterius vitae quoddam initium ordimur. Iam quidam qui

90 nos absentis defenderunt incipiunt praesentibus occulte irasci, aperte invidere. Vehementer te requirimus.

LETTER 10

Cicero to Publius Cornelius Lentulus Spinther.
13 January 56

The first nine letters in the first of the sixteen volumes of the *epistulae ad familiares* are all addressed to Spinther, and date from the years 56 to 54, when Spinther was governing the province of Cilicia (where Cicero himself was to go as governor in 51). As consul in 57 Spinther had played a crucial role in stage-managing the moves that led to Cicero's recall on 4 August with the passage of the law that stood in Spinther's name. This put Cicero deeply in Spinther's debt. Spinther was desperately anxious in 56 to secure the commission to restore the Pharaoh of Egypt to his throne; and it was incumbent on Cicero to show his gratitude by doing all he could to help. But the issue was very delicate and tangled, and aroused strong and conflicting ambitions and fears, because the Egyptian commission could in certain circumstances offer a powerful man the prospect of money and patronage on a vast scale, and Roman politics were heavily based on these two commodities. Pompey was himself keen to be given the job, which made a number of people equally keen to see that he did not get it. In the end the whole affair got bogged down in a stalemate. (Later, in 55, Gabinius, governor of Syria since his consulship in 58, moved in on his own initiative and restored the exiled monarch.)

This letter (like the others addressed to Spinther) bears all the marks of careful and polished, and sometimes intricate, composition, and the style contrasts markedly with the looser and more colloquial syntax and vocabulary of the genuinely intimate letters Cicero wrote to really close friends like Atticus and Caelius Rufus and his brother Quintus.

Scr. Romae Id. Ian. an. 56.

M. CICERO S. D. P. LENTVLO PROCOS.

1 Ego omni officio ac potius pietate erga te ceteris satis
facio omnibus, mihi ipse numquam satis facio; tanta enim
magnitudo est tuorum erga me meritorum, ut, quod tu nisi 5
perfecta re de me non conquiesti, ego quia non idem in tua
causa efficio, vitam mihi esse acerbam putem. In causa
haec sunt: Hammonius, regis legatus, aperte pecunia nos
oppugnat; res agitur per eosdem creditores, per quos, cum
tu aderas, agebatur; regis causa si qui sunt qui velint, qui 10
pauci sunt, omnes rem ad Pompeium deferri volunt, senatus
religionis calumniam non religione, sed malevolentia et illius
2 regiae largitionis invidia comprobat. Pompeium et hortari
et orare et iam liberius accusare et monere, ut magnam
infamiam fugiat, non desistimus; sed plane nec precibus 15
nostris nec admonitionibus relinquit locum, nam cum in
sermone cotidiano tum in senatu palam sic egit causam
tuam, ut neque eloquentia maiore quisquam nec gravitate
nec studio nec contentione agere potuerit, cum summa
testificatione tuorum in se officiorum et amoris erga te sui. 20
Marcellinum tibi esse iratum scis; is hac regia causa ex-
cepta ceteris in rebus se acerrimum tui defensorem fore
ostendit. Quod dat, accipimus; quod instituit referre de
religione et saepe iam retulit, ab eo deduci non potest.
3 Res ante Idus acta sic est (nam haec Idibus mane scripsi): 25
Hortensi et mea et Luculli sententia cedit religioni de
exercitu; teneri enim res aliter non potest; sed ex illo
senatus consulto, quod te referente factum est, tibi decernit,
ut regem reducas, quod commodo rei p. facere possis, ut
exercitum religio tollat, te auctorem senatus retineat. 30
Crassus tris legatos decernit nec excludit Pompeium, censet
enim etiam ex iis, qui cum imperio sint; Bibulus tris legatos
ex iis, qui privati sunt. Huic adsentiuntur reliqui consulares

praeter Servilium, qui omnino reduci negat oportere, et
35 Volcacium, qui Lupo referente Pompeio decernit, et Afranium, qui adsentitur Volcacio. Quae res auget suspicionem
Pompei voluntatis, nam advertebatur Pompei familiaris
adsentiri Volcacio. Laboratur vehementer; inclinata res est.
Libonis et Hypsaei non obscura concursatio et contentio
40 omniumque Pompei familiarium studium in eam opinionem
rem adduxerunt, ut Pompeius cupere videatur; cui qui
nolunt, idem tibi, quod eum ornasti, non sunt amici; nos 4
in causa auctoritatem eo minorem habemus, quod tibi
debemus, gratiam autem nostram exstinguit hominum
45 suspicio, quod Pompeio se gratificari putant. Ut in rebus
multo ante, quam profectus es, ab ipso rege et ab intimis ac
domesticis Pompei clam exulceratis, deinde palam a consularibus exagitatis et in summam invidiam adductis ita versa-
mur. Nostram fidem omnes, amorem tui absentis praesentes
50 tui cognoscent. Si esset in iis fides, in quibus summa esse
debebat, non laboraremus.

LETTER 11

Cicero to his brother Quintus. 12–15 February 56

This is one of the most fascinating letters in the whole corpus of
Cicero's correspondence. It tells of the exciting and turbulent events
at Rome in the first half of February 56 in a breathless and staccato
style, and with a vividness and gusto that two thousand years are
powerless to dim. The projected trial of Milo brought Pompey into
a head-on collision with Clodius and Crassus. The partnership
cemented by Caesar in 59 lay in ruins, and Roman politics seemed to
be teetering on the brink of a totally new alignment. Gangs clashed in
the streets, and Pompey began to summon up his supporters from the
country. Cicero can scarcely contain his excitement. His Micawberish
side once again takes control, and he is convinced that 'something is

bound to turn up'. In these racy paragraphs he gives his absent brother, and us, a ringside seat from which to watch the show.

Scr. Romae prid. Id. Febr. et data xv Kal. Mart. an. 56.

MARCVS QVINTO FRATRI SALVTEM.

1 Scripsi ad te antea superiora; nunc cognosce postea quae sint acta. Kal. Febr. legationes in Id. Febr. reiciebantur; eo die res confecta non est. A. d. IIII Non. Febr. Milo adfuit; ei Pom- 5 peius advocatus venit; dixit M. Marcellus a me rogatus; honeste discessimus; prodicta dies est in VII Id. Febr. Interim reiectis legationibus in Idus referebatur de provinciis quaestorum et de ornandis praetoribus; sed res multis querelis de re publica interponendis nulla transacta est. C. Cato legem promulgavit 10 de imperio Lentuli abrogando; vestitum filius mutavit.

2 A. d. VII Id. Febr. Milo adfuit. Dixit Pompeius sive voluit; nam, ut surrexit, operae Clodianae clamorem sustulerunt, idque ei perpetua oratione contigit, non modo ut acclama- tione sed ut convicio et maledictis impediretur. Qui ut per- 15 oravit (nam in eo sane fortis fuit; non est deterritus; dixit omnia atque interdum etiam silentio, cum auctoritate per- vicerat)—sed ut peroravit, surrexit Clodius. Ei tantus clamor a nostris (placuerat enim referre gratiam) ut neque mente nec lingua neque ore consisteret. Ea res acta est, cum hora sexta 20 vix Pompeius perorasset, usque ad horam octavam, cum omnia maledicta, versus denique obscenissimi in Clodium et Clodiam dicerentur. Ille furens et exsanguis interrogabat suos in clamore ipso quis esset qui plebem fame necaret; respon- debant operae 'Pompeius'. Quis Alexandriam ire cuperet; re- 25 spondebant 'Pompeius'. Quem ire vellent; respondebant 'Crassum' (is aderat tum, Miloni animo non amico). Hora fere nona quasi signo dato Clodiani nostros consputare coeperunt; exarsit dolor. Vrgere illi ut loco nos moverent; factus est a nostris impetus; fuga operarum; eiectus de rostris Clodius, 30

ac nos quoque tum fugimus, ne quid in turba. Senatus vo-
catus in curiam; Pompeius domum; neque ego tamen in
senatum, ne aut de tantis rebus tacerem aut in Pompeio
defendendo (nam is carpebatur a Bibulo, Curione, Favonio,
35 Servilio filio) animos bonorum virorum offenderem; res in
posterum dilata est. Clodius in Quirinalia prodixit diem.

A. d. vi Id. Febr. senatus ad Apollinis fuit, ut Pompeius 3
adesset; acta res est graviter a Pompeio; eo die nihil per-
fectum est. A. d. v. Id. Febr. senatus ad Apollinis; senatus
40 consultum factum est ea quae facta essent a. d. vii Id. Febr.
contra rem publicam esse facta. Eo die Cato vehementer est
in Pompeium invectus et eum oratione perpetua tamquam
reum accusavit; de me multa me invito cum mea summa laude
dixit, cum illius in me perfidiam increparet; auditus est
45 magno silentio malevolorum. Respondit ei vehementer Pompeius Crassumque descripsit dixitque aperte se munitiorem
ad custodiendam vitam suam fore quam Africanus fuisset,
quem C. Carbo interemisset. Itaque magnae mihi res iam 4
moveri videbantur. Nam Pompeius haec intellegit nobis-
50 cumque communicat, insidias vitae suae fieri, C. Catonem a
Crasso sustentari, Clodio pecuniam suppeditari, utrumque et
ab eo et a Curione, Bibulo, ceterisque suis obtrectatoribus
confirmari; vehementer esse providendum ne opprimatur,
contionario illo populo a se prope alienato, nobilitate inimica,
55 non aequo senatu, iuventute improba; itaque se comparat,
homines ex agris accersit. Operas autem suas Clodius confirmat; manus ad Quirinalia paratur. In ea multo sumus
superiores ipsius Milonis copiis; sed magna manus ex Piceno
et Gallia exspectatur, ut etiam Catonis rogationibus de
60 Milone et Lentulo resistamus.

A. d. iiii Id. Febr. Sestius ab indice Cn. Nerio Pupinia 5
de ambitu est postulatus et eodem die a quodam M. Tullio
de vi. Is erat aeger. Domum, ut debuimus, ad eum statim
venimus eique nos totos tradidimus idque fecimus praeter

hominum opinionem, qui nos ei iure suscensere putabant, 65
ut humanissimi gratissimique et ipsi et omnibus videremur,
itaque faciemus. Eodem die senatus consultum factum est ut
sodalitates decuriatique discederent lexque de iis ferretur, ut
qui non discessissent ea poena quae est de vi tenerentur.

6 A. d. III Id. Febr. dixi pro Bestia de ambitu apud prae- 70
torem Cn. Domitium in foro medio maximo conventu incidique in eum locum in dicendo, cum Sestius multis in
templo Castoris vulneribus acceptis subsidio Bestiae servatus
esset. Hic προῳκονομησάμην quiddam εὐκαίρως de iis quae
in Sestium adparabantur crimina, et eum ornavi veris lau- 75
dibus magno adsensu omnium; res homini fuit vehementer
grata. Quae tibi eo scribo, quod me de retinenda Sesti gratia
litteris saepe monuisti.

7 Prid. Id. Febr. haec scripsi ante lucem; eo die apud
Pomponium in eius nuptiis eram cenaturus. Cetera sunt in 80
rebus nostris cuius modi tu mihi fere diffidenti praedicabas,
plena dignitatis et gratiae; quae quidem tua, mi frater,
patientia, virtute, pietate, suavitate etiam tibi mihique sunt
restituta. Domus tibi ad lacum Pisonis Liciniana conducta est,
sed, ut spero, paucis mensibus post Kal. Quint. in tuam com- 85
migrabis; tuam in Carinis mundi habitatores Lamiae conduxerunt. A te post illam Vlbiensem epistulam nullas litteras
accepi; quid agas et ut te oblectes scire cupio maximeque te
ipsum videre quam primum. Cura, mi frater, ut valeas et,
quamquam est hiems, tamen Sardiniam istam esse cogites. 90
xv Kal. Mart.

LETTER 12

Cicero to Atticus. Late June 56

A lot has happened since February. As relations between Pompey and
Crassus worsened, Cicero became increasingly confident that the
'First Triumvirate' had broken beyond repair, and he moved in to the

attack. Defending Sestius at his trial *de vi*, he took the chance offered by the cross-examination of the prosecution witness Vatinius to inveigh against the violence and irregularities of the year 59, when Vatinius as tribune had been one of Caesar's prominent assistants. Sestius was acquitted by a unanimous verdict, which further encouraged Cicero in his hopes of another *annus mirabilis* like 63; and he began to see himself as the leader of an optimate revival. Pompey's apparently complacent attitude also strengthened him. On 5 April, Cicero proposed in the senate that the question of the Campanian Land (and hence of Caesar's agrarian legislation of 59) be discussed on 15 May. Still Pompey gave no hint of displeasure. But Pompey was only using Cicero to put pressure on Caesar. Caesar reacted quickly, and the alliance of himself and Pompey and Crassus was re-cemented at Lucca in north Italy in mid-April, with Pompey securing generous concessions as the price of coming back into line. Pompey promptly made it clear to Cicero that he must stop being awkward and behave himself. Disillusioned and powerless, Cicero capitulated. As he writes in this letter, 'Finis sit'. April 56 marks a clear watershed in Cicero's career. Henceforth we are confronted with Cicero the realist, who recognizes that he cannot hope to be a controlling influence in politics and resigns himself increasingly to the role of observer and commentator. Only after Caesar's murder in March 44 does he re-emerge to assume the political leadership of the fight to save the Republic.

(I have discussed the controversial issue of Cicero's political position and behaviour in 57 and 56 in detail in 'Cicero and the *Ager Campanus*', *TAPA* 93 (1962) 471–89.)

In this letter Cicero tells Atticus about the decision he has taken, and about his formal recantation of his independent position. He is perhaps not being entirely honest with Atticus, or with himself.

Scr. Anti mense Iun. (ut vid.) an. 56.

CICERO ATTICO SALVTEM.

Ain tandem? me existimas ab ullo malle mea legi pro- 1 barique quam a te? Cur igitur cuiquam misi prius? Vrgebar 5 ab eo ad quem misi, et non habebam exemplar. Quin etiam

(iam dudum enim circumrodo quod devorandum est) subturpicula mihi videbatur esse παλινῳδία. Sed valeant recta
vera honesta consilia. Non est credibile quae sit perfidia in
istis principibus, ut volunt esse et ut essent si quicquam
haberent fidei. Senseram noram inductus relictus proiectus 10
ab iis; tamen hoc eram animo, ut cum iis in re publica con-
sentirem. Idem erant qui fuerant; vix aliquando te auctore
2 resipivi. Dices eatenus te suasisse qua tacerem, non etiam ut
scriberem. Ego me hercule mihi necessitatem volui imponere
huius novae coniunctionis, ne qua mihi liceret labi ad illos qui 15
etiam tum cum misereri mei debent non desinunt invidere.
Sed tamen modici fuimus 'ἀποθεώσει', ut scripsisti:
erimus uberiores si et ille libenter accipiet et ii subringentur
qui villam me moleste ferunt habere quae Catuli fuerat, a
Vettio emisse non cogitant; qui domum negant oportuisse me 20
aedificare, vendere aiunt oportuisse (sed quid ad hos?); et
quibus sententiis dixi quod ei ipsi probarent, laetati sunt
tamen me contra Pompei voluntatem dixisse. Finis sit;
quoniam qui nihil possunt ii me nolunt amare, demus operam
3 ut ab iis qui possunt diligamur. Dices 'vellem iam pridem'. 25
Scio te voluisse et me asinum germanum fuisse. Sed iam tempus
est me ipsum a me amari, quando ab illis nullo modo possum.

Domum meam quod crebro invisis est mihi valde gratum.
Viaticam Crassipes praeripit. Tu 'de via recta in hortos?'
Videtur commodius; ad te postridie scilicet; quid enim tua? 30
sed viderimus. Bibliothecam mihi tui pinxerunt cum
structione et sillybis; eos velim laudes.

LETTER 13

Cicero to Atticus. 22 April 55

The best part of a year has gone by since Cicero capitulated to the
realities of power politics (Letter 12). This present letter is fairly

typical of his mood at this time: detached and reflective, disillusioned
but interested in what is going on at Rome, and devoting much of his
time to literary activity in which he can find occupation and a release
for his energies. In 55 he finished the three books of the *de oratore*, and
another work on rhetoric, *oratoriae partitiones*, probably dates from
the following year; and the *de optimo genere oratorum* saw the light in
52. Apart from works on rhetoric, the six books *de re publica* were
published in 51, and the *de legibus* had been begun in 52.

Scr. in Cumano ix Kal. Mai. an. 55.

⟨CICERO ATTICO SALVTEM.⟩

Puteolis magnus est rumor Ptolomaeum esse in regno; 1
si quid habes certius velim scire.

5   Ego hic pascor bibliotheca Fausti. Fortasse tu putabas
his rebus Puteolanis et Lucrinensibus; ne ista quidem desunt,
sed me hercule ut ceteris oblectationibus deseror et taedet
voluptatum propter rem publicam, sic litteris sustentor et
recreor, maloque in illa tua sedecula quam habes sub imagine
10 Aristotelis sedere quam in istorum sella curuli tecumque
apud te ambulare quam cum eo quocum video esse ambulan-
dum. Sed de illa ambulatione fors viderit aut si quis est qui
curet deus: nostram ambulationem et Laconicum eaque 2
quae Cyrea sint velim quod poterit invisas et urgeas Philo-
15 timum ut properet, ut possim tibi aliquid in eo genere
respondere.

Pompeius in Cumanum Parilibus venit; misit ad me
statim qui salutem nuntiaret. Ad eum postridie mane vade-
bam, cum haec scripsi.

LETTER 14

Cicero to Marcus Marius. October 55

This letter is of a markedly different type from any of the preceding
letters in this collection, which are all genuine letters which it so happened were subsequently collected and published. True, two of them
(Letters 3 and 10) are studied compositions written in a formal style;
but for all that they were written to convey information and points
of view on matters of current importance and immediate relevance
to writer and recipient—they were real letters and not literary exer-
cises. But a literary exercise is precisely what we have here: an elegant
little essay on a conventional theme cast in the form of a letter
(apparently at the request of Marius: see section 6). It thus looks forward to the verse *Epistles* of Horace, the patently artificial and studied
Epistulae of Seneca, and the polished productions of the Younger Pliny
(on which see Sherwin-White, *Fifty Letters of Pliny* (Oxford, 1967)
xv–xviii). Without in any way disparaging the literary qualities and
social interest and very real charm of the later genre of literary letters,
we must count it our great good fortune that overwhelmingly in the
Ciceronian letters we discover that lively and uncontrived freshness
and vivid sense of immediate participation which can come only from
the day-to-day correspondence of an important political figure and
his close friends and acquaintances, written without thought for
publication or literary immortality.

In this letter to Marius, Cicero uses the occasion of the games given
by Pompey in autumn 55 as a hook on which to hang his little essay
on the tawdriness and banality of such entertainments when contrasted
with the civilized refinement of literary and intellectual pleasures.
Marcus Marius came, like Cicero himself, from Arpinum. He was
clearly a member of the family of that other famous citizen of
Arpinum, Gaius Marius, the conqueror of Jugurtha and of the Ger-
mans and bitter enemy of Sulla. Cicero's own family was connected
by marriage with the Marii. The first four letters of Book vii of
the *epistulae ad familiares* are addressed to Marius. He was a retiring
character of weak health (perhaps something of a hypochondriac),
but Cicero was genuinely fond of him.

Scr. Romae m. Oct. an. 55.

M. CICERO S. D. M. MARIO.

Si te dolor aliqui corporis aut infirmitas valetudinis tuae 1
tenuit quo minus ad ludos venires, fortunae magis tribuo
5 quam sapientiae tuae; sin haec, quae ceteri mirantur, con-
temnenda duxisti et, cum per valetudinem posses, venire
tamen noluisti, utrumque laetor, et sine dolore corporis te
fuisse et animo valuisse, cum ea, quae sine causa mirantur
alii, neglexeris, modo ut tibi constiterit fructus oti tui; quo
10 quidem tibi perfrui mirifice licuit, cum esses in ista amoenitate paene solus relictus. Neque tamen dubito quin tu in
illo cubiculo tuo, ex quo tibi Stabianum perforasti et patefecisti sinum, per eos dies matutina tempora lectiunculis
consumpseris, cum illi interea, qui te istic reliquerunt, spe-
15 ctarent communis mimos semisomni. Reliquas vero partis
diei tu consumebas iis delectationibus quas tibi ipse ad
arbitrium tuum compararas; nobis autem erant ea per-
petienda, quae Sp. Maecius probavisset. Omnino, si quae- 2
ris, ludi apparatissimi, sed non tui stomachi; coniecturam
20 enim facio de meo. Nam primum honoris causa in scae-
nam redierant ii, quos ego honoris causa de scaena decessisse
arbitrabar. Deliciae vero tuae, noster Aesopus, eius modi
fuit ut ei desinere per omnis homines liceret. Is iurare
cum coepisset, vox eum defecit in illo loco: 'Si sciens
25 fallo.' Quid tibi ego alia narrem? nosti enim reliquos
ludos; qui ne id quidem leporis habuerunt, quod solent
mediocres ludi. Apparatus enim spectatio tollebat omnem
hilaritatem, quo quidem apparatu non dubito quin animo
aequissimo carueris. Quid enim delectationis habent ses-
30 centi muli in 'Clytaemestra' aut in 'Equo Troiano'
creterrarum tria milia aut armatura varia peditatus et equitatus in aliqua pugna? quae popularem admirationem
habuerunt, delectationem tibi nullam attulissent. Quod si 3

tu per eos dies operam dedisti Protogeni tuo, dum modo
is tibi quidvis potius quam orationes meas legerit, ne tu 35
haud paulo plus quam quisquam nostrum delectationis
habuisti. Non enim te puto Graecos aut Oscos ludos
desiderasse, praesertim cum Oscos vel in senatu vestro
spectare possis, Graecos ita non ames ut ne ad villam
quidem tuam via Graeca ire soleas. Nam quid ego te 40
athletas putem desiderare, qui gladiatores contempseris? in
quibus ipse Pompeius confitetur se et operam et oleum
perdidisse. Reliquae sunt venationes binae per dies quin-
que, magnificae, nemo negat; sed quae potest homini esse
polito delectatio, cum aut homo imbecillus a valentissima 45
bestia laniatur aut praeclara bestia venabulo transverberatur?
Quae tamen, si videnda sunt, saepe vidisti; neque nos, qui
haec spectamus, quicquam novi vidimus. Extremus ele-
phantorum dies fuit. In quo admiratio magna vulgi atque
turbae, delectatio nulla exstitit; quin etiam misericordia 50
quaedam consecuta est atque opinio eius modi, esse quan-
dam illi beluae cum genere humano societatem.

4 His ego tamen diebus ludis scaenicis, ne forte videar tibi
non modo beatus sed liber omnino fuisse, dirupi me paene
in iudicio Galli Canini, familiaris tui. Quod si tam facilem 55
populum haberem quam Aesopus habuit, libenter me hercule artem desinerem tecumque et cum similibus nostri
viverem. Nam me cum antea taedebat, cum et aetas et
ambitio me hortabatur, et licebat denique, quem nolebam,
non defendere, tum vero hoc tempore vita nulla est. Neque 60
enim fructum ullum laboris exspecto et cogor non numquam homines non optime de me meritos rogatu eorum, qui
5 bene meriti sunt, defendere. Itaque quaero causas omnis
aliquando vivendi arbitratu meo teque et istam rationem
oti tui et laudo vehementer et probo, quodque nos minus 65
intervisis, hoc fero animo aequiore, quod, si Romae esses,
tamen neque nos lepore tuo neque te, si qui est in me,

meo frui liceret propter molestissimas occupationes meas.
Quibus si me relaxaro (nam, ut plane exsolvam, non pos-
70 tulo), te ipsum, qui multos annos nihil aliud commentaris,
docebo profecto quid sit humaniter vivere. Tu modo
istam imbecillitatem valetudinis tuae sustenta et tuere, ut
facis, ut nostras villas obire et mecum simul lecticula concursare possis.

75   Haec ad te pluribus verbis scripsi quam soleo, non oti 6
abundantia sed amoris erga te, quod me quadam epistula
subinvitaras, si memoria tenes, ut ad te aliquid eius modi
scriberem, quo minus te praetermisisse ludos paeniteret.
Quod si adsecutus sum, gaudeo; sin minus, hoc me tamen
80 consolor, quod posthac ad ludos venies nosque vises neque
in epistulis relinques meis spem aliquam delectationis tuae.

LETTER 15

Cicero to Gaius Julius Caesar. April 54

Cicero writes to recommend his young friend Gaius Trebatius for an
appointment on Caesar's staff in Gaul. Roman society had many
features in common with our own up to well into the nineteenth
century, here we may note the fact that public appointments and advancement—and indeed wide tracts of public and business life—depended heavily on patronage and influence, on *gratia* and reciprocal
services. Cicero wrote a great many letters of recommendation on
behalf of friends (and friends of friends) and men of business asking
that the addressee (frequently a provincial governor or quaestor) give
them an appointment or treat them with some special consideration.
This particular letter exemplifies this facet of Roman life (still going
strong 150 years later, as the letters of the Younger Pliny show),
although it is fuller and warmer than most such letters, since
Trebatius was a close friend.

   Gaius Trebatius was a rising young jurisconsult, who was hoping to
gain experience, advancement, and (not least important) money in

Gaul and Britain from the activity and profits of conquest. In all, seventeen letters survive from Cicero to Trebatius (*ad famm.* vii. 6–22), stretching from 54 to 44. Early in 49, after the outbreak of civil war, he acted as an intermediary between Cicero and Caesar. To him, in 44, Cicero addressed his rhetorical work *Topica*; and the first Satire in the second book of Horace's Satires is a dialogue between Horace and Trebatius. He developed into a leading jurisconsult whose advice was sought by both Julius Caesar and Augustus, and he was the teacher of Antistius Labeo, one of the most famous jurisconsults of the early principate.

Scr. Romae m. Apr. an. 54.

CICERO CAESARI IMP. S. D.

1 Vide quam mihi persuaserim te me esse alterum non modo in iis rebus, quae ad me ipsum, sed etiam in iis, quae ad meos pertinent. C. Trebatium cogitaram, quocumque 5 exirem, mecum ducere, ut eum meis omnibus studiis, bene-ficiis quam ornatissimum domum reducerem; sed, postea quam et Pompei commoratio diuturnior erat quam putaram, et mea quaedam tibi non ignota dubitatio aut impedire profectionem meam videbatur aut certe tardare (vide quid 10 mihi sumpserim), coepi velle ea Trebatium exspectare a te, quae sperasset a me, neque me hercule minus ei prolixe de tua voluntate promisi quam eram solitus de mea polliceri. 2 Casus vero mirificus quidam intervenit quasi vel testis opinionis meae vel sponsor humanitatis tuae. Nam cum de 15 hoc ipso Trebatio cum Balbo nostro loquerer accuratius domi meae, litterae mihi dantur a te, quibus in extremis scriptum erat: 'M. Titinium, quem mihi commendas, vel regem Galliae faciam, vel hunc Leptae delega, si vis. Tu ad me alium mitte quem ornem.' Sustulimus manus et ego 20 et Balbus. Tanta fuit opportunitas, ut illud nescio quid non fortuitum, sed divinum videretur. Mitto igitur ad te Trebatium atque ita mitto ut initio mea sponte, post autem 3 invitatu tuo mittendum duxerim. Hunc, mi Caesar, sic

25 velim omni tua comitate complectare, ut omnia, quae per
me possis adduci ut in meos conferre velis, in unum hunc
conferas. De quo tibi homine haec spondeo non illo vetere
verbo meo, quod cum ad te de Milone scripsissem, iure
lusisti, sed more Romano, quo modo homines non inepti
30 loquuntur, probiorem hominem, meliorem virum, pudentiorem esse neminem; accedit etiam, quod familiam ducit in
iure civili singulari memoria, summa scientia. Huic ego
neque tribunatum neque praefecturam neque ullius benefici
certum nomen peto, benevolentiam tuam et liberalitatem peto
35 neque impedio quo minus, si tibi ita placuerit, etiam hisce
eum ornes gloriolae insignibus; totum denique hominem
tibi ita trado, 'de manu', ut aiunt, 'in manum' tuam istam
et victoria et fide praestantem. Simus enim putidiusculi,
quamquam per te vix licet; verum, ut video, licebit. Cura
40 ut valeas, et me, ut amas, ama.

LETTER 16

Cicero to Gaius Trebatius. May 54

This, and the following letter, carry the story of Trebatius' service in
Gaul and Britain a little further. It is evident that Trebatius, like
Cicero himself a few years later in Cilicia, found provincial service
distasteful and was homesick for Rome.

Scr. in Cumano aut Pompeiano m. Mai. an 54.

CICERO S. D. TREBATIO.

In omnibus meis epistulis, quas ad Caesarem aut ad 1
Balbum mitto, legitima quaedam est accessio commenda-
5 tionis tuae, nec ea vulgaris sed cum aliquo insigni indicio
meae erga te benevolentiae. Tu modo ineptias istas et
desideria urbis et urbanitatis depone et, quo consilio

profectus es, id adsiduitate et virtute consequere. Hoc tibi
tam ignoscemus nos amici, quam ignoverunt Medeae,

   'Quaé Corinthum arcem áltam habebant mátronae opu- 10
   lentae, óptimates,'

quibus illa manibus gypsatissimis persuasit ne sibi vitio illae
verterent, quod abesset a patria; nam

   'Múlti suam rem béne gessere et públicam patriá procul;
   Múlti, qui domi aétatem agerent, própterea sunt ímpro- 15
   bati.'

2 Quo in numero tu certe fuisses, nisi te extrusissemus. Sed
plura scribemus alias. Tu, qui ceteris cavere didicisti, in
Britannia ne ab essedariis decipiaris caveto et (quoniam
Medeam coepi agere) illud semper memento: 20

   'Qui ípse sibi sapiéns prodesse nón quit, nequiquám sapit.'
Cura ut valeas.

LETTER 17

Cicero to Gaius Trebatius. Late June 54

Scr. Romae ex. m. Iun. an. 54.

CICERO TREBATIO.

1 Ego te commendare non desisto, sed quid proficiam ex
te scire cupio. Spem maximam habeo in Balbo, ad quem
de te diligentissime et saepissime scribo. Illud soleo mirari, 5
non me totiens accipere tuas litteras, quotiens a Quinto
mihi fratre adferantur. In Britannia nihil esse audio neque
auri neque argenti. Id si ita est, essedum aliquod capias
2 suadeo et ad nos quam primum recurras. Sin autem sine
Britannia tamen adsequi quod volumus possumus, perfice 1
ut sis in familiaribus Caesaris. Multum te in eo frater ad-
iuvabit meus, multum Balbus, sed, mihi crede, tuus pudor et
labor plurimum. Habes imperatorem liberalissimum, aetatem

opportunissimam, commendationem certe singularem, ut tibi
15 unum timendum sit ne ipse tibi defuisse videare.

LETTER 18

Cicero to his brother Quintus. June 54

Early in 54 Quintus resigned his legateship under Pompey and transferred to Gaul to serve as legate to Caesar. It is possible that to begin
with the transfer was to some degree intended to serve as a guarantee
to Caesar for Marcus' good behaviour; but Quintus soon won
Caesar's friendship and favour, and Marcus himself quickly fell under
the spell of Caesar's charm and courtesy. Of course Cicero was aware
that what he wrote in his letters to his brother in Gaul might come to
the notice of Caesar, but the growing warmth of his feelings towards
Caesar can also be seen in the letters he wrote to Atticus.

Scr. Romae in. mense Iun. an. 54.

MARCVS QVINTO FRATRI SALVTEM.

A. d. IIII Non. Iun., quo die Romam veni, accepi tuas 1
litteras datas Placentia, deinde alteras postridie datas Blan-
5 denone cum Caesaris litteris refertis omni officio, diligentia,
suavitate. Sunt ista quidem magna vel potius maxima
(habent enim vim magnam ad gloriam et ad summam dignitatem); sed, mihi crede quem nosti, quod in istis rebus ego
plurimi aestimo, id iam habeo, te scilicet primum tam inser-
10 vientem communi dignitati, deinde Caesaris tantum in me
amorem, quem omnibus iis honoribus quos me a se exspectare
vult antepono. Litterae vero eius una datae cum tuis, quarum
initium est quam suavis ei tuus adventus fuerit et recordatio
veteris amoris, deinde se effecturum ut ego in medio dolore
15 ac desiderio tui te, cum a me abesses, potissimum secum esse
aetarer, incredibiliter delectarunt. Qua re facis tu quidem 2

fraterne quod me hortaris, sed me hercule currentem nunc
quidem, ut omnia mea studia in istum unum conferam. Ego
vero ardenti quidem studio, ac fortasse efficiam quod saepe
viatoribus cum properant evenit, ut, si serius quam voluerint 20
forte surrexerint, properando etiam citius quam si de nocte
vigilassent perveniant quo velint; sic ego, quoniam in isto
homine colendo tam indormivi diu te me hercule saepe ex-
citante, cursu corrigam tarditatem cum equis tum vero
(quoniam tu scribis poema ab eo nostrum probari) quadrigis 25
poeticis; modo mihi date Britanniam quam pingam coloribus
tuis, penicillo meo. Sed quid ago? quod mihi tempus, Romae
praesertim (ut iste me rogat) manenti, vacuum ostenditur?
Sed videro; fortasse enim, ut fit, vincet unus amor omnis
difficultates. 30

3 Trebatium quod ad se miserim persalse et humaniter etiam
gratias mihi agit; negat enim in tanta multitudine eorum qui
una essent quemquam fuisse qui vadimonium concipere posset. M. Curtio tribunatum ab eo petivi (nam Domitius se
derideri putasset, si esset a me rogatus; hoc enim est eius 35
cottidianum, se ne tribunum militum quidem facere; etiam
in senatu lusit Appium conlegam propterea isse ad Caesarem
ut aliquem tribunatum auferret), sed in alterum annum; id
et Curtius ita volebat.

4 Tu quem ad modum me censes oportere esse et in re 40
publica et in nostris inimicitiis, ita et esse et fore oricula
5 infima scito molliorem. Res Romanae se sic habebant: erat
non nulla spes comitiorum sed incerta, erat aliqua suspicio
dictaturae, ne ea quidem certa, summum otium forense sed
senescentis magis civitatis quam adquiescentis, sententia autem 45
nostra in senatu eius modi magis ut alii nobis adsentiantur
quam nosmet ipsi.

   Τοιαῦθ' ὁ τλήμων πόλεμος ἐξεργάζεται.

LETTER 19

Cicero to his brother Quintus. August 54

Cicero writes to tell his brother how very busy he is just now, and
to give him the latest news about what is going on in the senate and
in the lawcourts. He congratulates Quintus on his safe arrival in
Britain, and asks him for a frank report of Caesar's opinion about a
poem he has written.

Scr. Romae ex. mense Sext. an. 54.

MARCVS QVINTO FRATRI SALVTEM.

Cum a me litteras librari manu acceperis, ne paulum **1**
quidem me oti habuisse iudicato, cum autem mea, paulum;
5 sic enim habeto, numquam me a causis et iudiciis districtiorem fuisse, atque id anni tempore gravissimo et caloribus
maximis. Sed haec, quoniam tu ita praescribis, ferenda sunt,
neque committendum ut aut spei aut cogitationi vestrae ego
videar defuisse, praesertim cum, si id difficilius fuerit, tamen
10 ex hoc labore magnam gratiam magnamque dignitatem sim
conlecturus. Itaque, ut tibi placet, damus operam ne cuius
animum offendamus, atque ut etiam ab iis ipsis qui nos cum
Caesare tam coniunctos dolent diligamur, ab aequis vero aut
etiam a propensis in hanc partem vehementer et colamur et
15 amemur. De ambitu cum atrocissime ageretur in senatu mul- **2**
tos dies, quod ita erant progressi candidati consulares ut non
esset ferendum, in senatu non fui; statui ad nullam medicinam
rei publicae sine magno praesidio accedere.

Quo die haec scripsi Drusus erat de praevaricatione a tri- **3**
20 bunis aerariis absolutus in summa quattuor sententiis, cum
senatores et equites damnassent. Ego eodem die post meri-
diem Vatinium eram defensurus; ea res facilis est. Comitia in
mensem Septembrem reiecta sunt. Scauri iudicium statim
exercebitur, cui nos non deerimus. Συνδείπνους Σοφοκλέους,

quamquam a te factam fabellam video esse festive, nullo modo 25
probavi.

4   Venio nunc ad id quod nescio an primum esse debuerit.
O iucundas mihi tuas de Britannia litteras! Timebam Ocea-
num, timebam litus insulae; reliqua non equidem contemno,
sed plus habent tamen spei quam timoris, magisque sum sollici- 30
tus exspectatione ea quam metu. Te vero ὑπόθεσιν scribendi
egregiam habere video: quos tu situs, quas naturas rerum et
locorum, quos mores, quas gentis, quas pugnas, quem vero
ipsum imperatorem habes! Ego te libenter, ut rogas, quibus
rebus vis, adiuvabo et tibi versus quos rogas, γλαῦκ᾽ εἰς Ἀθή- 35
5 νας, mittam. Sed heus tu! celari videor a te. Quomodonam,
mi frater, de nostris versibus Caesar? Nam primum librum se
legisse scripsit ad me ante, et prima sic ut neget se ne Graeca
quidem meliora legisse; reliqua ad quendam locum ῥαθυμότερα
(hoc enim utitur verbo). Dic mihi verum, num aut res eum 40
aut χαρακτὴρ non delectat? Nihil est quod vereare; ego enim
ne pilo quidem minus me amabo. Hac de re φιλαληθῶς et, ut
soles scribere, fraterne.

LETTER 20

Cicero to his brother Quintus. November 54

Quintus has just got over a brief bout of irritation and complaining
brought on by his distaste for military life. Marcus assures him that he
need be patient only a little longer, and warns him to be careful what
he says in his letters. He says that he will try to finish his poem for
Caesar, and then goes on to give the latest news about the unsettled
state of politics at Rome.

Scr. Romae ex. mense Nov. an. 54.

MARCVS QVINTO FRATRI SALVTEM.

Superiori epistulae quod respondeam nihil est, quae plena **1**
stomachi et querelarum est, quo in genere alteram quoque
5 te scribis pridie Labieno dedisse, quae adhuc non venerat;
delevit enim mihi omnem molestiam recentior epistula. Tantum te et moneo et rogo ut in istis molestiis et laboribus et
desideriis recordere consilium nostrum quod fuerit profecti-
onis tuae. Non enim commoda quaedam sequebamur parva
10 ac mediocria. Quid enim erat quod discessu nostro emendum
putaremus? Praesidium firmissimum petebamus ex optimi et
potentissimi viri benevolentia ad omnem statum nostrae
dignitatis. Plura ponuntur in spe quam petimus; reliqua ad
iacturam reserventur. Qua re, si crebro referes animum tuum
15 ad rationem et veteris consili nostri et spei, facilius istos
militiae labores ceteraque quae te offendunt feres et tamen
cum voles depones; sed eius rei maturitas nequedum venit et
tamen iam adpropinquat. Etiam illud te admoneo, ne quid **2**
ullis litteris committas quod si prolatum sit moleste fera-
20 mus; multa sunt quae ego nescire malo quam cum aliquo
periculo fieri certior. Plura ad te vacuo animo scribam cum,
ut spero, se Cicero meus belle habebit. Tu velim cures ut
sciam quibus nos dare oporteat eas quas ad te deinde litteras
mittemus, Caesarisne tabellariis ut is ad te protinus mittat, an
25 Labieni; ubi enim isti sint Nervii et quam longe absint nescio.

De virtute et gravitate Caesaris, quam in summo dolore **3**
adhibuisset, magnam ex epistula tua cepi voluptatem. Quod
me institutum ad illum poema iubes perficere, etsi distentus
cum opera tum animo sum multo magis, tamen quoniam ex
30 epistula quam ad te miseram cognovit Caesar me aliquid esse
exorsum, revertar ad institutum idque perficiam his supplicationum otiosis diebus, quibus Messalam iam nostrum
reliquosque molestia levatos vehementer gaudeo; eumque

quod certum consulem cum Domitio numeratis nihil a nostra
opinione dissentitis. Ego Messalam Caesari praestabo. Sed 35
Memmius in adventu Caesaris habet spem; in quo illum puto
errare; hic quidem friget. Scaurum autem iam pridem Pom-
4 peius abiecit. Res prolatae; ad interregnum comitia adducta.
Rumor dictatoris iniucundus bonis, mihi etiam magis quae
loquuntur; sed tota res et timetur et refrigescit. Pompeius 40
plane se negat velle; antea mihi ipse non negabat. Hirrus
auctor fore videtur, o di, quam ineptus, quam se ipse amans
sine rivali! Crassum Iunianum, hominem mihi deditum, per
me deterruit. Velit nolit scire difficile est; Hirro tamen agente
nolle se non probabit. Aliud hoc tempore de re publica nihil 45
5 loquebantur; agebatur quidem certe nihil. Serrani Domestici
fili funus perluctuosum fuit a. d. VIII Kal. Dec.; laudavit
pater scripto meo.
6 Nunc de Milone. Pompeius ei nihil tribuit et omnia Guttae
dicitque se perfecturum ut in illum Caesar incumbat; hoc 50
horret Milo nec iniuria et, si ille dictator factus sit, paene
diffidit. Intercessorem dictaturae si iuverit manu et praesidio
suo, Pompeium metuit inimicum; si non iuverit, timet ne
per vim perferatur. Ludos adparat magnificentissimos, sic,
inquam, ut nemo sumptuosiores, stulte bis terque non postu- 55
latos, vel quia munus magnificum dederat vel quia facultates
non erant vel quia potuerat magistrum se non aedilem
putare. Omnia fere scripsi. Cura, mi carissime frater, ut
valeas.

LETTER 21

Marcus Caelius Rufus to Cicero. Late May 51

In 52 Pompey as consul (for the third time) passed a law changing the
system of provincial appointments. Henceforth consuls and praetors
were to go out to govern provinces only after the lapse of an interval
of five years from their tenure of their magistracies at Rome. For the

time being, until the new system could come into operation, ex-consuls and ex-praetors who had in the past declined to accept governorships were to be posted to provinces. So it was that Cicero found himself appointed to govern Cilicia in southern Asia Minor (Cyprus also came under his authority). He had been preceded as governor by his friend Lentulus Spinther (consul in 57) and by App. Claudius Pulcher (consul in 54).

Caelius Rufus was asked by Cicero to write to him while he was away to keep him *au fait* with what was going on at Rome. Seventeen letters written by him to Cicero make up the eighth book of the *epistulae ad familiares*, the first fourteen dating from this period of Cicero's governorship.

Caelius was a very close personal friend of Cicero's, though a good bit younger. Something of a gay young spark, he had at one time been an admirer of Catiline, was a friend of Catullus, and fell under the spell of Clodia, who turned against him and inspired his trial on a charge of attempted poisoning in 56. Cicero spoke in his defence with savage brilliance (the *pro Caelio*) and he was acquitted. Tribune in 52, he backed Milo against Pompey and was anything but friendly towards Caesar. He became aedile in 50, and chose Caesar's side when war broke out in 49. Rewarded with a praetorship, he met his death in a characteristically rash attempt to lead a popular insurrection along with his old friend Milo.

Cicero chose his correspondent well. Caelius' letters are marked by a strong taste for slang and mixed metaphors and an extraordinary liveliness and pungency. But behind his irreverence and apparent frivolity lay a shrewd and discerning mind and a tough appreciation of the realities of the political game. Cicero (Letter 22) said that Caelius had more flair for politics than anyone else he knew.

This is the first letter he wrote in his role as Cicero's personal political correspondent. It is a very good sample of his style and approach.

Scr. Romae ix. K. Iun. aut paulo post an. 51.

CAELIVS CICERONI S.

Quod tibi discedens pollicitus sum me omnis res urbanas **1** diligentissime tibi perscripturum, data opera paravi qui sic

omnia persequeretur, ut verear ne tibi nimium arguta haec 5
sedulitas videatur; tametsi tu scio quam sis curiosus et
quam omnibus peregrinantibus gratum sit minimarum quoque rerum, quae domi gerantur, fieri certiores. Tamen in
hoc te deprecor ne meum hoc officium adrogantiae condemnes, quod hunc laborem alteri delegavi, non quin mihi 10
suavissimum sit et occupato et ad litteras scribendas, ut tu
nosti, pigerrimo tuae memoriae dare operam, sed ipsum
volumen, quod tibi misi, facile, ut ego arbitror, me excusat.
Nescio quoius oti esset non modo perscribere haec sed
omnino animadvertere; omnia enim sunt ibi senatus con- 15
sulta, edicta, fabulae, rumores. Quod exemplum si forte
minus te delectarit, ne molestiam tibi cum impensa mea
exhibeam, fac me certiorem. Si quid in re p. maius actum
2 erit, quod isti operarii minus commode persequi possint, et
quem ad modum actum sit et quae existimatio secuta quae- 20
que de eo spes sit diligenter tibi perscribemus. Ut nunc
est, nulla magno opere exspectatio est. Nam et illi rumores
de comitiis Transpadanorum Cumarum tenus caluerunt,
Romam cum venissem, ne tenuissimam quidem auditionem
de ea re accepi; praeterea Marcellus, quod adhuc nihil 25
rettulit de successione provinciarum Galliarum et in K. Iun.,
ut mihi ipse dixit, eam distulit relationem, sane quam eos
sermones expressit, qui de eo tum fuerant cum Romae nos
essemus. Tu si Pompeium, ut volebas, offendisti, qui tibi
3 visus sit et quam orationem habuerit tecum quamque osten- 30
derit voluntatem (solet enim aliud sentire et loqui neque
tantum valere ingenio, ut non appareat quid cupiat), fac
mihi perscribas. Quod ad Caesarem, crebri et non belli de
4 eo rumores, sed susurratores dumtaxat, veniunt. Alius
equitem perdidisse, quod, opinor, certe factum est, alius 35
septimam legionem vapulasse, ipsum apud Bellovacos cir-
cumsederi interclusum ab reliquo exercitu; neque adhuc
certi quicquam est, neque haec incerta tamen vulgo iactan-

tur, sed inter paucos quos tu nosti palam secreto narrantur;
40 at Domitius, cum manus ad os apposuit. Te a. d. VIIII
K. Iun. subrostrani (quod illorum capiti sit!) dissiparant
perisse. Urbe ac foro toto maximus rumor fuit te a
Q. Pompeio in itinere occisum. Ego qui scirem Q. Pompeium Baulis embaeneticam facere et usque eo ut ego
45 miserer eius esurire, non sum commotus et hoc mendacio, si qua pericula tibi impenderent, ut defungeremur
optavi. Plancus quidem tuus Ravennae est et magno congiario donatus a Caesare nec beatus nec bene instructus est.
Tui politici libri omnibus vigent.

LETTER 22

Cicero to Caelius Rufus. 6 July 51

Cicero writes from Athens insisting that he does not want to hear from
Caelius about trivial details of no importance or interest, nor even
about major political events at Rome (unless they affect him personally). He wants Caelius' own informed opinions about the pattern
of politics at Rome, how it is shaping, what is likely to happen.

Cicero himself practised what he preached. Writing to Lentulus
Spinther in February 56, when Spinther was away in Cilicia, he had
had this to say: 'What is happening here at Rome, and what has happened, I imagine you already know through letters and reports from
a lot of people. But as to what is matter for conjecture or looks like
happening, these are the things I think *I* ought to write to you about'
(*ad fam.* i. 5b. 1). As with himself in 56, so now it is Caelius' proper
task to add the cream of speculation from an informed source.

Scr. Athenis prid. Non. Quint. an. 51.

M. CICERO PROCOS. S. D. M. CAELIO.

Quid? tu me hoc tibi mandasse existimas, ut mihi
gladiatorum compositiones, ut vadimonia dilata et Chresti 1

compilationem mitteres et ea, quae nobis, cum Romae sumus, 5
narrare nemo audeat? Vide, quantum tibi meo iudicio
tribuam (nec me hercule iniuria; πολιτικώτερον enim te adhuc neminem cognovi). Ne illa quidem curo mihi scribas,
quae maximis in rebus rei publicae geruntur cotidie, nisi
quid ad me ipsum pertinebit; scribent alii, multi nuntia- 10
bunt, perferet multa etiam ipse rumor. Qua re ego nec
praeterita nec praesentia abs te, sed ut ab homine longe in
posterum prospiciente futura exspecto, ut, ex tuis litteris cum
formam rei publicae viderim, quale aedificium futurum sit
2 scire possim. Neque tamen adhuc habeo quod te ac- 15
cusem; neque enim fuit quod tu plus providere posses
quam quivis nostrum in primisque ego, qui cum Pompeio
compluris dies nullis in aliis nisi de re publica sermonibus
versatus sum; quae nec possunt scribi nec scribenda sunt;
tantum habeto, civem egregium esse Pompeium et ad 20
omnia, quae providenda sunt in re publica, et animo et
consilio paratum. Qua re da te homini; complectetur, mihi
crede. Iam idem illi et boni et mali cives videntur, qui
nobis videri solent.

3   Ego cum Athenis decem ipsos dies fuissem multumque 25
mecum Gallus noster Caninius, proficiscebar inde pridie
Nonas Quintilis, cum hoc ad te litterarum dedi. Tibi cum
omnia mea commendatissima esse cupio tum nihil magis
quam ne tempus nobis provinciae prorogetur; in eo mihi
sunt omnia. Quod quando et quo modo et per quos agen- 30
dum sit, tu optime constitues.

LETTER 23

Cicero to Atticus. About 10 August 51

Cicero reached his province on the last day of July. He is now travelling from Synnada to Philomelium. In this hurried letter written

en route he tells Atticus of the sorry state in which he has found the province. He himself is being a model of correctness, and the local inhabitants entertain the highest hopes of their new governor. Appius Claudius is still active in the province. There is still no reliable news of Parthian movements and intentions. For a brief account of Cicero's governorship, see my essay 'Cicero's Year in Cilicia' in *History Today* (August, 1954) 548–55.

Scr. in itinere inter Synnada et Philomelium c. iv. Id. Sext. an. 51.

CICERO ATTICO SALVTEM.

Etsi in ipso itinere et via discedebant publicanorum tabel- **1**
larii et eramus in cursu, tamen surripiendum aliquid putavi
5 spati, ne me immemorem mandati tui putares. Itaque sub-
sedi in ipsa via, dum haec, quae longiorem desiderant
orationem, summatim tibi perscriberem.

Maxima exspectatione in perditam et plane eversam in **2**
perpetuum provinciam nos venisse scito prid. Kal. Sext.,
10 moratos triduum Laodiceae, triduum Apameae, totidem dies
Synnade. Audivimus nihil aliud nisi imperata ἐπικεφάλια
solvere non posse, ὠνὰς omnium venditas, civitatum gemitus
ploratus, monstra quaedam non hominis sed ferae nescio
cuius immanis; quid quaeris? taedet omnino eos vitae.
15 Levantur tamen miserae civitates quod nullus fit sumptus **3**
in nos neque in legatos neque in quaestorem neque in quemquam; scito non modo nos faenum aut quod e lege Iulia
dari solet non accipere sed ne ligna quidem, nec praeter
quattuor lectos et tectum quemquam accipere quicquam,
20 multis locis ne tectum quidem et in tabernaculo manere
plerumque. Itaque incredibilem in modum concursus fiunt
ex agris, ex vicis, ex oppidis omnibus; et omnes me hercule etiam adventu nostro reviviscunt, iustitia abstinentia
clementia tui Ciceronis cognita, quae opiniones omnium
25 superavit.

Appius ut audivit nos venire, in ultimam provinciam se **4** coniecit Tarsum usque; ibi forum agit. De Partho silentium est, sed tamen concisos equites nostros a barbaris nuntiabant ii qui veniebant. Bibulus ne cogitabat quidem etiam nunc in provinciam suam accedere; id autem facere ob eam causam 30 dicebant, quod tardius vellet decedere. Nos in castra properabamus, quae aberant bidui.

LETTER 24

Marcus Porcius Cato to Cicero. Late April or early May 50

The senate had voted that a decree be passed authorizing a solemn public thanksgiving (*supplicatio*) to honour Cicero's military achievements in Cilicia. Cato had voted against the decree, but he now writes to congratulate Cicero and at the same time to explain the reasoning behind his own opposition to the decree. The whole letter is painfully stiff and awkward, and in its way tells us a lot about Cato's stiff and awkward character. Cicero's reply follows next in this selection as Letter 25.

Scr. Romae vel ex. m. Apr. vel in. Mai. an. 50.

M. CATO S. D. M. CICERONI IMP.

1   Quod et res p. me et nostra amicitia hortatur, libenter facio ut tuam virtutem, innocentiam, diligentiam cognitam in maximis rebus domi togati, armati foris pari industria 5 administrare gaudeam. Itaque, quod pro meo iudicio facere potui, ut innocentia consilioque tuo defensam provinciam, servatum Ariobarzanis cum ipso rege regnum, sociorum revocatam ad studium imperi nostri voluntatem 2 sententia mea et decreto laudarem, feci. Supplicationem 10 decretam, si tu, qua in re nihil fortuito sed summa tua ratione et continentia rei p. provisum est, dis immortalibus

gratulari nos quam tibi referre acceptum mavis, gaudeo;
quod si triumphi praerogativam putas supplicationem et
15 idcirco casum potius quam te laudari mavis, neque supplica
tionem sequitur semper triumphus, et triumpho multo
clarius est senatum iudicare potius mansuetudine et innocentia imperatoris provinciam quam vi militum aut
benignitate deorum retentam atque conservatam esse; quod
20 ego mea sententia censebam.

Atque haec ego idcirco ad te contra consuetudinem 3
meam pluribus scripsi ut, quod maxime volo, existimes me
laborare ut tibi persuadeam me et voluisse de tua maies-
tate quod amplissimum sim arbitratus et quod tu maluisti
25 factum esse gaudere. Vale et nos dilige et instituto itinere
severitatem diligentiamque sociis et rei p. praesta.

LETTER 25

Cicero to Marcus Porcius Cato. Late July 51

Cato's letter was some time in reaching Cilicia and then catching up
with Cicero. In his reply Cicero cleverly masks his disappointment
under a show of formal politeness, but not without a delicate irony
which he probably knew would glance off Cato's thick skin making scarcely a scratch. The true depth and intensity of his annoyance
he reserved for his intimate letters to close friends. For the sake of
interest, I subjoin an extract from a letter to Atticus on this subject
(letter 25A).

Scr. Tarsi paulo ante iii K. Sext. an. 50.

M. CICERO S. D. M. CATONI.

'Laetus sum laudari me', inquit Hector, opinor, apud 1
Naevium, 'abs te, pater, a laudato viro.' Ea est enim pro-
5 fecto iucunda laus, quae ab iis proficiscitur, qui ipsi in

laude vixerunt. Ego vero vel gratulatione litterarum tuarum
vel testimoniis sententiae dictae nihil est quod me non
adsecutum putem, idque mihi cum amplissimum tum gratissimum est, te libenter amicitiae dedisse quod liquido
veritati dares. Et, si non modo omnes verum etiam multi 10
Catones essent in civitate nostra, in qua unum exstitisse
mirabile est, quem ego currum aut quam lauream cum tua
laudatione conferrem? Nam ad meum sensum et ad illud
sincerum ac subtile iudicium nihil potest esse laudabilius
quam ea tua oratio, quae est ad me perscripta a meis neces- 15
2 sariis. Sed causam meae voluntatis, non enim dicam
'cupiditatis', exposui tibi superioribus litteris; quae etiam si
parum iusta tibi visa est, hanc tamen habet rationem, non
ut nimis concupiscendus honos sed tamen, si deferatur
a senatu, minime aspernandus esse videatur. Spero autem 20
illum ordinem pro meis ob rem p. susceptis laboribus me
non indignum honore, usitato praesertim, existimaturum.
Quod si ita erit, tantum ex te peto, quod amicissime scribis,
ut, cum tuo iudicio quod amplissimum esse arbitraris
mihi tribueris, si id quod maluero acciderit, gaudeas. 25
Sic enim fecisse te et sensisse et scripsisse video, resque
ipsa declarat tibi illum honorem nostrum supplicationis
iucundum fuisse, quod scribendo adfuisti; haec enim senatus consulta non ignoro ab amicissimis eius, cuius de honore
agitur, scribi solere. Ego, ut spero, te propediem videbo, 30
atque utinam re p. meliore quam timeo!

LETTER 25A

Cicero to Atticus. Late November 50

Section 7 of *ad Att.* vii. 2 provides a remarkable contrast with Cicero's
letter to Cato. Here he tells Atticus how he *really* felt about Cato's

behaviour. 'I am eager to know what Hortensius has been doing, and what Cato is doing. Cato! His behaviour towards me has been disgracefully spiteful. He bore witness to my honesty, my clemency, my loyalty—but that was not what I was after. What I *was* asking him for, he refused. So, when Caesar writes to congratulate me [on the vote of a supplication] and promise me the earth, how he exults in his letter over the injustice this most ungrateful Cato has done me! Yet this same Cato proposed a twenty-day supplication for Bibulus. Forgive me: I cannot tolerate these things, nor shall I.'

The hollowness of Cato's professions and the insincerity of his remarks about 'supplications' was demonstrated when he himself supported the voting of a twenty-day supplication in honour of Bibulus—of whom Cicero remarked bitterly that 'so long as there was a single enemy soldier abroad in Syria he no more put his foot outside his front door than he did at Rome when he was consul' (*ad Att.* vi. 8. 5). It is perhaps churlish to point out that Bibulus was Cato's son-in-law.

Hortensius quid egerit aveo scire, Cato quid agat, qui **7** quidem in me turpiter fuit malevolus: dedit integritatis iustitiae clementiae fidei mihi testimonium, quod non quaerebam; quod postulabam negavit. Itaque Caesar iis 5 litteris quibus mihi gratulatur et omnia pollicetur quo modo exsultat Catonis in me ingratissimi iniuria! At hic idem Bibulo dierum xx. Ignosce mihi; non possum haec ferre nec feram.

LETTER 26

Marcus Caelius Rufus to Cicero. Early August 50

Caelius insists that Cicero is missing a great deal of fun by being away from Rome just now: he should have seen Ahenobarbus' face when Mark Antony beat him in the augurship election! War between Pompey and Caesar now seems unavoidable, since neither will make concessions: Caelius is wondering which horse to back. Meanwhile, there is Appius Claudius of all people trying to play the part of a strict and puritanical censor! Were it not for the great dangers involved, it would really be the most delightful show to watch.

Such is the spirit in which the eternally irrepressible Caelius views the rapidly approaching crisis which is to destroy the Roman Republic after nearly five hundred years of vigorous life. Caelius shows that it still had a lot of life and vigour left.

Scr. Romae in. m. Sext. an. 50.

CAELIVS CICERONI S.

1 Tanti non fuit Arsacen capere et Seleuceam expugnare, ut earum rerum quae hic gestae sunt spectaculo careres; numquam tibi oculi doluissent, si in repulsa Domiti vultum 5 vidisses. Magna illa comitia fuerunt, et plane studia ex partium sensu apparuerunt; perpauci necessitudinem secuti officium praestiterunt. Itaque mihi est Domitius inimicissimus ut ne familiarem quidem suum quemquam tam oderit quam me, atque eo magis quod per iniuriam sibi 10 putat ereptum auguratum, quoius ego auctor fuerim. Nunc furit tam gavisos homines suum dolorem inque ius vocat unum quemque studiosiorem Antoni; nam Cn. Saturninum adulescentem ipse Cn. Domitius reum fecit sane quam superiore a vita invidiosum; quod iudicium nunc in exspectatione 15 est, etiam in bona spe post Sex. Peducaei absolutionem.

2 De summa re publica saepe tibi scripsi me in annum pacem non videre et, quo propius ea contentio quam fieri necesse est accedit, eo clarius id periculum apparet. Propositum hoc est, de quo qui rerum potiuntur sunt dimi- 20 caturi, quod Cn. Pompeius constituit non pati C. Caesarem consulem aliter fieri nisi exercitum et provincias tradiderit, Caesari autem persuasum est se salvum esse non posse si ab exercitu recesserit; fert illam tamen condicionem, ut ambo exercitus tradant. Sic illi amores et invidiosa con- 25 iunctio non ad occultam recidit obtrectationem, sed ad bellum se erupit; neque mearum rerum quid consili capiam

reperio; quod non dubito quin te quoque haec deliberatio sit perturbatura. Nam mihi cum hominibus his et
30 gratiae et necessitudines sunt: causam illam amo unde homines odi. Illud te non arbitror fugere quin homines in dis- 3
sensione domestica debeant, quam diu civiliter sine armis
certetur, honestiorem sequi partem, ubi ad bellum et castra
ventum sit, firmiorem et id melius statuere quod tutius sit.
35 In hac discordia video Cn. Pompeium senatum quique res
iudicant secum habiturum, ad Caesarem omnis qui cum
timore aut mala spe vivant accessuros; exercitum conferendum non esse. Omnino satis spati est ad considerandas
utriusque copias et eligendam partem.
40 Prope oblitus sum quod maxime fuit scribendum. Scis 4
Appium censorem hic ostenta facere, de signis et tabulis,
de agri modo, de aere alieno acerrime agere ? persuasum
est ei censuram lomentum aut nitrum esse. Errare mihi
videtur; nam sordis eluere vult, venas sibi omnis et viscera
45 aperit. Curre, per deos atque homines ! et quam primum
haec risum veni, legis Scantiniae iudicium apud Drusum
fieri, Appium de tabulis et signis agere; crede mihi, est
properandum. Curio noster sapienter id, quod remisit de
stipendio Pompei, fecisse existimatur. Ad summam, quaeris
50 quid putem futurum. Si alter uter eorum ad Parthicum
bellum non eat, video magnas impendere discordias, quas
ferrum et vis iudicabit; uterque et animo et copiis est
paratus. Si sine summo periculo fieri posset, magnum et
iucundum tibi Fortuna spectaculum parabat.

Cicero (and his family) to Marcus Tullius Tiro.
3 November 50

Tiro, Cicero's freedman secretary, had gone out to Cilicia with Cicero. They were now on their way home, but Tiro fell ill and had to be left behind at Patrae (in the Gulf of Corinth). Cicero went on, and wrote this letter to Tiro while *en route* from Patrae to Alyzia (a town on the north-west coast of Greece). Ten further letters followed in quick succession up to the end of January 49, a good indication of Cicero's genuine concern and affection for his servant. In all we have twenty-seven letters addressed to (or concerning) Tiro; they make up the sixteenth and last volume of the *epistulae ad familiares*.

Slavery at Rome was a very complex institution embracing an enormous range of conditions. At one end we find chain-gangs driven to brutalizing labour, galley-slaves, or cheap prostitutes. There is also the trusted family slave working alongside his small-farmer owner, the free-ranging 'cowboy' of the great ranches of southern Italy, the skilled craftsman employed in a small workshop. At the top of the pyramid were the highly intelligent and well-educated slaves who served as confidential secretaries or business-managers for their owners. The most skilful and intelligent slaves were usually given their freedom at an early age and frequently became the confidants and personal friends of their masters. Some freedmen, like Petronius' Trimalchio, amassed huge fortunes; some, like the great secretaries of the Emperor Claudius, wielded enormous political power; some, even while remaining slaves, enjoyed a standard of living beyond the wildest dreams of most free men. We happen to have an inscription set up to commemorate a certain Musicus, a slave of the Emperor Tiberius, who at his death held a post in the financial department of the province of Gallia Lugdunensis at Lyons (Dessau, *ILS* 1514). It was erected by his personal household staff, which totalled sixteen, and comprised: a business agent, a majordomo, two cooks, two footmen, two personal servants, two butlers, a valet, three secretaries, a personal doctor, and a lady whose duties are left undefined.

Marcus Tullius Tiro belonged to this 'slave aristocracy'. He was given his freedom by his master Cicero in 53, when he was still very young, and (as was customary) took his master's name. Aulus Gellius (*Noctes Atticae* vi. 3. 8) tells us that 'he had been liberally educated from his earliest years, and Cicero used him as an assistant, almost a partner, in his literary work'. He began to make a collection of Cicero's correspondence even while Cicero was alive. He wrote at least four books about his master, and is credited with having produced 'The Humour of Cicero' in three volumes. He himself wrote widely on the Latin language. Cicero's concern for his health at this time was misplaced; Tiro lived to be ninety-nine.

Scr. in itinere Patris Alyziam iii Non. Nov. an. 50.

TVLLIVS TIRONI SVO S. P. D. ET CICERO MEVS ET
FRATER ET FRATRIS F.

Paulo facilius putavi posse me ferre desiderium tui, sed 1
5 plane non fero et, quamquam magni ad honorem nostrum
interest quam primum ad urbem me venire, tamen peccasse
mihi videor qui a te discesserim; sed quia tua voluntas ea
videbatur esse, ut prorsus nisi confirmato corpore nolles
navigare, approbavi tuum consilium neque nunc muto, si
10 tu in eadem es sententia; sin autem, postea quam cibum
cepisti, videris tibi posse me consequi, tuum consilium est.
Marionem ad te eo misi, ut aut tecum ad me quam primum
veniret aut, si tu morarere, statim ad me rediret. Tu 2
autem hoc tibi persuade, si commodo valetudinis tuae fieri
15 possit, nihil me malle quam te esse mecum; si autem intel-
leges opus esse te Patris convalescendi causa paulum com-
morari, nihil me malle quam te valere. Si statim navigas,
nos Leucade consequere; sin te confirmare vis, et comites
et tempestates et navem idoneam ut habeas diligenter vide-
20 bis. Unum illud, mi Tiro, videto, si me amas, ne te
Marionis adventus et hae litterae moveant. Quod valetudini
tuae maxime conducet si feceris, maxime obtemperaris

3 voluntati meae. Haec pro tuo ingenio considera. Nos ita
te desideramus, ut amemus; amor ut valentem videamus
hortatur, desiderium ut quam primum; illud igitur potius. 25
Cura ergo potissimum ut valeas. De tuis innumerabilibus in
me officiis erit hoc gratissimum. iii Non. Nov.

LETTER 28

Pompey to Lucius Domitius Ahenobarbus.
17 February 49

On the morning of 11 January 49 Caesar was south of the Rubicon
with the town of Ariminum (Rimini) in his hands. His advance continued with the *celeritas* for which he was famous. On 17 January
Pompey left Rome to take command of his two veteran legions in
Apulia; and the next day the consuls and the other magistrates also
quitted the capital. Pompey's strategy was to abandon Italy to Caesar
(whose generalship he did not underrate, nor the fighting qualities of
his veteran troops), blockade Italy with his fleets, and eventually
crush Caesar with the vastly superior resources of Spain, Africa, and
the East.

Unhappily for Pompey, Caesar's old enemy Lucius Domitius
Ahenobarbus, who had been appointed by the senate proconsular
governor of Transalpine Gaul in succession to Caesar, did not follow
Pompey's advice and retire in good order on Brundisium. He had
just over thirty cohorts (equivalent to three legions) under his command, and he thought he could stand and hold at Corfinium in central Italy, and perhaps even crush his old rival who was advancing
with only one legion, the Thirteenth. But Caesar, reinforced by the
arrival of the Eighth Legion and considerable levies from Gaul,
quickly tied Domitius up in knots: he blockaded him at Corfinium,
where Domitius surrendered on 21 February after his troops had
mutinied. Domitius' soldiers were taken into Caesar's service and
sent under Curio to secure Sicily and Africa. The officers were set at
liberty, so that Domitius survived to direct the defence of Marseilles

and to fall commanding Pompey's left wing at Pharsalus in August 48.

This letter written by an anxious Pompey from Luceria (in Apulia, some 150 miles north-west of Brundisium) to Domitius at Corfinium is preserved for us in the Atticus collection. In it Pompey urges Domitius to slip away from Corfinium and effect a junction with himself before Caesar's reinforcements arrive and make such a move impossible.

Scr. Luceriae xiii Kal. Mart. an. 49.

CN. MAGNVS PROCOS. S. D. L. DOMITIO PROCOS.

Litterae mihi a te redditae sunt a. d. XIII Kal. Mart., in I
quibus scribis Caesarem apud Corfinium castra posuisse.
5 Quod putavi et praemonui fit, ut nec in praesentia committere tecum proelium velit et omnibus copiis conductis
te implicet, ne ad me iter tibi expeditum sit atque istas
copias coniungere optimorum civium possis cum his legionibus de quarum voluntate dubitamus. Quo etiam magis
10 tuis litteris sum commotus; neque enim eorum militum quos
mecum habeo voluntate satis confido ut de omnibus fortunis
rei publicae dimicem neque etiam qui ex dilectibus con-
scripti sunt consulibus convenerunt.

Qua re da operam, si ulla ratione etiam nunc efficere potes, 2
15 ut te explices, huc quam primum venias, ante quam omnes
copiae ad adversarium conveniant. Neque enim celeriter
ex dilectibus huc homines convenire possunt et, si convenirent, quantum iis committendum sit qui inter se ne
noti quidem sunt contra veteranas legiones non te praeterit.

LETTER 29

Caesar to Cicero. March 49

Cicero spent the first weeks of 49 in a state of painful vacillation. It
was not that he was in any real doubt about his preference for Pompey

over Caesar. He always saw in Caesar the threat of despotism and the
death of the Republic which he so greatly admired, and he felt that
Caesar's early moderation and restraint and clemency in 49 were far
too good to last. While he recognized Caesar's charm and intellectual
distinction, he had nothing but loathing and contempt for most of his
leading supporters: 'Now who is he using as his colleagues and
assistants ? Are these men to rule the provinces, to rule Rome, not one
of whom could manage his own inheritance for two months together ?'
(*ad Att.* x. 8. 6: 1 May 49). On the other hand, failing to appreciate
Pompey's long-term strategy, he tended to see his old hero with feet
of clay, faint-hearted and irresolute, while Caesar was afire with
energy and fast consolidating support in Italy. As for Pompey's optimate colleagues, Cicero was horrified by their bloodthirsty talk of
proscriptions and revenge. A man of peace, a constitutionalist, Cicero
saw devastation and despotism whichever side won. A natural middle-
of-the-roader, he suffered the fate Aneurin Bevan used to predict for
those who stood in that position: he got knocked down and run over.

Caesar had a soft spot for Cicero and an unbounded admiration for
his literary genius. He was also desperately anxious to secure the
cachet of the public support of so respectable and influential a figure
to give respectability to his own *coup de main*. So he studiously courted
Cicero. In this brief note, dashed off while he was on the march from
Arpi (near Luceria) to Brundisium, he entreats Cicero to come to
Rome and lend him his aid and advice.

Scr. in itinere Arpis Brundisium in. mense Mart. an. 49.

CAESAR IMP. S. D. CICERONI IMP.

Cum Furnium nostrum tantum vidissem neque loqui neque
audire meo commodo potuissem, cum properarem atque
essem in itinere praemissis iam legionibus, praeterire tamen   5
non potui quin et scriberem ad te et illum mitterem gratias-
que agerem, etsi hoc et feci saepe et saepius mihi facturus
videor; ita de me mereris. In primis a te peto, quoniam
confido me celeriter ad urbem venturum, ut te ibi videam,
ut tuo consilio, gratia, dignitate, ope omnium rerum uti   10

possim. Ad propositum revertar; festinationi meae brevitatique litterarum ignosces. Reliqua ex Furnio cognosces.

LETTER 30

Cicero to Atticus. 14 May 47

Cicero and Caesar met on 28 March 49. But nothing Caesar could threaten or promise allayed Cicero's doubts and reservations. He finally left Italy on 7 June 49 and joined Pompey in Illyricum. Here he was appalled by the Sullan violence of Pompey's leading associates. His confidence in the leadership of his cause was quickly eroded, his mood became querulous and pessimistic. He took no part in the battle of Pharsalus in August 48, being in ill health at the time. Cato invited him as the senior consular to assume command of the Republican remnants at Corcyra, but Cicero declined and eventually returned to Italy in October 48, taking up residence at Brundisium.

He had believed that the war was over after Pharsalus. But the Pompeians regrouped and reorganized in Africa and in Spain, and fought on. Meanwhile, throughout the winter of 48/47 Caesar was cut off with a small force under siege and attack by vastly superior Egyptian forces in the palace quarter of Alexandria. The ever volatile Cicero now plunged deeper into despair as he convinced himself that the anti-Caesarian cause would triumph after all, and that his own premature defection after Pharsalus and return to Italy would find no forgiveness from the victors. Such is his mood, and such his thoughts, as he writes this letter to Atticus (who had remained at Rome), still unaware that on 27 March Caesar had broken out and won a decisive victory in Egypt.

Scr. Brundisi prid. Id. Mai. an. 47.

CICERO ATTICO SALVTEM.

Quoniam iustas causas adfers cur te hoc tempore videre 1 non possim, quaeso quid sit mihi faciendum. Ille enim ita
5 videtur Alexandria teneri ut eum scribere etiam pudeat de

illis rebus, hi autem ex Africa iam adfuturi videntur, Achaici, item ex Asia redituri ad eos aut libero aliquo loco commoraturi. Quid mihi igitur putas agendum ? Video difficile esse consilium. Sum enim solus aut cum altero cui neque ad illos reditus sit neque ab his ipsis quicquam ad spem ostendatur. 10 Sed tamen scire velim quid censeas; idque erat cum aliis cur te, si fieri posset, cuperem videre.

2 Minucium x̄īī sola curasse scripsi ad te antea. Quod superest velim videas ut curetur. Quintus non modo non cum magna prece ad me sed acerbissime scripsit, filius vero mirifico odio. 15 Nihil fingi potest mali quo non urgear. Omnia tamen sunt faciliora quam peccati dolor, qui et maximus est et aeternus. Cuius peccati si socios essem habiturus ego quos putavi, tamen esset ea consolatio tenuis. Sed habet aliorum omnium ratio exitum, mea nullum. Alii capti, alii interclusi non 20 veniunt in dubium de voluntate, eo minus scilicet cum se expedierint et una esse coeperint. Ii autem ipsi qui sua voluntate ad Fufium venerunt nihil possunt nisi timidi existimari. Multi autem sunt qui, quocumque modo ad illos se recipere volent, recipientur. Quo minus debes mirari non posse me 25 tanto dolori resistere. Solius enim meum peccatum corrigi non potest et fortasse Laeli. Sed quid me id levat ? Nam C. quidem Cassium aiunt consilium Alexandriam eundi mutavisse.

3 Haec ad te scribo, non ut queas tu demere sollicitudinem sed ut cognoscam ecquid tu ad ea adferas quae me conficiunt; 30 ad quae gener accedit et cetera quae fletu reprimor ne scribam. Quin etiam Aesopi filius me excruciat. Prorsus nihil abest quin sim miserrimus. Sed ad primum revertor, quid putes faciendum, occultene aliquo propius veniendum an mare transeundum. Nam hic maneri diutius non potest. 35

4 De Fufidianis qua re nihil potuit confici ? Genus enim condicionis eius modi fuit in quo non solet esse controversia, cum ea pars quae videtur esse minor licitatione expleri posset. Hoc ego non sine causa quaero. Suspicor enim coheredes

40 dubiam nostram causam putare et eo rem in integro esse
malle. Vale. Prid. Id. Mai.

LETTER 31

Servius Sulpicius Rufus to Cicero. March 45

Sulpicius, one of the great jurisconsults of his day, was a very old
friend of Cicero's. As consul in 51 he had consistently advocated
moderation and compromise; and during the Civil War he had
followed a neutral course. Towards the end of 47 Caesar appointed
him governor of Achaea, whence he now writes to console Cicero on
the death of his daughter Tullia.

Sulpicius' letter is one of the most famous in the corpus of Cicero's
correspondence. It is composed with great care and elegance, but this
does not detract from its sincerity. For all that he had won distinction
from Caesar, Sulpicius shared Cicero's republican, constitutionalist
views; and for him the present regime is the negation of all he believes
in. Sulpicius represents, in an unaggressive fashion, those resentments
and dissatisfactions with the authoritarian aspects of Caesar's rule
which were twelve months later to move men to murder him as a
tyrant.

When Caesar's bitter enemy, Marcus Claudius Marcellus, Sulpicius' colleague as consul in 51, was pardoned by Caesar, Cicero had
become optimistic and broken his long silence in the senate; and his
letters of 46 are marked by a cheerful note. But the letters of 45 show
a great change. Cicero had been encouraged to begin a letter of advice
to Caesar; but he thought it prudent to show it to Caesar's intimates
first, and they made so many alterations that he quite lost heart and
dropped the idea. Coming on top of his disillusion, Tullia's death was
a shattering blow for her devoted father.

Scr. Athenis circ. medio m. Mart. an. 45.

SERVIVS CICERONI S.

1 Postea quam mihi renuntiatum est de obitu Tulliae, filiae
tuae, sane quam pro eo ac debui, graviter molesteque tuli
communemque eam calamitatem existimavi; qui, si istic 5
adfuissem, neque tibi defuissem coramque meum dolorem
tibi declarassem. Etsi genus hoc consolationis miserum
atque acerbum est, propterea quia, per quos ea confieri
debet, propinquos ac familiaris, ii ipsi pari molestia ad-
ficiuntur neque sine lacrimis multis id conari possunt, uti 10
magis ipsi videantur aliorum consolatione indigere quam
aliis posse suum officium praestare, tamen, quae in praesentia in mentem mihi venerunt, decrevi brevi ad te perscribere, non quo ea te fugere existimem, sed quod forsitan
dolore impeditus minus ea perspicias.   15

2 Quid est quod tanto opere te commoveat tuus dolor
intestinus? Cogita, quem ad modum adhuc fortuna nobiscum egerit; ea nobis erepta esse, quae hominibus non
minus quam liberi cara esse debent, patriam, honestatem,
dignitatem, honores omnis. Hoc uno incommodo addito 20
quid ad dolorem adiungi potuit? aut qui non in illis rebus
exercitatus animus callere iam debet atque omnia minoris

3 existimare? An illius vicem, cedo, doles? Quotiens in
eam cogitationem necesse est et tu veneris et nos saepe
incidimus, hisce temporibus non pessime cum iis esse 25
actum, quibus sine dolore licitum est mortem cum vita com-
mutare! Quid autem fuit quod illam hoc tempore ad
vivendum magno opere invitare posset? quae res, quae spes,
quod animi solacium? ut cum aliquo adulescente primario
coniuncta aetatem gereret? Licitum est tibi, credo, pro 30
tua dignitate ex hac iuventute generum deligere, cuius
fidei liberos tuos te tuto committere putares. An ut ea
liberos ex sese pareret, quos cum florentis videret laetaretur,

qui rem a parente traditam per se tenere possent, honores
35 ordinatim petituri essent in re publica, in amicorum negotiis
libertate sua usuri? Quid horum fuit quod non prius-
quam datum est ademptum sit? At vero malum est
liberos amittere. Malum; nisi hoc peius sit, haec sufferre
et perpeti. Quae res mihi non mediocrem consolationem 4
40 attulit, volo tibi commemorare, si forte eadem res tibi
dolorem minuere possit.

Ex Asia rediens cum ab Aegina Megaram versus navi-
garem, coepi regiones circumcirca prospicere. Post me
erat Aegina, ante me Megara, dextra Piraeus, sinistra
45 Corinthus, quae oppida quodam tempore florentissima
fuerunt, nunc prostrata et diruta ante oculos iacent. Coepi
egomet mecum sic cogitare: 'Hem! nos homunculi in-
dignamur, si quis nostrum interiit aut occisus est, quorum
vita brevior esse debet, cum uno loco tot oppidum cadavera
50 proiecta iacent? Visne tu te, Servi, cohibere et meminisse
hominem te esse natum?' Crede mihi, cogitatione ea non
mediocriter sum confirmatus. Hoc idem, si tibi videtur,
fac ante oculos tibi proponas. Modo uno tempore tot viri
clarissimi interierunt, de imperio populi Romani tanta
55 deminutio facta est, omnes provinciae conquassatae sunt;
in unius mulierculae animula si iactura facta est, tanto
opere commoveris? Quae si hoc tempore non diem suum
obisset, paucis post annis tamen ei moriendum fuit,
quoniam homo nata fuerat. Etiam tu ab hisce rebus 5
60 animum ac cogitationem tuam avoca atque ea potius
reminiscere, quae digna tua persona sunt, illam, quam
diu ei opus fuerit, vixisse, una cum re publica fuisse,
te, patrem suum, praetorem, consulem, augurem vidisse,
adulescentibus primariis nuptam fuisse, omnibus bonis
65 prope perfunctam esse, cum res publica occideret vita
excessisse. Quid est quod tu aut illa cum fortuna hoc
nomine queri possitis? Denique noli te oblivisci Ciceronem

esse et eum, qui aliis consueris praecipere et dare
consilium, neque imitare malos medicos, qui in alienis
morbis profitentur tenere se medicinae scientiam, ipsi se 70
curare non possunt, sed potius, quae aliis tute praecipere
soles, ea tute tibi subiace atque apud animum propone.
6 Nullus dolor est, quem non longinquitas temporis minuat
ac molliat. Hoc te exspectare tempus tibi turpe est ac non
ei rei sapientia tua te occurrere. Quod si qui etiam inferis 75
sensus est, qui illius in te amor fuit pietasque in omnis
suos, hoc certe illa te facere non vult. Da hoc illi
mortuae, da ceteris amicis ac familiaribus, qui tuo dolore
maerent, da patriae, ut, si qua in re opus sit, opera et
consilio tuo uti possit. Denique, quoniam in eam for- 80
tunam devenimus, ut etiam huic rei nobis serviendum sit,
noli committere ut quisquam te putet non tam filiam quam
rei publicae tempora et aliorum victoriam lugere.

Plura me ad te de hac re scribere pudet, ne videar
prudentiae tuae diffidere. Qua re, si hoc unum proposuero, 85
finem faciam scribendi: Vidimus aliquotiens secundam
pulcherrime te ferre fortunam magnamque ex ea re te
laudem apisci; fac aliquando intellegamus adversam
quoque te aeque ferre posse neque id maius, quam debeat,
tibi onus videri, ne ex omnibus virtutibus haec una tibi 90
videatur deesse.

Quod ad me attinet, cum te tranquilliorem animo esse
cognoro, de iis rebus, quae hic geruntur, quemadmodum-
que se provincia habeat, certiorem faciam. Vale.

LETTER 32

Cicero to Manius Curius. Early January 44

The final battle of the civil war took place at Munda in southern Spain
on 17 March 45, when Caesar shattered the last Pompeian army, and

his old lieutenant Titus Labienus fell on the field. Caesar was back in Italy in September. Hitherto it had been possible for the sanguine to believe that the authoritarian and peremptory character of his rule since 49 was dictated by the exigencies of the moment, and that the final end of the war might see some move towards relaxation and even the partial restoration of normal government. Any such hopes soon died. Caesar gave no hint of any such amelioration: rather the reverse, for in many ways his behaviour can only be explained either by supposing that he was deliberately and rashly flouting moderate opinion and trampling on the cherished assumptions of the nobility, or by the thought that long habit of supreme command and trust in his good luck had deadened his sensibilities so that he was unaware of the widespread resentment building up against him even among a considerable number of his own principal followers. Early in 44 he underlined his autocracy by assuming the title of *dictator perpetuus*.

One example of the sort of behaviour that many people found offensive and intolerable is reported by Cicero in this letter. When one of the consuls died on the very last day of 45, Caesar at once proceeded, without even a cursory respect for the proper religious preliminaries, to secure the election of a suffect (substitute) consul for the last few hours of the year. The needs of state did not demand that this be done; and clearly many people like Cicero saw Caesar's action as an insult, casual or calculated, to the dignity of the consular office and to Republican precedents. Why Caesar acted as he did we can only guess, but Tacitus is surely right in holding that he saw a heaven-sent opportunity to advance one of his deserving supporters to consular rank: 'nam consul uno die et ante fuerat Caninius Rebilus C. Caesare dictatore, cum belli civilis praemia festinarentur' (*Histories* iii. 37).

Manius Curius, to whom this letter is addressed, was a knight prominent in business at Patrae in Achaea, a close personal friend of both Cicero and Atticus. He had been very kind to Cicero's freedman Tiro when he fell sick in 50 and had to be left behind on Cicero's return journey to Italy (Letter 27).

Scr. Romae in. m. Ian. an. 44.

CICERO CVRIO S. D.

1 Ego vero iam te nec hortor nec rogo ut domum redeas;
quin hinc ipse evolare cupio et aliquo pervenire, 'ubi nec
Pelopidarum nomen nec facta audiam'. Incredibile est 5
quam turpiter mihi facere videar, qui his rebus intersim.
Ne tu videris multo ante providisse quid impenderet, tum
cum hinc profugisti. Quamquam haec etiam auditu acerba
sunt, tamen audire tolerabilius est quam videre. In campo 10
certe non fuisti, cum hora secunda comitiis quaestoriis
institutis sella Q. Maximi, quem illi consulem esse dicebant,
posita esset; quo mortuo nuntiato sella sublata est. Ille
autem, qui comitiis tributis esset auspicatus, centuriata
habuit, consulem hora septima renuntiavit, qui usque ad 15
K. Ian. esset quae erant futurae mane postridie. Ita
Caninio consule scito neminem prandisse. Nihil tamen eo
consule mali factum est; fuit enim mirifica vigilantia, qui
2 suo toto consulatu somnum non viderit. Haec tibi ridicula
videntur; non enim ades. Quae si videres, lacrimas non 20
teneres. Quid, si cetera scribam? sunt enim innumerabilia
generis eiusdem; quae quidem ego non ferrem, nisi me in
philosophiae portum contulissem et nisi haberem socium
studiorum meorum Atticum nostrum. Cuius quoniam proprium te esse scribis mancipio et nexo, meum autem usu et 25
fructu, contentus isto sum. Id enim est cuiusque proprium,
quo quisque fruitur atque utitur. Sed haec alias pluribus.
3 Acilius, qui in Graeciam cum legionibus missus est,
maximo meo beneficiost (bis enim est a me iudicio capitis
rebus salvis defensus) et est homo non ingratus meque vehe- 30
menter observat. Ad eum de te diligentissime scripsi eamque
epistulam cum hac epistula coniunxi. Quam ille quo modo
acceperit et quid tibi pollicitus sit velim ad me scribas.

LETTER 33

Cicero to Atticus. 22 April 44

It was now some five weeks since Caesar had been stabbed to death at the foot of Pompey's statue. Any brief elation Cicero may have felt quickly gave way to gloom and pessimism. Mark Antony, Caesar's colleague in the consulship of 44, remained alive and active; and the 'liberators' (as Cicero termed Caesar's assassins) had failed to follow up their murder of Caesar by winning control of the state and setting about a restoration of normal government. Already Antony is beginning to order affairs under the cloak of the authority of the dead Caesar.

Writing from Puteoli in Campania to Atticus in Rome, Cicero expresses his forebodings about the turn events are taking. He also reports his first meeting with young Octavius, the future Emperor Augustus, who had hurriedly returned to Italy to claim his inheritance; for in a codicil to his will Caesar had adopted his great-nephew and made him his principal heir. Little more than eighteen months later the boy who now treats Cicero with such amicable deference will put his name along with Antony's to Cicero's death-warrant.

Scr. Puteolis x Kal. Mai. an. 44.

CICERO ATTICO SALVTEM.

O mi Attice, vereor ne nobis Idus Martiae nihil dederint 1
praeter laetitiam et odi poenam ac doloris. Quae mihi istim
5 adferuntur ! quae hic video ! Ὦ πράξεως καλῆς μέν, ἀτελοῦς δέ.
Scis quam diligam Siculos et quam illam clientelam honestam
iudicem. Multa illis Caesar, neque me invito (etsi Latinitas
erat non ferenda. Verum tamen—). Ecce autem Antonius
accepta grandi pecunia fixit legem 'a dictatore comitiis latam'
10 qua Siculi cives Romani; cuius rei vivo illo mentio nulla.
Quid ? Deiotari nostri causa non similis ? Dignus ille quidem
omni regno, sed non per Fulviam. Sescenta similia. Verum
illuc referor: tam claram tamque testatam rem tamque

iustam, Buthrotiam, non tenebimus aliqua ex parte? et eo
quidem magis quo ista plura?   15

2   Nobiscum hic perhonorifice et peramice Octavius. Quem
quidem sui Caesarem salutabant, Philippus non, itaque ne
nos quidem. Quem nego posse esse bonum civem—ita multi
circumstant, qui quidem nostris mortem minitantur, negant
haec ferri posse. Quid censes cum Romam puer venerit, ubi   20
nostri liberatores tuti esse non possunt? Qui quidem semper erunt clari, conscientia vero facti sui etiam beati; sed nos,
nisi me fallit, iacebimus. Itaque exire aveo 'ubi nec Pelopidarum', inquit. Haud amo vel hos designatos, qui etiam
declamare me coegerunt, ut ne apud aquas quidem acquie-   25
scere liceret. Sed hoc meae nimiae facilitatis. Nam id erat
quondam quasi necesse, nunc, quoquo modo se res habet,
non est item.

3   Quam dudum nihil habeo quod ad te scribam! Scribo
tamen, non ut delectem his litteris sed ut eliciam tuas. Tu   30
si quid erit de ceteris, de Bruto utique quicquid. Haec con-
scripsi x Kal., accubans apud Vestorium, hominem remotum
a dialecticis, in arithmeticis satis exercitatum.

LETTER 34

Gaius Matius to Cicero. Late August 44

Gaius Matius was a Roman knight, some ten years younger than
Cicero and a very old friend. Little is known of him of public note: in
his old age he wrote a work on gastronomy, and he may just perhaps
be the Gaius Matius who (Pliny, *nat. hist.* xii. 6. 13) introduced topiary
(*nemora tonsilia*) into Italian gardens—both of them activities which
seem well suited to his amiable nature. An intimate personal friend of
Caesar, though not a political supporter, he courageously persisted
in his loyalty to his dead friend. Matius had been told that Cicero had
been making slighting comments about his behaviour in this regard,

and when this was in turn reported to Cicero he hastened to write to
Matius to reassure him (*ad famm.* xi. 27). Matius here replies to Cicero.
For all its cragginess of style and expression (which necessitates a fair
bit of exegesis), it was not without justice that Rice Holmes said of
this letter (*The Roman Republic* iii. 349) that it 'seems to me the noblest
that has come from antiquity'.

Scr. Romae ex. Sext. an. 44.

MATIVS CICERONI S.

Magnam voluptatem ex tuis litteris cepi, quod quam **1**
speraram atque optaram habere te de me opinionem co-
5 gnovi; de qua etsi non dubitabam, tamen, quia maximi
aestimabam, ut incorrupta maneret laborabam. Conscius
autem mihi eram nihil a me commissum esse quod boni
cuiusquam offenderet animum. Eo minus credebam plurimis atque optimis artibus ornato tibi temere quicquam
10 persuaderi potuisse, praesertim in quem mea propensa et
perpetua fuisset atque esset benevolentia. Quod quoniam
ut volui scio esse, respondebo criminibus, quibus tu pro
me, ut par erat tua singulari bonitate et amicitia nostra,
saepe restitisti.

15   Nota enim mihi sunt quae in me post Caesaris mortem **2**
contulerint. Vitio mihi dant quod mortem hominis necessari graviter fero atque eum quem dilexi perisse indignor;
aiunt enim patriam amicitiae praeponendam esse, proinde
ac si iam vicerint obitum eius rei p. fuisse utilem. Sed
20 non agam astute; fateor me ad istum gradum sapientiae
non pervenisse; neque enim Caesarem in dissensione civili
sum secutus sed amicum; quamquam re offendebar, tamen
non deserui, neque bellum umquam civile aut etiam causam
dissensionis probavi, quam etiam nascentem exstingui summe
25 studui. Itaque in victoria hominis necessari neque honoris
neque pecuniae dulcedine sum captus, quibus praemiis reliqui, minus apud eum quam ego cum possent, immoderate

sunt abusi. Atque etiam res familiaris mea lege Caesaris deminuta est, cuius beneficio plerique, qui Caesaris morte lae-
tantur, remanserunt in civitate. Civibus victis ut parceretur 30
aeque ac pro mea salute laboravi.

3   Possum igitur qui omnis voluerim incolumis eum a quo
id impetratum est perisse non indignari ? cum praesertim
idem homines illi et invidiae et exitio fuerint. 'Plecteris
ergo' inquiunt 'quoniam factum nostrum improbare audes.' 35
O superbiam inauditam alios in facinore gloriari, aliis ne
dolere quidem impunite licere ! At haec etiam servis semper
libera fuerunt, ut timerent, gauderent, dolerent suo potius
quam alterius arbitrio; quae nunc, ut quidem isti dictitant,
4 'libertatis auctores' metu nobis extorquere conantur. Sed 40
nihil agunt; nullius umquam periculi terroribus ab officio
aut ab humanitate desciscam; numquam enim honestam
mortem fugiendam, saepe etiam oppetendam putavi. Sed
quid mihi suscensent, si id opto ut paeniteat eos sui facti ?
Cupio enim Caesaris mortem omnibus esse acerbam.   45

    'At debeo pro civili parte rem p. velle salvam.' Id qui-
dem me cupere, nisi et ante acta vita et reliqua mea spes
5 tacente me probat, dicendo vincere non postulo. Qua re
maiorem in modum te rogo ut rem potiorem oratione ducas
mihique, si sentis expedire recte fieri, credas nullam com- 50
munionem cum improbis esse posse. An quod adulescens
praestiti, cum etiam errare cum excusatione possem, id
nunc aetate praecipitata commutem ac me ipse retexam ?
Non faciam neque quod displiceat committam, praeterquam quod hominis mihi coniunctissimi ac viri amplissimi 55
doleo gravem casum. Quod si aliter essem animatus, numquam quod facerem negarem, ne et in peccando improbus
et in dissimulando timidus ac vanus existimarer.

6   'At ludos quos Caesaris victoriae Caesar adulescens
fecit curavi.' At id ad privatum officium, non ad statum 60
rei p. pertinet; quod tamen munus et hominis amicissimi

memoriae atque honoribus praestare etiam mortui debui
et optimae spei adulescenti ac dignissimo Caesare petenti
negare non potui. Veni etiam consulis Antoni domum **7**
65 saepe salutandi causa; ad quem qui me parum patriae
amantem esse existimant rogandi quidem aliquid aut au-
ferendi causa frequentis ventitare reperies. Sed quae haec
est adrogantia, quod Caesar numquam interpellavit quin
quibus vellem atque etiam quos ipse non diligebat tamen iis
70 uterer, eos qui mihi amicum eripuerunt carpendo me efficere
conari ne quos velim diligam ?

Sed non vereor ne aut meae vitae modestia parum **8**
valitura sit in posterum contra falsos rumores aut ne etiam
ii, qui me non amant propter meam in Caesarem constan-
75 tiam, non malint mei quam sui similis amicos habere. Mihi
quidem si optata contingent, quod reliquum est vitae in
otio Rhodi degam; sin casus aliquis interpellarit, ita ero
Romae ut recte fieri semper cupiam. Trebatio nostro
magnas ago gratias, quod tuum erga me animum simplicem
80 atque amicum aperuit et quod eum, quem semper libenter
dilexi, quo magis iure colere atque observare deberem fecit.
Bene vale et me dilige.

LETTER 35

Cicero to Gaius Trebonius. About 2 February 43

This seemed an appropriate letter with which to close this selection.
In it we find Cicero coming out of his long political retirement,
which had begun nearly thirteen years earlier (Letter 12), to assume
the leadership of the fight to save the Republic.

By July 44, Octavian's popularity had begun to shake Antony's
confidence. He was on good terms with Cicero, who judged that the
young man would be of priceless value in splitting the Caesarian
loyalties and bringing about the collapse of Antony—Octavian could

then be dealt with separately: 'laudandum adulescentem, ornandum, tollendum' (*ad famm.* xi. 20. 1). By 2 September Cicero felt sufficiently confident to deliver a major political speech in the senate: this, the *First Philippic*, was a powerful but restrained attack on Antony's policies. In October the breach between Antony and Octavian came to a head when the latter appeared in Rome at the head of a large body of veterans and delivered a public harangue against Antony. During these weeks Cicero was lying low, busy with the composition of his astonishing *Second Philippic*. On 29 November Antony marched north to take over his province of Cisalpine Gaul. Almost immediately Cicero published the *Second Philippic*, and on 20 December he openly threw his hat into the ring in a bid for political leadership with the delivery of the *Third Philippic*, the speech he refers to in section 2 of this letter.

Gaius Trebonius, to whom it is addressed, was governor of Asia. Tribune in 53, and a Caesarian legate in Gaul, he fought for Caesar in the Civil War, becoming praetor in 49 and suffect (substitute) consul in 45. He was one of the group that conspired to assassinate his old chief.

Trebonius never read this letter. He had been murdered by Cicero's former son-in-law Dolabella in Asia a week or so before Cicero wrote it. And Cicero's own sands were running out. In the autumn of 43 the 'boy' Octavian, now consul, met Antony and Lepidus near Bononia, and the 'Second Triumvirate' was born. Cicero's was one of the first names on the list of those to be proscribed. On 7 December 43 he abandoned his half-hearted attempts to escape from Italy and stoically offered his neck to a soldier's sword. His head and hands were severed, and sent to Antony's wife Fulvia (Letter 33, section 1), who after subjecting them to indignities had them displayed on the Rostra in the Forum.

Scr. Romae circ. iv Non. Febr. an. 43.

CICERO TREBONIO S.

1   Quam vellem ad illas pulcherrimas epulas me Idibus Martiis invitasses! reliquiarum nihil haberemus. At nunc cum iis tantum negoti est, ut vestrum illud divinum in 5

rem p. beneficium non nullam habeat querelam. Quod vero
a te, viro optimo, seductus est tuoque beneficio adhuc vivit
haec pestis, interdum, quod mihi vix fas est, tibi subirascor;
mihi enim negoti plus reliquisti uni quam praeter me
10 omnibus. Ut enim primum post Antoni foedissimum discessum senatus haberi libere potuit, ad illum animum
meum reverti pristinum, quem tu cum civi acerrimo, patre
tuo, in ore et amore semper habuisti. Nam cum senatum 2
a. d. xiii K. Ian. tr. pl. vocavissent deque alia re referrent,
15 totam rem p. sum complexus egique acerrime senatumque
iam languentem et defessum ad pristinam virtutem consuetudinemque revocavi magis animi quam ingeni viribus.
Hic dies meaque contentio atque actio spem primum
populo R. attulit libertatis reciperandae; nec vero ipse
20 postea tempus ullum intermisi de re p. non cogitandi solum
sed etiam agendi.

   Quod nisi res urbanas actaque omnia ad te perferri arbi- 3
trarer, ipse perscriberem, quamquam eram maximis occu-
pationibus impeditus. Sed illa cognosces ex aliis; a me
25 pauca, et ea summatim. Habemus fortem senatum, consularis partim timidos, partim male sentientis; magnum
damnum factum est in Servio; L. Caesar optime sentit sed,
quod avunculus est, non acerrimas dicit sententias; consules
egregii, praeclarus D. Brutus, egregius puer Caesar, de quo
30 spero equidem reliqua; hoc vero certum habeto, nisi ille
veteranos celeriter conscripsisset legionesque duae de exercitu Antoni ad eius se auctoritatem contulissent atque is
oppositus esset terror Antonio, nihil Antonium sceleris, nihil
crudelitatis praeteriturum fuisse. Haec tibi, etsi audita esse
35 arbitrabar, volui tamen notiora esse. Plura scribam, si plus
oti habuero.

NOTES

LETTER 1

1. 3. Petitionis nostrae, 'my candidature'. *Petere consulatum* = 'to seek election to, stand for, the consulship'. *Nos, noster*, and the first person plural of verbs are frequently used in place of the singular forms by Cicero.

tibi summae curae esse, 'is in the forefront of your thoughts'. *Curae* is an example of the predicative use of the dative; *tibi* is the so-called 'dative of interest', 'dative of the person concerned' (compare 'mihi et fratri magno usui' in section 3, below).

4. ratio. A word with a wide range of meaning, with the basic notion of planning, ordering, calculating. Here translate: 'the position about, the outlook for, my candidature'.

coniectura. Ablative case. *Coniectura* is not so much a 'guess' as an opinion based on (necessarily imperfect) evidence or inference.

possit. The subjunctive is regularly used after 'quod' when 'quod' is being used in its limiting sense, as virtually equivalent to 'quoad' or 'quantum' ('so far as'): this usage is common in Cicero's letters.

5. Prensat unus, 'is the only one who is actively canvassing'. *Prenso* is a syncopated form of *prehenso*, and the idea is of taking hold of people to solicit their support. Publius Sulpicius Galba was a noble and a patrician, who had probably been a colleague of Cicero's as praetor in 66.

sine fuco ac fallaciis. Probably a proverbial expression = (literally) 'without artificial colouring or dissemblings'. Translate: 'He is getting a plain, unvarnished, old-fashioned No.'

6. aliena rationi nostrae, 'disadvantageous to my plans'.

7–8. nam illi . . . dicant. This delicate and elegant construction with *ita . . . ut* is one of which Cicero is particularly fond: 'Their refusal to support him involves their admitted commitment to me'—'For generally their refusals take the form of saying that there is a commitment to me'.

9–10. **plurimos . . . amicos,** 'very numerous' (*not* 'in the majority'). As nowadays, there was a considerable 'band-wagon' element in Roman elections: people liked to be on the winning side. There was too a great deal of patronage and influence in Roman politics. If you supported X, you would expect in return to have a call on his good offices and influence, both public and private. So Cicero is encouraged by the swell of support for himself which Galba's premature canvass is revealing: it will encourage others to switch their support to himself.

10. **cogitabamus.** The epistolary use of the imperfect tense: 'I am thinking'. This usage arises from looking at what is being said from the point of view of the recipient of the letter, for whom it will all be past when he reads about it. Thus also *dicebat, videbantur,* etc., below.

11. **puerum,** 'boy': here, as usually, in the sense of 'slave'. Letters were carried either by servants of the writers or addressees, or by friends' servants, or by the agents of men of business; though provincial governors and the like might have a regular dispatch service.

12. **Cincius.** A business agent of Atticus, often mentioned in the letters.

campo. The Campus Martius, frequently called simply 'the Campus', where elections were regularly held.

comitiis tribuniciis, 'at the tribunician elections', at which the *tribuni plebis* were elected for the coming year. They were no doubt the first in the series of elections held this July. The crowds attending would provide a good starting-point for Cicero's own canvass.

12–13. **a. d. XVI Kal. Sext.** 17 July.

14. **Antonius.** Gaius Antonius, uncle of Mark Antony, who was in fact elected with Cicero to the consulship of 63. He went on to govern Macedonia. He was a 'bad hat'; he had been expelled from the senate by the censors of 70, but had climbed back up the ladder of office. He eventually ran for election in combination with Catiline, whom he narrowly edged into third place. In 59 he was convicted of malpractices as a provincial governor, and forced into exile. Ironically enough, he survived to be appointed censor in 42.

Q. Cornificius. Apparently a worthy but dull man. It may be that it is at the idea of Cornificius' being a candidate that Atticus will either laugh or cry; but possibly Atticus was expected to do so at the prospect of all three candidates named—how ridiculous or distressing that this should be the best Rome could manage as consular candidates!

15. **ut frontem ferias,** 'to make you really beat your brow' (or, as we

say, 'tear your hair'): a typically theatrical Latin gesture to this day.

Caesonium. Marcus Caesonius had been a colleague of Cicero's as aedile and praetor. To judge from this passage, he was far too light-weight for the consulship. At this time there were twenty quaestors elected each year and eight praetors, but only two consuls—so competition got progressively stiffer as men climbed the ladder of office.

16. **putent.** Generic subjunctive, 'there are some who actually think'. On the origin and development of the generic subjunctive see E. C. Woodcock, *A New Latin Syntax*, §§ 155-9.

Aquilium. Gaius Aquilius Gallus, one of the most eminent jurisconsults of his day. Cicero speaks of him with respect in *pro Caecina* 77. (A jurisconsult was an 'academic' as opposed to a practising lawyer, one who gave legal advice and was regarded as an authority without necessarily practising as an advocate.)

17. **iuravit . . . opposuit.** Technical legal phraseology, used for light irony here: 'has entered a plea of ill-health and offered his dominating position at the Bar as rebutting argument'. Shackleton Bailey rightly sees here a gentle dig at Aquilius: 'No doubt Aquilius had let it be understood that ill-health and professional preoccupations made him unwilling to stand, but Cicero regarded such excuses as rather superfluous from a person who was scarcely consular timber anyway.'

18. **Catilina.** Lucius Sergius Catilina, the future revolutionary. After being praetor in 68 he had governed the province of Africa (roughly, the modern Tunisia), returning late in 66. He was now faced with a prosecution *de rebus repetundis* for extortion and maladministration in Africa. If convicted, he would be debarred from public life. His guilt (as Cicero says) was 'as plain as daylight'; but the way Cicero says it implies that he thinks Catiline may none the less get off and stand for the consulship. He was in fact acquitted, thanks (it was plausibly alleged) to financial help from Crassus, a collusive prosecutor, and a bribed jury: see further, Letter 2, section 1, and notes.

19. **Aufidio . . . Palicano.** Titus Aufidius had governed Asia in the mid sixties. He lived to a great age and was 'a good, honest man' (so Cicero, *Brutus* 179). Marcus Lollius Palicanus had been tribune in 71, when he was active in helping some of the Sicilian victims of Verres; he also co-operated with Pompey and Crassus and was energetic in support of the restoration of the full powers of the tribunes in 70. He was so disliked by the conservatives that in 67 the consul Piso said that even if Palicanus won a majority of the votes he would refuse to declare him

consul. He was of humble origins, coming from Picenum in north-west Italy (a region where Pompey was dominant). Sallust called him 'loquax magis quam facundus'.

19–20. **non puto . . . scribam.** That is, they are so unlikely that Atticus will rule them out of consideration himself without any need of a letter from Cicero. In the event, the final line-up of candidates at the July 64 election was: Cicero, Antonius, Catiline, Galba, Cornificius, and two others not here mentioned: Lucius Cassius Longinus and Gaius Licinius Sacerdos.

2. 20. **Caesar.** Lucius Julius Caesar, a distant relation of the famous Gaius Julius Caesar. His sister was the mother of Mark Antony. A quietly conservative character, he narrowly escaped being proscribed in 43, thanks to his sister's intercession with her son. He was in fact elected consul for 64, at the head of the poll.

21. **Thermus cum Silano . . .,** 'the second consulship is reckoned to be a fight between Thermus and Silanus'. Thermus is a bit of a puzzle, but he must pretty certainly be identified with Gaius Marcius Figulus, who was elected consul for 64 along with Lucius Caesar. It is quite incredible that so close to election day Cicero should fail to so much as mention the name of the candidate who got in with Caesar. Thermus must be assumed to have been adopted into the Marcian family shortly after this (or even shortly before, for Cicero may have gone on using his old name after adoption), and to have taken his adoptive father's name, probably under a will. (This was a regular Roman practice, and adult adoptions were common, to keep a family's name alive. Atticus was adopted by his uncle Caecilius in this way, and Octavius by his great-uncle Julius Caesar; other examples will be found in the notes to these letters.) Decimus Junius Silanus failed to get in this year, but was elected consul for 62 at the 63 elections. As consul designate late in 63, he lost his nerve in the debate on the Catilinarian conspirators, after having first urged that they be executed.

21–2. **sic inopes . . . sunt,** 'they are so hard up for both friends and reputation'.

23. **ἀδύνατον,** 'impossible', 'out of the question'. Cicero often slips into Greek, which came naturally to the pen or tongue of an educated Roman. Greek was the great literary language of the Mediterranean world, and the lingua franca of the Empire east of the Adriatic and of much of southern and south-central Italy and Sicily as well.

Turium obducere, 'to slip Turius in ahead of them'. In fact this outsider that Cicero half fancied nearly came home, for Turius missed election only by a narrow margin (*Brutus* 237).

24. **Nostris rationibus maxime conducere,** 'it seems it would serve my interests best', 'suit my calculations best'.

25. **fieri.** That is, *fieri consulem*.

26. **in nostrum annum reciderit,** 'if he falls over, is left over, as a candidate for my year'—that is, to stand against me in 64.

27. **curator . . . viae Flaminiae.** The Via Flaminia was the great trunk road running north to Ariminum (Rimini). Repairs and extensions to such roads were special commissions (*curae*) entrusted to *curatores*. Thermus could be expected to garner political support, for he would be in a position to favour riparian interests and important communities along the route.

28–9. **eum libenter . . . accuderim.** The manuscripts' text is corrupt, and this is the neatest correction: it certainly yields the required sense: 'I should be only too pleased to rivet him on to Caesar as consul this year.' *Accuderim* is a perfect potential subjunctive of the rare verb *accudo*.

29. **informata.** This does not mean 'without shape' but rather 'not fully shaped', 'beginning to take shape', 'first impression'.

31–2. **in suffragiis . . . Gallia,** 'Gaul looks like weighing heavily in the voting'. Gaul here (as often) means specifically Cisalpine Gaul, that part of Italy which was south of the Alps and north of the River Rubicon. It fell into two halves: Transpadane and Cispadane Gaul, the areas north and south respectively of the River Po (*Padus*). Cispadane Gaul, though part of a province, was composed entirely of prosperous communities of Roman citizens. In Transpadane Gaul the communities had only Latin status (see Letter 33, section 1, note), but the ruling families were full Roman citizens. The support of the well-to-do burgesses of the two regions was very important, since at the consular elections which took place in the centuriate assembly at Rome the votes of the wealthier citizens weighed far more heavily than those of the poor (see further below, Letter 9, section 4, note).

32–3. **cum Romae . . . refrixerit,** 'when the Forum here at Rome gets a breather (cools off) after the courts close down'. The Forum was the centre of Roman legal activity. During the last three or four months of the year the courts were mostly closed during a long series of festivals and public games (cf. *Verrines* I. 31).

33. **excurremus . . . Pisonem,** 'I shall run off to Piso to join his staff'. 'Legati' is in apposition to the implied subject of 'excurremus': on the post of *legatus*, see Letter 9, section 7, note. Gaius Calpurnius Piso, consul in 67, and an old enemy of Pompey's, was now governor of the conjoined provinces of Transalpine and Cisalpine Gaul. By offering Cicero this temporary and honorary appointment on his staff to facilitate his electioneering in north Italy Piso put Cicero under an obligation (*officium*), whether or not Cicero actually took up the offer (which we do not know). So when in 63 Piso is prosecuted by Julius Caesar we are not surprised to find Cicero successfully leading for the defence. (See further below, section 4, note on l. 58.)

34. **ut . . . revertamur,** 'planning to return' (in such a way as to return).

35. **prolixa,** 'plain sailing' (cf. *laxus*).

35-6. **his . . . competitoribus.** It is not clear just what Cicero means by this. It might be (*a*) 'with these competitors here at Rome, at any rate (*dumtaxat*)'; (*b*) 'with these unmilitary competitors . . .'; or (*c*) 'with these city Romans as competitors . . .'. The first two renderings are probably preferable, with their suggestion that Pompey (at present in Asia fighting Mithridates) might send back one of his lieutenant-generals to stand with his backing, thus altering Cicero's calculations. (*c*) would imply that a man like Cicero, himself from a *municipium* background, might find more favour with the well-to-do non-urban voters of his own class.

36. **manum,** 'that crew of Pompey's'.

cura ut praestes, 'be sure to answer for, look after, see to'. This *cura . . . ut* construction is common in the letters. Cicero is of course only joking here, as is shown by 'propius abes': Atticus was in Epirus in north-west Greece, nearer Asia than Rome but still a very long way off. So too 'nega me . . . iratum fore' is not serious: there was no question of Pompey's coming back to Rome specially to support Cicero.

3. 40. **pervelim.** Potential subjunctive. The prefix *per-* has a strengthening force: 'I should very much like'.

Caecilius. Quintus Caecilius was an enormously rich banker, a friend of Lucius Lucullus and reputedly 'a crusty character' ('difficillima natura': Valerius Maximus vii. 8. 5). He died in 58, leaving his fortune and his name to his nephew Atticus (whom Cicero went on calling Pomponius and not Caecilius).

42. **agere coepit cum,** 'has begun an action against'.

43. **dolo malo mancipio accepisse,** 'to have acquired (*mancipio accepisse*) fraudulently'. *Mancipium* (*manu capere*) is the technical legal term for acquiring by purchase. *Dolus malus* is the general term for any sort of fraud. Presumably Varius was alleged to have conveyed property to his cousin Satyrus (*frater* can mean either 'brother' or 'cousin') by selling it to him at an artificially low price in order to defraud Varius' creditors, who would otherwise have distrained on the property.

diceret. This use of the subjunctive is strictly illogical, though it is common in Cicero. In a subordinate clause the subjunctive may be employed (*inter alia*) to express another person's thought: the speaker or writer is disclaiming authority for the statement (cf. the use of 'interemisset': Letter 11, section 3, note on *Africanus*). This is in fact the rationale behind the use of the subjunctive in subordinate clauses in *oratio obliqua*. Thus, had Cicero written here *de iis rebus quas is accepisset* the meaning would be 'about that property which (so your uncle said) had been acquired by Satyrus'. Logically, if the verb of saying is inserted, as here, no subjunctive is needed, and the indicative *dicebat* would be correct. But *dicebat* is attracted into the subjunctive *diceret* by a sort of false analogy, or contamination, from the other usage. (See Handford, *The Latin Subjunctive*, para. 164.)

44. **L. Lucullus.** Consul 74, and subsequently C.-in-C. of the war against Mithridates until ousted by the manœuvres of Pompey and his friends. In 65 he was still waiting outside Rome for his long-delayed triumph, which he finally celebrated only in 63.

45. **P. Scipio.** Scipio Nasica, scion of the great house of the Cornelii Scipiones, and soon to be adopted by will by Q. Metellus Pius—hence acquiring the splendidly polyonymous address Quintus Caecilius Metellus Pius Scipio Nasica. His daughter, previously married to Publius Crassus, son of the famous Crassus, became the wife of Pompey in 53 after the death of Caesar's daughter Julia; and father-in-law and son-in-law shared the consulship in 52. One of the leading anti-Caesarian commanders in the Civil War, he took his own life after the Battle of Thapsus in 46.

magistrum. That is, *magistrum auctionis* = 'receiver'. Clearly Cicero did not think it would actually come to Satyrus' being sold up to satisfy the creditors. *Venirent* is the imperfect subjunctive of *veneo* = 'to be put on sale'.

46. **verum hoc . . . de magistro,** 'but this talk of a receiver'.

47. **adessem.** *Adesse* is regularly used of 'appearing' as a counsel or advocate.

49. **observat . . .,** 'Lucius Domitius has the greatest claim on his loyalties, but I come next'. This is Domitius Ahenobarbus ('Brassbeard'), father of Shakespeare's Enobarbus, and great-great-grandfather of the Emperor Nero. He was a brother-in-law of Marcus Cato, and like him an extreme optimate and a violent enemy of Caesar. In 65 he was in his early thirties, but his birth, immense wealth, and wide-ramifying political connections explain the importance of his support for Cicero. Pompey and Crassus kept him out of the consulship in his due year of 55, but he got in in 54 along with Appius Claudius Pulcher, the elder brother of Publius Clodius.

50. **Quinto fratri.** On Quintus, younger brother of Marcus Cicero, see *Introduction*, p. ix. He was married to Atticus' sister, Pomponia.

51. **petitionibus.** Marcus had been quaestor in 75, aedile in 69, praetor in 66. Quintus had been quaestor (69 or 68), and was aedile for the current year, 65.

4. 51–2. **cum . . . tum,** 'in view of my friendship both with Satyrus himself and with Domitius, on whom above all others my hopes of advancement depend'.

54. **illo.** Satyrus.

54–5. **me ei satis facturum fuisse.** This construction, future participle+*fuisse*, is the regular formula in Ciceronian Latin to express an unrealized condition in past time in *oratio obliqua*: 'I should have given him satisfaction'.

56–7. **suo nomine perhiberet,** 'might bring in on his own account'.

58. **et officio . . . tempori,** 'to have some thought for my obligations and my present position'. *Officium* is what one man owes another for services rendered (*beneficia*); the grantor of the favour acquires *gratia* ('influence' or 'pull') with the beneficiary. These are three key-words in the Roman political vocabulary, for public and private life were firmly based on the principle of *manus manum lavat*—'You scratch my back and I'll scratch yours'. Of course, from time to time, as here, *officia* owed to different individuals might pull a man in different directions. Cicero wrote a treatise on the subject, the *de officiis*.

58–9. **Durius . . . quam vellem,** 'less graciously than I could have wished'.

59–60. **homines belli,** 'gentlemen'.

60–1. **et postea . . . refugit,** 'and subsequently he has altogether re-coiled from the intimacy which had grown up between us during the past few days'.

62. **humanitate,** 'common decency'.

62–4. **ne . . . venirem,** 'from appearing against a friend whose whole reputation was at stake and in his darkest hour'. A conviction for fraud would have involved public disgrace (*infamia*) for Satyrus.

65. **durior,** 'somewhat unkind'.

66. **etiam si id sit,** 'even if this be so'.

67. **ἐπεὶ οὐχ ἱερήιον . . .** A tag from Homer, *Iliad* xxii. 159 (Cicero quotes from Homer far more than from any other author). The point of the original passage is that no ordinary prize is at stake, but the life or death of Hector. Achilles was pursuing Hector round the walls of Troy, hence Cicero continues the simile with 'in quo cursu'. Translate: 'For 'tis no common prize I strive for now'.

68. **gratias.** See note on l. 58 above.

5. 71. **Hermathena.** A bust of the goddess Athena set on a straight-sided pillar or 'herm'. A present from Atticus for the decoration of Cicero's Tusculan villa.

72. **totum gymnasium . . . videatur,** 'that the whole Gymnasium seems to be dedicated to its honour'. A gymnasium was strictly a place where men and boys took exercise, but because philosophers like Socrates frequented such places for discussion and argument the word came also to mean a place intended for intellectual or literary pursuits—often a hall or suchlike suitably adorned with busts and statuary, as here. ἀνάθημα means 'an offering to the gods', a 'dedication'; its specialized variant ἀνάθεμα (a New Testament word) gives us our word 'anathema', an 'accursed thing'.

LETTER 2

1. 3. **L. Iulio . . . coss.** At Rome years were dated not by consecutive numbering but by the names of the two consuls in office, usually in the ablative case: 'Lucius Julius Caesar and Gaius Marcius Figulus being consuls . . .' Cicero here, however, is jokingly using the names of the two men just elected consuls for the coming year (64) as if they constituted a regular dating formula. He thus conveys to Atticus (*a*) the fact and date—election day—of his son's birth; and (*b*) the result of the elections. [*coss.* = *consulibus.*]

filiolo. An affectionate diminutive—diminutive forms can of course also be used derisively. The whole sentence is in a deliberately mock-pompous vein: 'I have the honour to inform you that I have been blessed with a little son.' Cicero already had a daughter, his darling Tullia or Tulliola. His new son Marcus was given a consulship by Octavian in 30, but by and large he was to prove a disappointment to his father.

4. salva Terentia, 'Terentia came through it well': an ablative of attendant circumstances, akin in use to the ablative absolute (cf. the consular dating formulas). Cicero had married Terentia in 77, when he was 29 years old. He divorced her for a younger and richer wife in 46.

5–6. de meis . . . rationibus. See Letter 1 for Cicero's 'plans' or 'calculations'. Note here the contrived order of words to bring *meis* and *ad te* into close juxtaposition (hyperbaton).

6–7. Catilinam . . . defendere. This is a very intriguing piece of information. Cicero did not in fact undertake the brief, though some ancient commentators thought he did (see Asconius, p. 86 C). But the very fact that in summer 65 he was contemplating doing so, and (below) actually entertaining the idea of running in double harness with Catiline for the two consulships of 63, casts grave doubt on the traditional Ciceronian and Sallustian accounts of the 'first Catilinarian conspiracy' of 66/5. Had Catiline been believed, or even widely suspected, to be involved in a plan to murder consuls, seize power, and initiate a 'massacre of *optimates*', it is unthinkable that Cicero could have dreamed of publicly associating himself with such a man, especially since he was particularly anxious to conciliate conservative opinion among the nobility. As so often, a private letter reveals facts which are suppressed or glossed over in Cicero's public utterances, and are at variance with them.

7–8. Iudices . . . voluntate, 'we have the jury we wanted, thanks to the very ready co-operation of the prosecution'. There was a panel or pool of well-to-do citizens (senators, *equites*, and *tribuni aerarii*) from which the *iudices* were selected by lot for any particular trial; it was called the *album iudicum*. But both prosecution and defence had the right to strike individual jurors off by challenge (*reicere, reiectio*). If the prosecution colluded with the defence, a 'rigged' or 'packed' jury could result. Clearly the prosecutor here was guilty of collusion (*praevaricatio*) with the defence. He was in fact Publius Clodius, who was at this time on good terms with Cicero: in 63 he served as a volunteer member of Cicero's personal bodyguard at the height of the Catilinarian crisis (Plutarch, *Cicero* 29). Cicero some years later sneered at Clodius as 'Catilinae praevaricator' (*in Pisonem* 23), but he was happy enough about the prospect at the time.

8–9. si absolutus erit. Catiline was acquitted, but no collaboration with Cicero followed.

9–10. in ratione petitionis. See Letter 1, section 1, note.

10. humaniter. That is, as a man should: 'I shall not be too upset'.

2. 11. opus est. A Latin idiom of long standing: literally 'There is work for us to do with . . .' = 'I need your presence here as soon as possible'.

12. nobilis. The term *nobilis* has a precise connotation, and means a man of consular family, i.e. one who could count at least one consul among his direct male ancestors. Such men constituted an élite of birth and wealth and influence among the senatorial class. They tended very much to resent the intrusion of outsiders, *novi homines*, into the consulship, which they regarded as their private preserve. On this, see Sallust, *Jugurtha* 63.

13. honori nostro. 'Honos' here as often has the concrete sense of 'office' or 'magistracy'. The phrase *cursus honorum* described the ladder of office up which men climbed from junior magistracy to consulship.

LETTER 3

2. M. TVLLIVS M. F. . . . , 'Marcus Tullius Marci filius Cicero salutem dat Gnaeo Pompeio Gnaei filio Magno Imperatori'. This is a very formal address, and the letter itself is carefully composed in a style closer to that of Cicero's literary and oratorical works than is usual in the letters. (The full style of a Roman citizen was even longer than this, however, containing in addition the name of the man's paternal grandfather and of his tribe (voting district).) This formality indicates that Cicero and Pompey are not on terms of close intimacy, and also suggests that the letter was meant to circulate, through copies, in the Roman political world; certainly some of Cicero's letters were clearly written with this intention, as an informal way of advertising a point of view or justifying a line of policy.

3. **MAGNO.** The title 'Magnus' (Pompey the Great) was accorded Pompey by his troops in Africa in 81, when he was 25 years old, and apparently confirmed by Sulla, in whose behalf Pompey had been fighting. Pompey was frequently called 'Magnus' without any qualification.

IMPERATORI. Strictly 'imperator' denotes a military commander in possession of *imperium*. More particularly, it was with this title that a victorious Roman army saluted its commander. The use of the title as a permanent *praenomen* begins only with Augustus (*Imperator Caesar Augustus*), whence it comes to have the sense of the modern words derived from it: 'emperor', etc. (On the whole question, see Syme, *Historia* 7 (1958), 172–88.)

I. 4. S. T. E. Q. V. B. E., 'si tu exercitusque valetis, bene est': 'My best wishes to you and your army'.

Ex litteris tuis. These were the official dispatches sent by Pompey to the Senate and People of Rome to announce his final victory over Mithridates and his settlement of the Near East.

6. **oti.** *Otium* is best translated 'peace'. Probably Cicero is thinking chiefly of peace in Asia Minor, racked by decades of war and disturbance. But he may well also have had in mind peace and quiet at home, with the return of Pompey (he reached Italy at the very end of 62) restoring stability to affairs at Rome, which had been turbulent enough in his absence.

7. **pollicebar.** Cicero uses the imperfect, past continuous, tense because he had made such promises repeatedly. He refers most obviously to his own speech as praetor in 66 in support of Pompey's original appointment to Asia (*pro lege Manilia*); but he had in general followed a Pompeian line ever since the *Verrines* in 70, and his speeches as consul in 63, most notably in opposition to the Rullan agrarian bill (*de lege agraria*), stress the interests of Pompey.

7–8. **veteres hostis, novos amicos.** Cicero is careful to name no names. He must have had Caesar in mind. Caesar's activity in 63 Cicero saw as anti-Pompeian, but as praetor in 62 Caesar joined with Metellus Nepos in advocating the recall of Pompey to finish off Catiline and the transference to Pompey of the honour of dedicating the rebuilt Capitoline temple. He can scarcely mean Crassus, since there is no sign that Crassus now or later spoke or acted in a way that could be construed as friendly to Pompey. The plural perhaps includes besides Caesar and his friends a number of Pompey's old opponents from the early seventies who now found it expedient to pretend goodwill towards their victorious enemy.

8–9. **ex magna spe . . . iacere,** 'are prostrated by the confounding of their high hopes'.

2. 9. Ad me autem. After the suppression of the Catilinarians, Cicero had written a long letter (no longer extant) to Pompey to tell him all about it. It was somewhat high-handed in its tone ('aliquanto insolentius': Schol. Bob. 167); and twice later forensic opponents threw it in Cicero's face (*pro Sulla* 67; *pro Plancio* 85). It was this letter presumably that evoked Pompey's cool reply to Cicero; there are those who believe (I do not) that Pompey had hoped to be called back to Italy to deal with Catiline himself.

12. **meorum officiorum conscientia,** 'my personal conviction that I have done my duty'. On *officia* see Letter 1, section 4, note.

13–14. **quibus si quando . . . patior,** 'and if at times no reciprocal response is made, I am well content that the greater credit for services rendered should rest with me'.

15. **studia,** 'efforts', 'exertions'. See note on *pollicebar*, above.

15–16. **res publica.** Frequently used in this sense to denote not 'the state' but 'public affairs', 'public policy', or 'the public interest'.

3. 19. necessitudinis. This is a stronger word than 'amicitia', and refers to particularly close ties, sometimes to ties of kinship—though this latter does not apply here.

20. **exspectavi.** The indicative marks this as a plain statement of fact. A subjunctive would have meant: 'I might have expected'.

21. **vererere.** Here the subjunctive is used because Cicero is expressing the supposed grounds for Pompey's omission of congratulations.

26–7. **Africanus . . . Laelium.** Cicero is not consistent in his construction within the comparative clauses: *Africanus* is made the subject of a clause, *Laelium* is attracted into the accusative case by the *me* which precedes. Publius Cornelius Scipio Aemilianus, often known as Africanus or Africanus Minor in honour of his victory over Carthage in the Third Punic War, was the grandson by adoption of the earlier Scipio Africanus, the conqueror of Hannibal. He was a towering figure in Roman politics in the third quarter of the second century B.C., and a particular hero of Cicero's. Together with his close friend and confidant Gaius Laelius he features in Cicero's treatise *de re publica* as an ideal statesman or 'moderator rei publicae' (Book v, ch. 8). We see then that Cicero is toying with the idea of playing Laelius to Pompey's Africanus, influencing the 'moderator' himself with sage advice and political tuition.

LETTER 4

1. 3. putidum, 'disagreeable', 'distasteful': the basic meaning is 'rotten', and hence 'malodorous'.

4. distinebar. Epistolary imperfect: 'I am so distracted'.

tantulae epistulae, 'these few lines'—or, perhaps better, 'these hurried lines'; for the letter is not particularly brief, while it does bear the marks of hasty composition, being much looser and more colloquial in style, syntax, structure, and vocabulary than any of the preceding three in this selection.

7. contio. *Contio*—a syncopated form of *conventio* = 'a coming together'—meant a public assembly summoned by a magistrate or tribune to be addressed or harangued on matters of topical interest, as opposed to a formal assembly convened for electoral or legislative purposes (*comitia*). It was a handy way of airing arguments and sounding public opinion, and frequently was put to use as a sort of press conference at which leading politicians could be questioned about their views. By a natural process, *contio* comes also to mean a speech or address delivered at such a meeting. (The earlier letter here referred to, 'scripsi ad te antea', has not survived.)

8–9. non iucunda . . ., non gravis, 'it offered no comfort to the poor, no hope to the wicked, no pleasure to the rich, no reassurance to the solid citizens'. These somewhat emotive terms: *miseri* = 'poor', 'wretched'; *improbi* = 'scoundrels', 'rascals'; *beati* = 'fortunate', 'rich'; *boni* = 'the good people', 'those you approve of' (cf. *optimates* = 'the best people') are all common usage in Cicero's day. Compare the similar use in Greek of words like βέλτιστοι, χρηστοί, πονηροί.

9. frigebat, 'it was a frost', that is, 'it fell flat'.

Pisonis. Marcus Pupius Piso Frugi Calpurnianus. He is to be distinguished from Gaius Calpurnius Piso, the consul of 67 (Letter 1, section 2).

10. **levissimus,** 'irresponsible'. 'Levis' means 'light' or 'lightweight', lacking in *gravitas* ('responsibility').

Fufius. Quintus Fufius Calenus, later praetor (in 59), *legatus* under Caesar (51–49), and consul (in 47).

11. **circo Flaminio.** The Flaminian Circus was in the Campus Martius, outside the old city boundary of Rome, the *pomerium*. Pompey was hoping to celebrate a triumph, so he had to stay outside the *pomerium* since the rule was that if a promagistrate crossed it and entered the city he automatically lost his *imperium* and forfeited any chance of a triumph. So Calenus calls his *contio* at a convenient spot just outside so that Pompey may attend and speak, which he could do only at the invitation of the presiding officer. Similarly, though Cicero does not bother to mention it, the meeting of the senate attended by Pompey (below) must have been held in a building outside the *pomerium* for the same reason. The Temple of Apollo was sometimes used for this purpose: see Letter 11, section 3.

12. **nundinarum.** *Nundinae* = 'market-day'. The Romans worked on an eight-day 'week', from one *nundinae* to the next. (The root of the word is 'novem-dies', 'ninth day' by inclusive reckoning from one to the next.)

πανήγυρις. A 'panegyris' (cf. 'panegyric') in Greek was a solemn assembly or conclave. Cicero is being ironical, contrasting the pomp and circumstance of the Greek word with the everyday hustle and bustle of a market-day—the sublime and the ridiculous.

12–13. **Quaesivit . . . uteretur,** 'he asked Pompey whether he agreed that the jurors should be picked by the praetor himself for the selfsame praetor to use as his panel'. Technically, the *iudices* constituted the 'consilium'('council', 'panel of advisers') on whom the presiding officer relied for advice in trying a case; though in practice the vote of the *iudices* for acquittal or conviction was final and binding. The senate had decided that for Clodius' trial the *iudices* should not be selected from the pool (*album iudicum*) at random, as was customary, but hand-picked by the presiding praetor. The object of this was to secure as incorruptible a jury as possible. But Fufius, like the consul Piso a supporter of Clodius, carefully phrased his question to bring out the unfairness of this procedure. He hoped to elicit from Pompey, whose political influence was very great, public condemnation of the senate's plan, which would have to be voted into law by a citizen assembly before it could be effective.

14. **religione.** That is, the question of *religio*, the alleged sacrilege committed against *religio*.

2. 15. μάλ' ἀριστοκρατικῶς, 'in a truly aristocratic fashion'—that is, like a true optimate noble. Clearly, as a little later in the senate, Pompey adopted his customary trick of evading a direct answer and taking refuge in airy generalizations so as to avoid committing himself. We need to remember that he was not long back in Italy, and was feeling his way warily in political circumstances which had changed a great deal since he had left some six years earlier. On landing at Brindisi, he had ostentatiously disbanded his army, and had made overtures to the staunch optimate Cato for a marriage alliance. He was anxious to secure grants of land for his veteran soldiers and the formal ratification of his settlement of the Near East. While putting out feelers for a *modus vivendi* with his old enemies among the *optimates*, he was not risking a precipitate false step. He was justifiably irritated, no doubt, by being harried over the comparatively trivial Clodian affair. Clodius had worked in Pompey's interests in the early sixties when serving on the staff of the then commander in Asia Minor, his own brother-in-law Lucius Lucullus, by encouraging mutiny among Lucullus' troops and helping to pave the way for his supersession by Pompey. Now Lucullus and his optimate friends were out for Clodius' blood (which is why they were making so much fuss about the Bona Dea affair). Pompey did not want to cross the *optimates*, but no more did he want to alienate popular feeling, which was behind Clodius. Hence his evasiveness, for which Cicero shows such small sympathy.

16. **maximi.** Genitive of price or value: 'He held it in the highest respect', 'had the highest regard for . . .'

17. **et id multis verbis,** 'and that in many words'—i.e. 'and he was very long-winded about saying it'.

Messalla. Marcus Valerius Messalla, Piso's colleague as consul in 61 and his opponent in this matter. He was a sound optimate.

19. **de promulgata rogatione.** A *rogatio* is a proposal for legislation (an 'asking'), which if duly ratified by a citizen assembly became a *lex* or *plebiscitum*. The senate had decreed that a bill be prepared by the consuls and put to the people. It had first to be formally published (promulgated) some time in advance of the voting to allow time for reflection and discussion.

20. **illius ordinis consulta.** The *ordo* is the senate, frequently so referred

to. A *senatus consultum* was a decree of the senate. In many matters it was sufficient authority in itself; but in many others it had to be ratified by a citizen assembly before it could become effective, thus constituting (as here) only a recommendation for action backed by the authority of the senate.

γενικῶς, 'in general terms'. That is, he was evasive.

21. **de istis rebus.** Cicero is quoting Pompey's actual words to him as he resumed his seat: 'those affairs of yours'. Pompey was being sarcastic: was this Clodian business all that Rome had to worry about ?

3. 22. **Crassus.** Marcus Licinius Crassus, consul with Pompey in 70, and then again in 55. The two men never hit it off, and were generally in sharp rivalry. Caesar brought them together in the 'First Triumvirate' in 59, but they were only superficially reconciled to each other, though Caesar managed to get them to co-operate with himself.

22–4. **postea . . . placere,** 'after Crassus saw that Pompey had poached some approval because of the general impression that he thought well of my consulship'. *Excepisse* means to pick up something that might otherwise have gone elsewhere. *Quod* is frequently used in Ciceronian Latin to introduce a noun clause; similarly *quod esset senator* = 'the fact that he was a senator'. Pompey's general praise of all *senatus consulta* was taken to imply that he approved the actions of Cicero and the senate in 63 in suppressing and executing the Catilinarians.

26. **mihi acceptum.** A metaphor from book-keeping: 'All this he put down as owed to me'.

28. **Quid multa ?** A common idiom (understand some such verb as *dicam*): 'Need I say more ?'

29. **locum.** *Locus* is here used in the technical rhetorical sense of a 'topic' or 'theme'.

varie, 'gaudily'—the sense is of brightly contrasting colours: cf. 'varia' in Letter 14, section 2.

29. **Aristarchus.** The most famous of the Alexandrian critics, and especially noted for his stern rejection of many lines of Homer as unauthentic. (Cf. Horace, *ars poetica* 445–51.) Cicero regularly submitted his literary works (speeches included) to Atticus for comment and criticism before publication (see Letter 12, section 1). Here we might translate *Aristarchus* as 'my severest critic', 'my *Edinburgh Review*'.

30–1. **nosti illas λληκύθους,** 'you know how rich my palette is'. 'Lēcu-thoi', usually small oil-flasks, could also be used as flasks to hold paints.

31. **Proxime.** Superlative of *prope*, governing the accusative case = 'closest', 'right next to'.

32–4. **intellexi . . . laudarentur,** 'I saw that he was upset that Crassus should be coming in for the credit which he might have had for himself —or perhaps that my achievements were so momentous that the senate should be so delighted to hear them extolled'. The construction—accusative and infinitive—after *moveri* is used because *moveri* is a kind of 'emotional verb' which can be followed by the accusative and infinitive as verbs like *sentio* are. Being uncertain about the precise explanation for Pompey's being affected or upset, Cicero follows up his first explanation with a disjunctive question introduced by *an*—'or it may be . . .'. *Inire gratiam* (cf. *inire hereditatem*) conveys the notion that Crassus 'inherited', 'came into', the *gratia* which might in the first place have gone to Pompey.

35. **eo minus . . . quod,** 'all the less because': cf. 'eo brevior quod' below, section 4.

36. **litteris.** Here not 'letters' but 'published writings', chiefly the speeches *pro lege Manilia* and *de lege agraria*. In the former Pompey had been given the sole credit for the defeat of Spartacus, though Crassus had won the decisive battle; in the latter Crassus had been covertly but severely criticized for selfish and irresponsible scheming to damage the position of Pompey, whom Cicero portrayed as 'the true champion of the Roman people'.

perstrictus, 'belittled', 'slighted': 'He had been rather shabbily treated in the interest of extolling Pompey'. Adjectives like *Pompeianus* are commonly formed from proper names, where we should say 'of Pompey'.

4. 37. **adiunxit.** These warm feelings for Crassus did not last long: Cicero never really liked or trusted him.

illo, Pompey.

aperte tecte has been taken either (*a*) as an asyndeton = 'openly or covertly'; or (*b*) as an oxymoron (cf. 'bitter-sweet') = 'with ostentatious guardedness'. I think the run of the sentence and the general sense favour the former: 'But all the same, whatever Pompey gave me, whether explicitly or implicitly, I accepted the gift gratefully'.

39. **ἐνεπερπερευσάμην . . .,** 'how I flaunted myself before my new audience, Pompey.' (The dative *Pompeio* is governed by the Greek verb.)

Pompey and Crassus, both senior to Cicero as ex-consuls (*consulares*) had been called on to speak before him. Now it was his own turn, and Pompey (unlike the rest of the senate) had not been treated to Cicero's Catilinarian flights before.

40–1. περίοδοι... tempore, 'if ever rounded periods and rhythmical endings and proofs and demonstrations came to my bidding, it was then'. The Greek words are all technical terms of rhetoric, on the theory and analysis of which Greek scholars had laboured for centuries. Like other Romans of his class, Cicero had studied rhetoric under the leading Greek professors of his day. (The word ἐνθυμήματα strictly means 'rhetorical forms of argument'.)

41. **clamores.** The verb (*fuerunt*) is, as often, omitted. 'It brought the house down', or (more simply): 'Need I go on? Roars of applause'.

42. ὑπόθεσις. Not a 'hypothesis' but a 'theme' or 'topic'.

42–4. **de gravitate ordinis . . . de otio.** In a nutshell, the *leit-motifs* of Cicero's policy from 63 onwards: a responsible and respected senate, co-operating with and supported by the equestrian order, and backed by a united Italy; guaranteeing security, prosperity, and peace.

43. **intermortuis,** 'half-dead', 'moribund'—the extremists left over from the destruction of the Catilinarian movement were a spent force.

44. **vilitate,** 'the low price (cheapness) of corn', here advanced as evidence of stability and good government.

sonitus, 'boomings', 'thunderings'.

45. **usque istinc,** 'even as far away as where you are'—Atticus was in Epirus, in NW. Greece. *Exaudire* = 'to hear at a distance'.

5. 47. **Senatus Ἄρειος πάγος,** 'the senate is a veritable Areopagus'. The Areopagus, the ancient High Council of Athens, had become a byword for wisdom and resolution and unflinching probity.

48. **severius,** 'severus' means 'strict', 'stern', rather than 'severe'.

49. **rogationi . . . ferendae,** 'for carrying the bill in accordance with the senate's decree'. On this bill, see above, l. 19.

50. **barbatuli,** 'with their silly little beards'. In Cicero's day, a clean-shaven face was the norm; to wear a small, neatly-trimmed beard was the affectation of the young fop. Compare the uproarious section 33 of Cicero's *pro Caelio* where the smart beardlets of Clodia's friends are contrasted with the rich and shaggy growth that had decorated the chin of her distinguished ancestor, the Blind Censor.

grex Catilinae, 'all that crowd that used to trail after Catiline' (*grex* suggests silly sheep, easily led). A number of young bloods, many of them deep in debt, had openly favoured Catiline in 63; compare *pro Murena* 49: 'Catilinam . . . stipatum choro iuventutis', where the metaphor again suggests a similar idea.

50–1. **duce filiola Curionis,** 'with little Miss Curio at their head'. This is Gaius Scribonius Curio the younger, regularly referred to as *Curio filius* to distinguish him from his father of the same name, consul in 76. Young Curio was about 22 at this time. Generally anti-Caesarian until his startling defection to Caesar as tribune early in 50, he was a great personal friend of Publius Clodius. Despite the sneer 'filiola', which imputes not merely effeminacy but homosexual prostitution, he was generally on very friendly terms with Cicero.

51. **antiquaret,** 'reject', 'vote against'. Roman voters were handed two tablets (*tabellae*) marked respectively *V.R.* = *uti rogas* ('as you ask'), and *A.* = *antiquo* ('I am opposed to it'). They discarded one and deposited the other in a voting-urn or basket.

52. **lator . . . dissuasor.** As consul and president of the senate, Piso had to present the senate's proposal to the assembly, though personally he was opposed to it. He made no attempt to hide his opposition.

53. **pontis.** The narrow gangways leading from the voting-enclosures (*saepta*), where the tribes or centuries were marshalled, to the actual voting platforms were called *pontes*.

tabellae. See on *antiquaret*, above.

54. **tibi.** The so-called 'ethic dative', implying the interest of the person(s) in the dative case in what is being described or said. It often serves to enliven a narrative: 'Then, if you please, up rushes Cato on to the speakers' platform . . .' The *rostra*, the speakers' platform in the Forum, got its name from the ships' prows (*rostra*) which decorated it, the trophies of a Roman naval victory in the early Republic.

Cato. Marcus Porcius Cato, descendant of the famous Censor. In 63 he had rallied a wavering senate to vote for the death sentence on the arrested Catilinarian conspirators. Tribune in 62, praetor in 54, despite his comparative youth he was the most powerful and effective leader the *optimates* had, and a paragon of integrity (cf. Letter 18, section 4). He gained posthumous fame and near-sainthood for his unflinching opposition to Caesar in the Civil War and his defence of (and suicide at) Utica in Tunisia—whence he was often later called *Cato Uticensis*.

57. **salutis,** 'sanity'.

Hortensius. Consul in 69, and a staunch optimate. Cicero displaced him as Rome's leading orator and advocate in the early sixties; but Hortensius made a come-back from 63 onwards, and he and Cicero were engaged for all the leading cases (Cicero, *Brutus* 320–4).

58. **Favoni.** Marcus Favonius, a staunch admirer and disciple of Cato.

59. **dimittuntur . . . vocatur.** Compare *advolat* and *facit*, above. The shift into the present tense imparts pace and immediacy and variety to the narrative.

60. **frequenti senatu,** 'at a packed meeting of the senate'. A *frequens senatus* was either (*a*) a well-attended meeting of the senate; or (*b*) more technically, a meeting attendance at which was made mandatory on all available senators or at which a quorum (probably of 200) of members was necessary for certain business to be transacted. (See Balsdon, *JRS* 47 (1957), 18–20.)

63. **Curioni.** Father of 'little Miss Curio' (who was too young to be a member of the senate). A reliable optimate, and a determined opponent of Caesar's in the fifties, he shared his son's friendship and support for Clodius.

nullum . . . facienti, 'who was against any decree's being passed'— that is, Curio moved that no action be taken.

64. **ex altera parte,** 'on the other side'. The numbers involved are surprisingly large. The total number of senators at this period was between 500 and 600, but at any given time a good many would be absent on public service or private business, or ill, and so on. In a letter of December 57, Cicero speaks of 200 as a good turn-out: 'Sane frequentes fuimus: omnino ad ducentos' (*ad Q. fr.* ii. 1. 1). And in a crucial and well-attended debate shortly before the outbreak of Civil War, 392 senators voted (Appian, *BC* ii. 30). Here we have 'some 15' in favour of Curio's motion and 'a good 400' against: a striking indication of the intense interest and excitement aroused by the Clodius affair.

64–5. **Acta res est,** 'so that was the end of that'.

65. **Fufius . . . concessit.** The MSS. reading is very uncertain here, but this seems the best restoration: 'the tribune Fufius at this point gave in'. Fufius could have used his tribunician veto against the decree and so rendered it null and void; but he refrained. But he could still use his veto when the proposal came to the vote in the popular assembly, and it was his threat to do so that in the end forced Hortensius & Co. to

climb down (*ad Att.* 1. 16. 2) and accept a normally constituted panel of *iudices* for the trial of Clodius (who was acquitted only by a fairly narrow margin of votes).

66. **habebat.** Epistolary imperfect: 'is holding'.

Lucullum . . . Messalam. The four men named here were the hard core of the attack on Clodius, hoping that he would be convicted and thus barred from public life. Lucius Lucullus had an old grudge against Clodius (see above, note on μάλ᾽ ἀριστοκρατικῶς). On Gaius Piso, consul 67, see Letter 1, section 2, note; he is not to be confused with Clodius' supporter, the consul in office, Marcus Pupius Piso.

68. **'comperisse',** 'his sole charge against me is that "I have been fully apprised" '. This was a wicked dig at Cicero, an allusion to the year 63 when, without divulging his sources or his evidence, Cicero repeatedly claimed 'to have been apprised' of the plans of the conspirators. The jibe was by no means unique: 'nam *comperisse* me non audeo dicere, ne forte id ipsum verbum ponam quod abs te aiunt falso in me solere conferri' (*ad famm.* v. 5. 2: a letter addressed to Cicero's old colleague, Gaius Antonius).

68-9. **de provinciis praetorum,** 'the allocation of provinces to the praetors'.

69. **legationibus,** 'embassies' from the provinces and client states regularly given audience by the senate in February of each year.

decernebat. Apparently attracted from the perfect into the imperfect tense by the preceding epistolary imperfects. By this decree priority was accorded to the Clodius affair above all other public business. But it may have the meaning, 'is for decreeing'.

6. 73. **laudator amator imitator.** Note the triple jingle for effect.

Ille alter. Scornful: 'That partner of his' (Piso).

73-4. **uno vitio minus vitiosus quod,** 'a man of many vices, with the one saving vice that . . .'.

75. ἀπρακτότατος **. . .,** 'utterly ineffectual, but in disposition so distempered that . . .' ἀπρακτότατος is the superlative of the Greek adjective meaning 'inactive', 'ineffectual'; κακέκτης is a medical term for 'ill-disposed'. Incidentally, if Piso really had taken against Pompey, the mood did not last long, for the two were co-operating by July: *ad Att.* 1. 16. 2.

79. **studio perditarum rerum,** 'by his support for extremism'.

81. Cornuto . . . Pseudocatone, 'with Cornutus a reach-me-down Cato'. As praetor in 57, Gaius Caecilius Cornutus was to show himself active in helping to secure Cicero's recall from exile against the opposition of Clodius.

81–2. quid quaeris? Similar in use to *Quid multa?*: 'Is there anything more to add?'

7. 83. redeam. Cicero writes 'return' because his private affairs are a constant topic in his letters to Atticus.

Τεῦκρις . . ., 'Teucris has fulfilled her promise'. 'Teucris' was acting as an intermediary in the matter of a loan promised to Cicero by his former colleague as consul in 63, Gaius Antonius, to help him buy a house on the Palatine Hill at Rome. Who she was we do not know, and the name is probably a 'code-name' used to insure against a prying messenger; one guess is that she was Antonius' wife.

84. mandata . . , 'the job I gave you to do'. Probably a reference to a request Cicero had made of Atticus shortly before to deal with a scoundrelly and troublesome freedman of Cicero's called Hilarus (*ad Att.* 1. 12. 2).

84–5. Argiletani aedifici . . . emit, 'has bought the remaining three-quarters of the Argiletum building'. The Argiletum was a street in Rome near the Subura, noted for its booksellers. Quintus must have inherited a quarter share in the building, and has bought out the interest of the co-heirs. No doubt he wanted the building as an investment to provide rent income.

85. HS $\overline{\text{DCCXXV}}$, 'for 725,000 sesterces'. On the calculation of Roman money, see Appendix 2. The building (probably an apartment building with shops at street level) was thus worth altogether getting on for one million sesterces, an enormous sum when one considers that property to the value of 400,000 sesterces qualified a man to rank as an *eques*, while under the early principate property worth one million was required for membership of the senate.

85–6. Tusculanum venditat, 'he is trying to sell his place at Tusculum'. *Vendito* is a frequentative form of *vendo*.

86. Pacilianam domum, 'Pacilius' house'—but who Pacilius was is unknown.

87. Lucceio. Lucius Lucceius was enormously rich and something of a literary figure. Cicero tried to wheedle him into writing a fulsome account of his own conduct as consul in 63 in suppressing Catiline: *ad famm.* v. 12. He later ran (unsuccessfully) in combination with Julius Caesar for the consulship of 59.

88. **petiturire.** A desiderative form of *peto* = 'to seek election' (Cicero has a fondness for such coinages) with the sense of 'itching to be a candidate', 'can't wait to be a candidate'. Lucceius was already looking forward to the elections in 60 (see preceding note).

navabo operam, 'I shall turn to and help'.

LETTER 5

1. 3–4. **Ut scribis . . . tua,** 'I see it is as you write: the present political uncertainty is mirrored in your letter'.

4. **ista,** 'which you describe'.

sermonum, 'gossip', 'talk'.

6. **ut fit in tantis rebus,** 'as happens when such important issues are involved'.

7–8. **quidnam . . . agrariam,** 'what universally acceptable way can be found to provide enough land'. Caesar had passed an agrarian law earlier in the year in order to provide land-grants for Pompey's discharged veterans from the eastern wars and for some of the urban poor. Opposition could be expected from vested landed interests or from the *publicani* who farmed the revenues from state-owned land like that in Campania in central Italy. (Shortly after this letter was written, Cicero heard from Atticus that this rich land, the *ager Campanus*, was to be made available for further allotments.)

2. 9. **ista magnitudo animi,** 'that "unselfish courage" you speak of'— *ista* shows that Cicero is picking up the actual words used by Atticus in his letter.

in comitiorum dilatione, 'in putting off the elections'. In an attempt to block his colleague Caesar's reform programme, Bibulus had recourse to two devices: he decreed that all the remaining days in the year available for public business should be public holidays (*feriae*) and hence *not* available for public business; and he announced that he was continually 'watching the heavens' for unpropitious signs (*de caelo servare*), that is, interposing a religious bar to any such business. Caesar's response was simply to ignore all this technical obstruction, and go ahead regardless: thanks to Pompey, he had superior force on his side. But it did mean that, should his position become weak in the future, he was open to prosecution on a number of technical counts.

10. **ipsius iudicium,** 'a demonstration of his own opinion'.

correctione, 'remedy', 'rectification'. In other words, while conceding Bibulus' personal courage, Cicero thought his action no more than a gesture and certainly no solution to the problems confronting the state.

11. **Nimirum . . .,** 'believe me, our hope lies in Publius'. The mere fact that Cicero calls his *bête noire* Clodius 'Publius' is evidence of friendly feeling. (When in a nastier mood, he calls him simply *ille* or 'Clodius' or 'Pulchellus' = 'pretty boy'—Clodius was a Claudius Pulcher.) The patrician Clodius (he preferred this low-class version of 'Claudius') had been adopted into a plebeian family earlier in the year with the blessing of Caesar and Pompey, thus becoming eligible for the important tribunate of the plebs, which office he held in 58 and carried out a wide-ranging legislative programme. But just now he seems to have been taking an independent line, even threatening opposition to Caesar—hence Cicero's favourable view. However, he soon made his peace with Caesar, and began that harassing of Cicero which ended in the latter's exile in 58. (See further Letter 6, section 3, Letter 7, section 16, and notes.)

12. **Epiro.** Atticus was planning to leave Italy for his estate in Epirus in May.

13–14. **mecum . . . disputare.** See note on *nimirum*, above. Cicero is still wary, but evidently confident of holding his own with Clodius if it comes to a fight—an optimistic view which he was far too slow in discarding.

14–15. **si quid erit eius modi.** Cicero means any sort of attack by Clodius.

15. **sis advolaturus,** 'you will come flying to my side'.

ut hoc non sit, 'even if this does not happen'. The conditional-concessive use of *ut* (or *cum*) with the subjunctive, easy to spot since it is always followed by *tamen* or some such adversative conjunction.

15–16. **sive ruet sive eriget,** 'whether he runs riot or puts the country back on its feet again'. (*Ruet* is intransitive, and does not govern *rem publicam* as *eriget* does.)

16–17. **mihi propono,** 'I promise myself', 'envisage for myself'.

17. **modo,** 'provided that', 'so long as'.

te consessore, 'with you sitting by my side'.

3. 18. **maxime,** 'just this moment'.

ecce tibi, 'lo and behold'—the ethic dative again.

18–19. **Nondum plane ingemueram,** 'scarcely had I finished groaning (about Sebosus) when . . .'. Sebosus and Arrius were Cicero's neighbours at Formiae, and he found their company tedious. In an earlier letter (*ad Att.* ii. 14. 2) he calls Arrius 'my room-mate' (*contubernalis*), so difficult was he to shake off. He would not go to Rome because he wanted to stay philosophizing with Cicero all day and every day.

21. **'in montis . . .'.** A hexameter line. Ennius and Cicero himself have been canvassed as possible authors. The Revd. L. M. Styler has pointed out to me the parallel with Virgil, *Aeneid* iii. 105: 'mons Idaeus ubi et gentis cunabula nostrae'; saying (rightly) that this would seem to make Ennius the likelier source, as more likely to be imitated by Virgil. 'Incunabula nostra'—'the cradle of my birth'—means Cicero's home town of Arpinum, where he still retained his paternal estate.

22. **solus,** sc. *esse*.

23. **perurbanis,** 'over-civilized', 'over-sophisticated'. *Per* is an intensitive particle, as in *perterritus*, etc. It is a fairly common feature of colloquial Latin in particular, and is used a lot in these letters.

ita tamen ut . . ., 'but not without waiting for you at my place here at Formiae until 5 May, since your letter tells me nothing definite (about your own plans)'. Formiae was on the coast some 50 miles north-west of Naples.

4. 27. **controversia Mulviana,** 'the Mulvian dispute'. Cicero's wife Terentia occupies some public land which she claims should be rent-free, but on which some *publicani* (see below) maintain that a rent is payable to them as lessees from the state. *Mulviana* may refer either to an agent of the *publicani* named Mulvius with whom Terentia is dealing, or to the district (near the *pons Mulvius* just outside Rome) where the land was perhaps situated.

27–8. **communem causam.** Clearly this was a general issue, and Terentia's dispute was only one among a number of the same sort— Atticus was personally involved on his own account. Probably the dispute involved the interpretation of the Agrarian Law of 111, which had certainly freed some categories of public land from rent-charges; the position may well have been affected in some way by Caesar's agrarian legislation earlier in the year.

29. **sed . . . recusat,** 'but you do pay *something* to the tax-farmers, she

won't even do *that*'. The root meaning of *pendo* is 'to weigh out'; hence
it can be used to mean 'to ponder', 'calculate', or (as here) 'to pay out',
since in early times before coinage (or even after that so long as coins
were somewhat irregular in size and shape) precious metal or copper
would be weighed on a scale to ascertain its value.

publicanis. This was the name given to men who undertook state contracts. As well as farming the state taxes, for which they are best known
nowadays (the 'publicans' of the Gospels), they also undertook a wide
variety of other public contracts for services for which Rome lacked the
apparatus of a civil service: working state-owned quarries and wood-
land and mines, erecting public buildings, victualling armies, and so on.
Frequently they formed joint-stock companies (*societates publicanorum*)
to undertake big contracts. The *publicani* leased the right to collect
taxes, etc., from the state, or were paid a fixed sum to provide certain
services: they recouped the coast from the profits, together with something on top for themselves. It was not necessarily a bad system, so long
as it was properly controlled.

30. **Κικέρων, ἀριστοκρατικώτατος παῖς,** 'Cicero, most aristocratic of boys'—that is, a loyal little optimate. Cicero's young son was
now getting on for six years old. It is an attractive, though unprovable,
suggestion that the boy, beginning to learn Greek, added these three
words in his own hand.

LETTER 6

1. 3. subtiliter, 'in detail', 'painstakingly'. As often, the main verb
(*scribam*) is omitted.

Tota periit, 'it (the *res publica*) has perished root and branch'.

4. hoc. The ablative looks forward to *quod*: 'in that'.

5. dominatio. The irresistible control exercised by the 'First Triumvirate'.

6. ita molesta . . . pernicie, 'unpalatable without actually being fatal'.

7. quorsus, 'in what directions'.

8. horreamus, 'we shudder to think . . .'.

9. illorum. The 'First Triumvirate'.

Catoni irati. Cato aroused their particular anger because of his
stubborn leadership of the campaign of constitutional obstruction to
the legislation of 59.

10–11. **videremur . . . interire,** 'it seemed that our death might be a painless one'.

11. **nunc vero . . . exarserint,** 'but now, what with the grumblings of respectable people and the murmurings throughout Italy, I am afraid that they have become quite inflamed'.

2. 12. **sperabam.** This, and *solebam*, are genuine (not epistolary) imperfects: 'I used to hope', etc.

13–15. **sic orbem . . . possemus,** 'that the wheel of state had revolved so smoothly that we could scarcely hear it, scarcely discern the track it made'. In other words, Cicero had originally hoped that the political revolution produced by the coalition of three such immensely powerful men as Caesar, Pompey, and Crassus was turning out to be a quiet and bloodless one. But widespread hostility and open opposition have changed all that: he now fears violence and armed repression.

3. 19. **ille noster amicus.** Pompey.

insolens infamiae, 'unaccustomed to unpopularity'. Pompey's career had been unbrokenly successful since he was in his early twenties, and since 70 he had been a great popular idol and darling of the *equites*.

20. **deformatus corpore.** Possibly a reference to a nasty ulcer on Pompey's leg which he wore a special sort of puttee to cover (*ad Att.* ii. 3. 1); possibly to his generally strained and run-down physical appearance (*tabescat dolore*).

21. **quo se conferat,** 'where to turn'.

21–2. **progressum . . . videt,** 'he sees that to press on is dangerous, to retreat a sign of vacillation'. *Progressus* means continuing with Caesar to more extreme measures, *reditus* means breaking with Caesar.

23. **vide mollitiem animi,** 'see how soft-hearted I am'.

24. **a. d. VIII Kal. Sext.** 25 July.

24–5. **edictis Bibuli.** An *edictum* was an official pronouncement by a magistrate. Bibulus, forcibly prevented from using his *par potestas* to block his fellow consul Caesar, and virtually a prisoner in his own house, continued to post edicts outside, attacking Caesar in particular. For an example of the contents of these edicts, see Suetonius, *Divus Julius* 9.

25. **contionantem,** 'addressing a *contio*'. See Letter 4, section 1, note.

25. **iactare se magnificentissime,** 'to cut such a superb figure'.

27. **ut ille tum humilis,** 'how low he had now sunk'.

4. 29. **Crasso.** Despite the coalition, the personal relationship of Pompey and Crassus remained anything but friendly.

29–30. **nam quia deciderat ... videbatur,** 'for, falling as he did from the stars, he seemed rather to have slipped than moved by deliberate choice'. Cicero pictures Pompey as a star plummeting down from the sky—he had never planned to find himself in so humiliating a position.

31. **Apelles.** Apelles and Protogenes were famous painters who had flourished in the late fourth century B.C. Apelles was the favourite painter of Alexander the Great, and his painting of Aphrodite Anadyomene (Venus rising from the sea) was one of the most renowned works of antiquity. Ialysus was in Greek mythology the grandson of Helios (the Sun), and gave his name to the town of Ialysus in Rhodes.

33. **a me pictum.** In his public speeches.

35. **Clodianum negotium,** 'the Clodius business'. Pompey as *augur* along with Caesar as *pontifex maximus* had participated officially in the primarily religious ceremony at which Clodius had been adopted into a plebeian family. Although it would be ridiculously exaggerated to see the whole or even the main object of this exercise as being to free Clodius to become a tribune of the plebs in order to assail Cicero, none the less in view of Clodius' open hostility to Cicero after his trial for sacrilege (at which Cicero gave evidence to break his alibi) it did represent a clear and grave threat to Cicero. By his refusal to join Caesar when invited (in December 60), and by his stubborn opposition to the 'Triumvirate', Cicero certainly did nothing to encourage Caesar or Pompey to restrain Clodius.

37. **Archilochia.** Archilochus was an early Greek poet (the exact date is disputed, but he flourished round about 700 B.C.) noted for his cutting invective. Hence 'Archilochian' was used in the sense of 'caustic', 'bitingly critical', as we might say 'Swiftian'.

39. **ipsi,** 'Pompeio'.

40. **tabescat dolore,** 'he is wasting away with grief', 'haggard with worry'.

me hercule molesta. A common and fairly mild expletive: 'terribly upsetting'.

42. **acer in ferro.** A somewhat odd expression, which presumably means 'a keen fighter' (but the manuscripts are perhaps corrupt: Watt suggests 'acer in furore').

42–3. ne omni . . . pareat. The construction is: *timeo ne tam vehemens vir . . . pareat*. The effect of the delayed introduction of *ne* is virtually: 'I fear that with so violent a man . . . he may give way whole-heartedly to disappointment and rage'.

5. 44. Bibuli . . . exitus, 'the outcome for Bibulus', 'how Bibulus will end up'.

45–6. comitia . . . distulisset, 'had postponed the elections'.

46. populi voluntatem offendere, 'to upset the people', 'be un-popular'.

47–8. ut iret ad Bibulum, 'to go and demonstrate outside Bibulus' house'—to protest against the postponement.

48–9. vocem exprimere, 'raise a shout', 'raise a cheer'.

49–50. ullius partis, 'of any section of the community'.

6. 53. studia . . . summa, 'the complete support', 'enthusiastic support'.

54. ordinum, 'classes'.

Te cum ego . . . vocat, 'it is not just that I miss you, but the situation calls for your presence to meet this crisis'.

55. consili animi praesidi. Partitive genitives after *plurimum*.

56. Varro. Marcus Terentius Varro, not only a famous scholar (author of the *de lingua Latina* and the *de re rustica*) but also a soldier and poli-tician who had served under Pompey in Spain and against the pirates and held the praetorship in about 68. As well as being a confidant and political adviser of Pompey, he was also a close friend of Cicero's (Cicero dedicated the second and revised edition of his *Academica* to Varro). He was now being somewhat helpful in the Clodius business (but hardly more: *satis facit* is distinctly cool).

57. divinitus. An adverb: 'like an angel'. But, as Cicero very well knew, what Pompey *said* and what Pompey *thought* or *did* were not necessarily the same thing.

58. discessuros. A military metaphor: 'leave the field'.

59. Sicyoniis. The people of the town of Sicyon in the north-west Peloponnesus, not far from Corinth. It had run heavily into debt, and one of its major creditors was Atticus. Sicyon was a 'free city' (*civitas libera*) and its independence had been upheld (much to Atticus' disgust and annoyance) by a senatorial decree which forbade proconsuls from taking cognizance of any debts it might have incurred. So Atticus could not rely on the governor of Achaea to force the Sicyonians to pay up, and had to do the best he could to extract the money from them himself.

LETTER 7

15. 2. Rem publicam . . . funditus amisimus, 'the state has slipped right out of our grasp (control)'.

Cato. Usually taken to be Gaius Cato, whose precise relationship to the famous Marcus Cato is unknown, but was probably not close. As tribune in 56 he worked closely with Crassus against Pompey, and was very thick with Clodius. See Letter 11.

2–3. adulescens nullius consili . . . Cato, 'an erratic young fellow, but all the same a Roman citizen and a Cato'.

4. Gabinium. Aulus Gabinius, a former legate of Pompey's, and a very active tribune in 67 when *inter alia* he steered through the law giving Pompey the command against the pirates (*lex Gabinia de piratis persequendis*). He had been elected consul for 58 along with L. Calpurnius Piso Caesoninus, the father of Caesar's wife Calpurnia.

de ambitu . . . postulare, 'to indict for electoral corruption', in connection with his election to the consulship of 58. Had he been tried and convicted, he would have been unseated (as Sulla and Autronius had been in 66); but he was not.

praetores. They were the chief legal officers of the state.

5. adiri . . . facerent, 'could not be approached and refused to make themselves available'. As long as the praetors made themselves inaccessible, Cato was powerless to initiate a prosecution, which had to begin with a preliminary hearing before a praetor.

5–6. in contionem ascendit, 'got up and addressed a *contio*'. This must have been at somebody else's invitation, since Cato held no public office himself. See Letter 4, section 1, note.

6. 'privatum dictatorem', 'a self-appointed dictator'. A *privatus* is not quite 'a private citizen' in our sense but a man who holds no public office. Thus for example Cicero, though a senator and ex-consul and an active politician, was at this time a *privatus*. The point of the jibe was that the dictatorship *was* a public office, though (with the unique exception of Sulla) a long defunct one.

16. 11. animo, 'spirits'—'Believe me, my hopes are high and my spirits even higher'. Ablatives of description are regularly qualified by an adjective, as here; here they are picked up again by means of the unqualified nouns: 'hope, so that . . .'.

14. diem . . . dixerit. *Diem dicere alicui* = 'to initiate a prosecution against somebody'. The crux of the matter was that as consul in December 63 Cicero had ordered the execution of the Catilinarians who had been arrested at Rome. It was a capital offence to execute a Roman citizen without trial, and the preceding examination of witnesses and prisoners in the senate and the debate on their treatment did not constitute a formal trial. Cicero had a defence: that prompt and deterrent action had been essential for the public security, and that the senate had expressed itself as being of this view, so that Cicero had not acted irresponsibly. In the event Cicero was not brought to trial. As tribune in 58 Clodius introduced a bill to outlaw anyone who had executed a citizen without trial; Cicero panicked and ran; and then Clodius had a law passed specifically outlawing Cicero and confiscating his property.

tota Italia. One of Cicero's political slogans. Only since 87 had the whole of Italy south of the Po enjoyed full Roman citizenship, and even then it had to wait for the principate of Augustus to reap the full fruits of political equality. Cicero enjoyed widespread support among the solid, well-to-do classes of the Italian towns.

15. discedamus, 'I shall leave the court'.

vi agere, 'to resort to violence'.

fore. The construction is: *spero fore ut resistamus.*

17. clientis, 'clients' or 'dependants'. A difficult word to translate, since it has its roots in practices and ideas that are uniquely Roman. Very roughly, a *cliens* was a man who was dependent on, and owed support and loyalty to, another, his *patronus*. The *patronus* in his turn was expected to look after the interests of his *clientes*. In the world of Republican Rome the protection and assistance of more powerful men was vital to smaller people, and even whole communities and towns and provinces had their *patroni* to look out for them. By Juvenal's day, with the decline of free politics and the decay of the citizen assemblies, the system had lost its political importance and become little more than a means whereby the wealthy and influential gained kudos by a public display of philanthropy—though the help of the rich and powerful remained desperately important for the ordinary man.

libertos. A *libertus* was a 'freedman', an ex-slave who had been manu-mitted, a practice increasingly common in the late Republic, especially with the better-educated and more skilled slaves. (Horace's father was a *libertus*.) If freed by a Roman master, the ex-slave acquired Roman citizenship, though with certain restrictions. He continued to owe loyalty to his former master, and his relations with him were governed by a mixture of custom and law.

18. **antiqua manus bonorum,** 'my old band of loyalists'. Cicero means his old supporters of 63, the solid citizens who had rallied to his support during the Catilinarian crisis.

19–20. **alieniores . . . languidiores,** 'inclined to be antagonistic or luke-warm'. These are not true comparatives, but of the 'rather' or 'somewhat' type.

20. **regum,** 'despots'—the 'Triumvirate' is meant.

22. **ita credo ut . . .,** 'my trust in them is not such as to cause me to relax any of my precautions'.

23. **Tribuni pl. . . . amici.** We know the names of only six of the ten tribunes for 58. Of these Clodius was violently hostile to Cicero, and Aelius Ligus backed Clodius. Lucius Ninnius Quadratus and Quintus Terentius Culleo tried to protect Cicero; and Lucius Antistius and Lucius Novius were probably sympathetic.

consules. The consuls designate for 58, Piso and Gabinius.

24. **praetores.** Again, the praetors designate for 58 are meant. Of the four named, we have already met Domitius Ahenobarbus (Letter 1, section 3, note). The others were Publius Nigidius Figulus, Gaius Memmius, and Lucius Cornelius Lentulus Crus. Memmius (to whom Lucretius dedicated his *de rerum natura*) was active with Ahenobarbus in attacking Caesar and his co-operative tribune of 59, Vatinius.

26. **alios,** 'some of the others' (not 'the others', which would be *ceteros*). Of these others, Lucius Flavius certainly clashed with Clodius in 58.

singularis, 'outstanding'.

26–7. **fac habeas . . . bonam,** 'see tha tyou keep your spirits up and your hopes high'.

LETTER 8

1. 3. **Amabo te . . . ne,** 'as you love me, I entreat you not to . . .'.

4. **mei,** 'my family', 'my dear ones'.

corruistis, 'you have been ruined', 'shared my downfall'.

4–5. improbitati . . . miseriaeque. The two pairs of nouns are best taken as examples of hendiadys: 'criminal irresponsibility' and 'miserable shortsightedness'.

5–7. Nullum est meum peccatum . . . arbitrabar, 'my only crime was that I put my trust in those who I had thought would never stain their honour by deceiving me, or at any rate who I used to suppose would not find it to their advantage to do so'. *Nefas* has its root in *ne-fari*, that which is not to be spoken, unmentionable, hence contrary to divine law, against morality, sinful. Cicero has Pompey very much in mind as having broken the sacred laws of friendship (cf. 'subita defectio Pompei', below); but also no doubt other friends who he thought had let him down disgracefully. The bitter addition of 'ne id expedire quidem' is a measure of his feeling about these false friends.

8. Intimus . . . quisque, 'all my nearest and dearest'.

9. fidem, 'loyalty'.

10. cautum meum consilium, 'sound judgement on my own part'.

2. 11. innocentia, 'blamelessness'.

vindicat, 'is keeping you safe'.

12–13. perspicis profecto . . . relinquatur, 'it must be very clear to you whether any hope at all of rescue is left to me'. By *salus* in these contexts Cicero means 'recall from exile'.

13. Pomponius. Atticus, whose full name was Titus Pomponius Atticus.

Sestius. Publius Sestius was tribune designate for 57 and was very energetic in the campaign for Cicero's recall. Along with Titus Annius Milo (also tribune in 57) he took on and beat Clodius. In 63 as quaestor he had been a great help to Cicero against the Catilinarians. In 56 he was prosecuted for offences in connection with his activities in 57, and successfully defended by Cicero.

Piso. Gaius Calpurnius Piso Frugi, who was married to Cicero's daughter Tullia. In this year (58) he was quaestor, and though assigned to the province of Bithynia–Pontus resigned this post to stay at Rome to help secure his father-in-law's recall. He died in 57, before Cicero's return.

14–15. longius discedere, 'to continue my flight further'.

15. **propter nescio quos motus,** 'on account of some developments or other'. Cicero's friends anticipated some political movements at Rome, perhaps disagreement between Pompey and Crassus, which might lead to his recall. But the weary *nescio quos* shows that Cicero was not disposed to put much hope in all this.

15–16. **verum ego . . . exspectabam,** 'the truth is, it is more because of their letters than through any real hope that I await [epistolary imperfect] the outcome'—the outcome of the *motus* just referred to.

17. **quid sperem.** Potential subjunctive: 'What have I to hope for?'. The following ablatives are ablatives of attendant circumstances.

inimico. Clodius.

obtrectatorem. *Obtrectare* (whence *obtrectator*) means to 'disparage', 'decry', 'carp at'.

3. 18–19. **novis . . . tribunis.** The tribunes recently elected to hold office in 57.

19. **officiosissimus,** 'most anxious to help'.

20. **Curtius.** Manius Curtius Peducaeus. Cicero had served as quaestor to Curtius' father when the latter was governor of Sicily in 75.

Milo. See above note on *Sestius*. Milo fought Clodius with his own weapons, organizing gangs of toughs on his own account to meet those of Clodius. His career as a right-wing rabble-rouser and gang-leader culminated in the murder of Clodius in a brawl early in 52, and Milo's subsequent exile despite Cicero's advocacy (*pro Milone*). He returned to the political fray in 48 in company with Cicero's friend Caelius Rufus in an armed rising that led to their deaths.

Fadius. Titus Fadius had been Cicero's personal quaestor in 63.

Fabricius. Quintus Fabricius led an abortive attempt in January 57 to pass a bill for Cicero's recall.

21. **privatus,** 'out of office'. See Letter 7, section 15, note.

manu, 'gang'. Rome had no police force until Augustus provided a *praefectus urbi* with cohorts under his command to act as a commissioner of police for the capital: 'qui coerceret servitia et quod civium audacia turbidum, nisi vim metuat' (Tacitus, *Annals* vi. 11). Hence organized gangs like those of Clodius and Milo could terrorize the city, and in an extreme emergency the only remedy was to call in the military (as Pompey was called in in 52).

22. **intercessor,** 'a vetoer'. Two of the tribunes for 57 were hostile to Cicero and could be expected to use their power of veto (*ius intercessionis*) to block any proposal to recall Cicero.

4. 22. Haec, 'all this'.

23. **proficiscenti,** 'when I was leaving Rome' to go into exile.

24. **'Quid tu igitur?',** 'why did you leave, then?'.

25. **convenerunt . . . meam,** 'combined to drive me out of my wits'. The subjunctive *exturbarent* is consecutive or generic.

26. **alienatio consulum.** Any hopes Cicero had had of Piso and Gabinius (Letter 7, section 16) had evaporated. Clodius intimidated them, and bought them off with special legislation giving them the highly desirable provinces of Macedonia and Syria. Cicero never forgave either of them, as can be seen clearly from his later speeches *de provinciis consularibus* and *in Pisonem* in particular, where he attacked them bitterly.

praetorum. See Letter 7, section 16.

27. **timor publicanorum.** Cicero usually reckoned to speak for the interests of the *publicani* and in return to be able to count on their support in politics. On the *publicani*, see Letter 5, section 4, note.

arma, 'open violence', 'brute force'—the activities of Clodius' gangs.

27-8. **ad mortem ire.** That is, to take his own life.

28. **honestatem,** 'honour' (*not* 'honesty').

29. **fuit.** *Fuisset* would mean 'would have been', but Cicero uses the perfect indicative to be emphatic: there was no might-have-been about it, suicide *had* been the best course to take. Cf. *moriendum fuit*: Letter 31, section 4, note.

30. **Phaethonti.** Phaethon was a freedman of Cicero's. (The letter was given to Phaethon to deliver to Quintus, not addressed to Phaethon.)

32. **communem.** Because Cicero's disgrace affected his brother's standing and prospects.

33-5. **sin plane occidimus . . . non eram,** 'but if we are lost beyond recall, then God help me! I shall have brought utter ruin on all my family— though never before had they any reason to be ashamed of me'. *dedecori non eram* is meiosis: Cicero means that his brilliant career had been a source of honour (*decus*) to his family.

5. 36. perspice rem et pertempta, 'look into the matter very closely and investigate it thoroughly'.

tempora nostra. Probably 'our predicament', though it could be 'my predicament'.

37. **fert,** 'demands'.

38. **tua interesse,** 'that your own interest is involved', 'that it is for your good'.

39–40. **tua causa velle,** 'is on your side': a fairly common idiom.

40. **Lentulum.** Publius Lentulus Spinther, consul in 57. His support for Cicero's recall in that year was invaluable, and put Cicero deeply in his debt. See further Letter 10.

40–1. **facta verbis difficiliora,** 'easier said than done'. This might mean either (*a*) that Spinther will find it harder to deliver results than to promise them; or (*b*) that it is easy for me (Cicero) to talk, the hard work of getting things done lies with you (Quintus).

41. **et quid opus sit et quid sit,** 'both what needs to be done and what the situation is'.

42–3. **si tuam solitudinem . . . poterit,** 'so long as no one rules you out of account because of your isolated position or our common ruin, then either it will be through you that something can be achieved or it will be hopeless'. Cicero means, not that Quintus can by himself rescue his brother, but that he is the essential intermediary. We know (*ad famm.* i. 9. 9) that in the end Quintus had to go bail to Pompey and Caesar that his brother would behave himself in future and cease his opposition before he was allowed to return.

44. **ne cessaris,** 'do not give way'—to their threats, as I did.

44–5. **non enim . . . agetur,** 'for with you it will be writs, not swords, that they will employ'. Cicero had feared physical violence should he not remove himself from Rome, but he is confident that this will not happen to Quintus. Just possibly it is of being able to help Quintus by composing speeches for delivery in court in the event of prosecution that Cicero was thinking when he said (above) that he would stay alive as long as he thought it would help his brother. In fact, Quintus was not attacked in the courts.

45. **haec absint velim,** 'I could wish there were none of this'. *Ut— velim (ut) haec absint*—is customarily omitted with *velle*.

48. **offici,** 'sense of duty', 'indebtedness'.

LETTER 9

1. 3. fuitque cui recte . . . darem, 'and found someone to whom I could properly entrust a letter to you'. (*Darem* is a generic subjunctive: 'the sort of person to whom I could give'.) The difficulty of finding a reliable letter-carrier who could be trusted to respect the confidential character of a letter is often mentioned by Cicero. Compare *ad Att.* i. 13. 1: 'Sed idcirco sum tardior, quod non invenio fidelem tabellarium ('letter-carrier'). Quotus enim quisque est qui epistulam paulo graviorem ferre possit nisi eam pellectione ('by perusal') relevarit?'

5. gratularer. That is, congratulate Atticus on the success of his efforts to secure Cicero's restoration.

5–7. Cognoram. . . . me ipsum. Cicero had found Atticus as cowardly and shortsighted as himself on the question of resisting Clodius' threats.

7. pro . . . observantia, 'considering my own unfailing concern for your interests'.

8. nimium...diligentem, 'so very conscientious', 'over-conscientious'.

eundemque te. *Eundem* is adversative in sense: 'And yet for all that you . . .'.

10. particeps. To be taken with *erroris* and *furoris* ('madness').

discidium, 'enforced separation'.

2. 14–15. unum . . . defuisse, 'the one thing that was missing to crown my happiness was . . .'.

15–17. quem semel nactus...exegero, 'and once I hold you fast again, should I ever let you go, or should I fail to exact (and in full) the arrears of the enjoyment of your delightful company for the time that has been lost . . .'. *Omnis* is accusative plural, not genitive singular, and qualifies 'fructus', its position in the sentence being chosen to give it emphasis.

18. profecto, 'then indeed'.

3. 20. in nostro statu, 'in the matter of my public position'.

quod looks forward to *splendorem* and *auctoritatem* and *gratiam,* the things which Cicero had thought would be hardest to recover. One might have expected 'quae' rather than 'quod', but all three are taken together in a lump as constituting the elements that in combination make up Cicero's public consequence.

21. splendorem . . . forensem, 'that public distinction I used to enjoy'.

Forensem can scarcely refer to Cicero's *legal* reputation since he had been back in Rome only a few days and had not appeared in court.

22. **auctoritatem.** *Auctoritas* is a very Roman word. It denotes the 'authority' or 'prestige' exercised by a man not in virtue of any public office or power ('potestas')—though that may be an ingredient of 'auctoritas'—but through his personal standing and reputation and ascendancy of character and political influence. Thus Augustus could contrast *potestas* and *auctoritas* in *res gestae* 34. 2: 'Post id tempus auctoritate omnibus praestiti, potestatis autem nihilo amplius habui quam ceteri qui mihi quoque in magistratu conlegae fuerunt.'

gratiam, 'influence'—cf. Letter 1, section 4, note.

23. **re . . . familiari,** 'private affairs', particularly financial affairs.

24. **fracta dissipata direpta.** Clodius had had Cicero's house at Rome torn down, and his villas had been looted. The compensation subsequently voted Cicero regarded as distinctly ungenerous: 'valde inliberaliter', *ad Att.* iv. 2. 5. (Note the stark asyndeton here.)

25. **valde laboramus,** 'I am in serious difficulties', 'seriously embarrassed'.

facultatum, 'resources'.

27. **reliquias,** 'fragments', 'bits and pieces'.

4. 28. **a tuis,** 'by your people'—Atticus' business agents at Rome, or his staff.

31. **Prid. Non. Sext.** 4 August.

32. **Non. Sext.** 5 August.

33. **Tulliola mea fuit praesto,** 'my dearest Tullia was there to meet me'. She had been recently widowed: Letter 8, section 2, note.

34. **natalis . . . Brundisinae coloniae.** That is, the day was also the anniversary of the foundation of the colony at Brundisium in 246 B.C., celebrated in the town as a public holiday.

tuae vicinae Salutis. The same day was also the anniversary of the dedication of the temple of *Salus* (the personification of 'Deliverance' or 'Welfare') on the Quirinal at Rome in 302 B.C. The goddess is called Atticus' 'neighbour' because he owned a house near the Temple which he had inherited from his rich uncle Caecilius.

35. **summa.** To be taken with *gratulatione*.

36. **A. d. III Id. Sext.** 11 August. The manuscripts read not 'III' but 'VI' or 'sex(t)', but this date, 8 August, seems too soon to allow time for news reached Brundisium from Rome (some 360 miles) especially since the messenger will hardly have started from Rome before the evening of 4 August. Still, it may have been a remarkably rapid journey, and the manuscripts may be right.

38. **Italiae.** See Letter 7, section 16, note.

39. **comitiis centuriatis,** 'in the Centuriate Assembly'. There were three legislative/electoral assemblies at Rome—excluding the *comitia curiata*, which hardly counted since it was only a rump survival dealing with odds and ends of routine business. The three were (i) the *concilium plebis*, presided over by the tribunes of the plebs and the plebeian aediles; (ii) the *comitia tributa populi Romani*, where consuls, praetors, curule aediles, and quaestors presided; (iii) the *comitia centuriata*, presided over by praetors and consuls. The first two were both organized by tribes (geographical electoral districts), a system which, while it weighted the conservative rural vote against the city vote, none the less gave each man in a tribe an equal vote regardless of wealth. In the Centuriate Assembly, however, the voters were so organized as very heavily to weight the votes of the richer citizens against those of the poorer. In Cicero's day it was not normally used for legislation but only for the election of consuls and praetors; and the fact that it was used to carry the law for Cicero's recall indicates that Clodius' influence in the more egalitarian tribal assemblies was still to be feared. (See also *Introduction*, pp. xxv–xxvi.)

39–40. **honestissime ornatus,** 'after having been loaded with honours'.

40. **iter ita feci ut,** 'my journey was such that'.

41. **legati,** 'deputations' from the towns of Italy.

5. 41. **Ad urbem ... veni,** 'I arrived outside Rome'. *Urbs* frequently = 'Rome', just as we may talk of 'going up to Town' and mean 'London'.

42. **nomenclatori.** A *nomenclator* was a servant whose job it was to know a very large number of people by name so that he could whisper to his master the name of anyone who approached him. Such services were naturally greatly in demand during an election campaign in particular. So what Cicero is saying amounts to 'Leaving aside open enemies, nobody who was anybody failed to make a point of coming out to meet and congratulate me'.

43–4. id ipsum . . . negare, 'who could not conceal or deny the simple fact that they *were* my enemies'.

45. portam Capenam. This gate was near the Circus Maximus, about half a mile north of the junction of the two great roads coming into Rome from the south, the Via Appia and the Via Latina.

infima plebe, 'the common people'.

47–8. me . . . celebravit, 'attended me', 'carried me along'.

6. 50. Non. Sept. 5 September. Here the abbreviation stands for the genitive: 'dies nonarum Septembrium'; and not for the ablative as in a simple dating formula.

51. gratias egimus. The speech is extant, the *oratio post reditum in senatu*.

Eo biduo, 'two days later'.

annonae summa caritas. 'a great scarcity of corn'.

52. ad theatrum. The 'ludi Romani' had begun—they lasted from 5 to 19 September.

53. mea opera, 'through my doing', 'my fault': presumably because the crowds that flocked to Rome to greet Cicero on his return were alleged to have caused the scarcity.

55. ad eius procurationem, 'to take charge of the corn supply'. Rome was by now a city of not far short of a million inhabitants, and the supply of grain, the basic staple of life, from the great overseas granaries of Sicily, Sardinia, and Egypt was of vital political importance. Shortages frequently led to riots: see P. A. Brunt's article in *Past and Present*, Number 35 (December 1966) on 'The Roman Mob'.

57. a me nominatim . . . postularet, 'called on me by name'.

decernerem. Strictly, Cicero could not 'decree' Pompey's appointment; the call was that he should initiate a motion in the senate to that effect.

58. accurate, 'in a carefully composed speech'.

sententiam. Members of the senate were invited to give their views by the presiding consul with the formula (e.g.) 'Dic, Marce Tulli, sententiam'. This *sententia* might involve moving that such and such should be done: it then remained to the consul to put it to the vote. If passed, the decree of the senate would be said to have been made on so-and-so's motion: cf. below: 'factum est senatus consultum in meam sententiam'.

abessent consulares. The consulars were as ex-consuls the senior and generally the most authoritative members of the senate. They made the violent mood of the mob an excuse (*negarent* is the subjunctive of the alleged reason) for non-attendance, but their real reason was hostility to and fear of Pompey and their unwillingness either to vote him new powers or to incur popular disfavour by opposing his appointment. (Cicero excludes himself, although he was also a consular.)

59. **Messallam.** Marcus Valerius Messalla Niger, consul in 61. He had been appointed a member of Caesar's agrarian commission in 59.

60. **Afranium.** Lucius Afranius, an old and staunch lieutenant of Pompey, who had boosted him into a consulship in 60. He was captured and executed after the battle of Thapsus in 46 at which he had commanded the forces still loyal to the dead Pompey.

61. **cum Pompeio ageretur ut,** 'that Pompey should be invited to'.

62. **lexque ferretur.** The *senatus consultum* by itself could not commission Pompey, who would need a grant of *imperium* which could be sanctioned only by a citizen assembly.

continuo, 'immediately'. As soon as the senate had concluded its business, the decree was read aloud to the crowds waiting outside.

63–4. **meo nomine recitando,** 'at the reading out of my name', presumably as proposer of and witness to the decree. Added to the preamble of a decree were the names of those who *scribendo adfuerunt* (witnessed to its authenticity). Such witnesses were drawn from those senators who had sponsored or favoured the decree (cf. Letter 25, section 2). The gerundive *recitando* virtually serves as a present passive participle, thus getting round the absence of such a participle in Latin.

64. **contionem.** On *contio* see Letter 4, section 1, note. If this was the extant speech to the people, the *post reditum ad Quirites*, it must have been considerably revised before publication, since the extant speech has no mention of corn shortages or Pompey's appointment. But it may well be that there were two separate speeches to the people by Cicero about this time.

65. **praetorem . . . tribunos.** The praetor was Appius Claudius Pulcher, elder brother of Publius Clodius, and later consul in 54 and Cicero's predecessor as governor of Cilicia. The tribunes were Quintus Numerius and Sextus Atilius Serranus. These three had stood out earlier against joining the other magistrates in backing Cicero's recall. Later, on 1 October, Serranus at first vetoed the decree compensating Cicero

for the loss of his property, but gave way and withdrew under heavy pressure: *ad Att.* iv. 2. 4.

7. 67. **senatus frequens.** See Letter 4, section 5, note.

68. **legatos,** 'lieutenants'. In the late Republic governors and generals were entitled to nominate 'legati' to assist them, the number of 'legati' varying with the importance of the governor's or general's responsibilities. The 'legati' were regularly senators, and frequently men of high rank and experience: Quintus Cicero, legate to both Pompey and Caesar, was an ex-praetor, and ex-consuls are also found as legates from time to time.

69. **principem,** 'named me first'—not as chief legate but first on the list. Quintus Cicero was also made a 'legatus'.

69–70. **alterum se,** 'his *alter ego*', 'second self'.

70. **conscripserunt,** 'drafted'.

70–2. **qua . . . daretur,** 'to grant', 'granting'. (Note how the generic and final uses of the subjunctive fade into each other so as to be indistinguishable.)

72. **alteram Messius,** 'Messius drafted an alternative bill'. Gaius Messius, tribune in 57, though now working in Pompey's interest, subsequently in 54 and later in 46 served as a legate under Caesar. Earlier in 57 he had proposed an abortive bill to recall Cicero from exile. Cicero defended him in the courts in 54.

72–3. **omnis pecuniae dat potestatem,** 'gives him *carte blanche* in the matter of finance'.

73–4. **maius imperium.** Pompey would need to be given *imperium pro consule* for the execution of his corn commission, which would involve widespread operations throughout the Mediterranean. He would have to operate in maritime provinces with their own governors invested with a similar *imperium*. By proposing that Pompey's *imperium* be designated *maius*, Messius meant to ensure that clashes of authority should be resolved in Pompey's favour. In 67 while operating against the pirates Pompey had not had *imperium maius* and this had led to a spectacular clash with the proconsul Metellus Creticus (consul in 69) in Crete. In 23 the *imperium* of Augustus was specifically designated *maius* to that of all other provincial governors; but under the *libera res publica* of the period before Caesar's coup in 49, such a thing was unknown, save for the special case of a dictator who outranked everybody. (See in general on this topic Hugh Last, *JRS* 37 (1947) 157–64).

75. **nostra lex consularis.** The bill resulting from the senate's decree on Cicero's motion would be put to the people by the consuls. Strictly it was not a *lex* until it had been carried by a citizens' assembly, but the Romans like ourselves quite often loosely referred to a proposed law simply as a 'law'.

76. **illam.** The consular proposal.   **hanc.** Messius' proposal.

familiares. A close, intimate friend is called a *familiaris*. The evasiveness and craft and 'poker-faced' side of Pompey is very often remarked by Cicero. Compare Letter 4, and in particular *ad Att.* iv. 9. 1: 'Nos hic cum Pompeio fuimus. Multa mecum de re publica, sane sibi displicens —ut *loquebatur*: sic est enim in hoc homine dicendum'—'So he *said*, for one must always add *that* when talking of Pompey.' The point is that it would be unbecoming to Pompey's dignity to grasp openly at the wider powers offered by Messius. It was up to his intimates to discern what he really wanted and act accordingly. Should they fail to get it for him, he would suffer no blow to his prestige such as would have resulted had he openly sought it for himself and been rebuffed.

77. **Consulares . . . fremunt,** 'the consulars are up in arms, with Favonius at their head'. On Favonius, see Letter 4, section 5, note. He was not himself a consular but only of quaestorian rank; but the consulars preferred to let him make the running for them (see note on *abessent consulares*, above, l. 58).

78. **quod de domo . . . responderunt,** 'because the Pontiffs have as yet given no decision about my house'. Cicero's town house had been confiscated by Clodius after his flight, pulled down, and the site consecrated for a temple to *Libertas*. The question of deconsecration was now before the college of Pontiffs. The Pontiffs were one of the three great priestly colleges of Rome (the other two being the college of Augurs and the *Quindecemviri Sacris Faciundis*), but they were not professional priests but leading and active politicians. Cicero was keeping quiet because he did not wish further to offend the conservative Pontiffs who were already put out by his proposal of a *cura annonae* for Pompey; nor did he want to upset Pompey by coming out against Messius' proposal.

79. **sustulerint religionem** ,'rule in favour of deconsecration'.

80. **superficiem . . . aestimabunt,** 'will prepare an estimate of the value of the building' (which was on the site before Clodius destroyed it).

81–2. aliter . . . aestimabunt. The soundness of the manuscripts' text here has been questioned, but is defended by Nisbet in *CR* 1961, p. 240. If sound, it must be taken to mean: 'Otherwise (if the site is not deconsecrated) they will demolish (the temple, as an unhappy reminder of Clodius' effrontery), let out a contract (for a new temple) in their own name, and make an estimate for the whole (for compensation to Cicero of the value of both house and site).' Personally I find this a shade too elliptic even for a letter of Cicero's, and am inclined to agree with those who hold that some words have dropped out in the manuscripts between *demolientur* and *suo nomine*.

8. 83–4. 'ut in secundis . . .'. An untraceable tag from an old play. The meaning is: looked at from the point of view of a man for whom everything has been going swimmingly, my position is somewhat unsettled; but for a man who has been having a very bad time of it, the position at present is pretty good. It all depends on one's point of view.

84. re familiari, 'my personal finances'.

perturbati, 'very embarrassed'.

85. quaedam domestica, 'certain family matters'—very likely trouble with his wife Terentia.

89. Alterius vitae . . . ordimur, 'it is as if I am beginning to build a new life'. His exile had been a political death, from which he has been resurrected.

90. praesentibus, sc. *nobis*.

LETTER 10

1. 3–4. Ego . . . omnibus, 'in the eyes of the world I fulfil all the claims of duty, or rather affection, which are due to you'. On *officium* see Letter 1, section 4, note. *Pietas* is the sort of feeling a man ought to owe to his father, or to the gods, or to his country: loyal and grateful affection.

5. meritorum, 'services'—see introduction to this letter.

5–6. nisi perfecta re. Ablative absolute: 'only when the task had been brought to completion'.

7. putem. Subjunctive following the *ut* two lines higher.

7–8. In causa haec sunt, 'the factors in the case are as follows'—i.e. the following can be said in my defence.

8. regis legatus. The ambassador of the Pharaoh Ptolemy XII, nicknamed Auletes (the flute-player), who was the father of the famous

Cleopatra. The great Ptolemaic kingdom of Egypt, carved out of the debris of Alexander's Empire by Alexander's general Ptolemy, had been fast running downhill for a century or more, and was in many respects virtually a Roman puppet. Crassus had cast longing eyes in that direction in the sixties; and it was only political rivalries at Rome that prevented its annexation during the last thirty or so years of the Republic. Ptolemy Auletes had been recognized by Rome as the legitimate Pharaoh in 59 at the price of a massive bribe to the 'Triumvirs'; but in 58 he was ejected from Alexandria by his dissident subjects, since when he had been intriguing vigorously to recover his throne with Roman assistance. (Octavian finally annexed Egypt after the Battle of Actium.)

9. **creditores.** One of these men who advanced money to Ptolemy's ambassador (to enable him to bribe freely among Roman politicians) was Gaius Rabirius Postumus, in whose defence Cicero in 54 delivered the speech, *pro Rabirio*, which is still extant.

10. **regis causa . . . velint.** Cf. *tua causa velle* (Letter 8, section 5) for the same idiom.

11. **rem . . . deferri,** 'that the business should be entrusted to Pompey'.

12. **religionis calumniam,** 'the chicanery of a religious objection'. A passage in the Sibylline Books (a sort of state oracle) was produced and interpreted by some interested parties as forbidding the use of military force to restore Ptolemy to his throne. The object was to baulk Pompey, either from fear that if he were given the job he would be too powerful if he had an army under his command again, or in the hope that without an army to go with it the job would lose its attractions for him.

malevolentia. Probably ill will towards Pompey, rather than Ptolemy, is meant.

2. 14. **liberius,** 'quite frankly'.

15. **infamiam.** Should Pompey fail to back Spinther, and openly throw his own hat into the ring, he would incur disrepute as showing ingratitude to the man who as consul had not only worked so hard for Pompey's protégé Cicero but also carried the law which gave Pompey his *cura annonae*.

16. **relinquit locum,** 'leaves room'. Pompey's conduct is admirable, making Cicero's pleas and warnings supererogatory.

18. **gravitate,** 'force', 'seriousness'. *Gravitas* (contrast *levitas*) was one of the canonical Roman virtues.

21. Marcellinum. Gnaeus Cornelius Lentulus Marcellinus, consul in this year 56. (The *cognomen* Marcellinus derives from his father, who had been born a Claudius Marcellus and adopted into the family of the Cornelii Lentuli.) The manuscripts' reading *iratum* is suspicious in view of the words that follow. Various suggestions have been made to correct the text, such as reading *gratum* or *non ingratum* for *iratum*. My own favourite is the suggestion of Cratander: 'tibicini esse iratum scis' (*tibicen, -inis* is the Latin for 'flute-player' = Auletes). It may not be right, but it is magnificent.

23. quod instituit, 'as to his having made up his mind . . .'.

referre. This is the technical term for raising a question in, referring a matter to, the senate.

24. religione. Above, section 1, note.

3. 25. ante Idus. 'up to the Ides' (13 January).

26. Hortensi. See Letter 4, section 5, note.

Luculli. As the more famous Lucius Lucullus (Mithridates' opponent) was pretty certainly dead by now (probably he died in the latter part of 57), this will be his younger brother Marcus, consul in 73. (Spinther of course would know who was meant.)

26–7. cedit . . . exercitu, 'concedes the religious objection to the use of an army'.

27. teneri enim . . . non potest, 'this is the only way to keep the issue open'.

27–8. ex illo s. c., 'in accordance with that s. c.'.

28. te referente, 'on your initiative'. As consul Spinther had got the senate to agree that the restoration of Ptolemy be entrusted to the governor of Cilicia, to which post he was himself destined.

tibi. Dative of interest: 'in your favour'. (On *decernit*, see Letter 9, section 6, note.)

29. quod commodo . . . possis, 'so far as you can do it without damage to the public interest'—that is, without using any army and thus running counter to *religio*. *Quod* is here used in the restrictive sense, and is virtually equivalent to *quantum* or *quoad*.

29–30. ut exercitum . . . retineat, 'with the result that while the religious objection rules out an army, the senate will retain you to oversee the operation'.

31. tris legatos, 'three ambassadors'. Pompey was *cum imperio* ('vested

with *imperium*') in virtue of his *cura annonae* (Letter 9, section 7, note)·
Others eligible as being *cum imperio* would be provincial governors like
Spinther in Cilicia and Gabinius in Syria, or even the consuls and
praetors in office at Rome. The object of Crassus' formula was to
secure that (i) if Pompey should get the job, he would not have a free
hand; and (ii) by choosing the ambassadors from those who were *cum
imperio* no special legislation (and hence probably special powers)
would be needed.

32. **Bibulus.** See Letter 6 for his anti-'triumviral' activity as consul in 59.

33. **privati.** See Letter 7, section 15, note. This proposal would of
course rule out both Pompey and Spinther.

34. **Servilium.** The grand old Publius Servilius Vatia Isauricus, consul
in 79, and senior living consular (he survived to 44). In the seventies he
had held a special command against the pirates.

omnino, 'at all'.

reduci, sc. 'regem reduci'.

35. **Volcacium.** Lucius Volcacius Tullus, who as consul in 66 had
refused to accept Catiline's candidature for the consulship of 65.

Lupo. Publius Rutilius Lupus, tribune this year (56). In the Civil War
he began on Pompey's side but later went over to Caesar. He was
praetor in 49.

35. **Afranium.** See Letter 9, section 6, note.

37. **voluntatis,** 'goodwill', hence here 'sincerity'. It was thought that
someone as close to Pompey as Afranius was must reflect by his actions
Pompey's true wishes.

38. **Laboratur . . . res est.** A military metaphor: 'It is a hot fight, and
of battle has turned against us.'

39. **Libonis.** Lucius Scribonius Libo, another tribune of 56. His daughter married Pompey's son, Sextus. He held the consulship in 34 along
with Mark Antony. His sister Scribonia married the future Emperor
Augustus, becoming the mother of the notorious Julia.

Hypsaei. Publius Plautius Hypsaeus, yet another tribune in the Pompeian interest. He had served as Pompey's quaestor in the East, and was
strongly backed by Pompey for one of the consulships of 52 against
Milo.

concursatio et contentio, 'the energetic to-ing and fro-ing'.

41. cupere, 'to be anxious for the appointment'.

41–2. cui qui nolunt, 'and those who are against him (Pompey)'.

42. quod eum ornasti, 'because of the distinction you accorded him' (in the matter of the *cura annonae*).

4. 43. auctoritatem. See Letter 9, section 3, note.

45. quod . . . putant, 'because they think that they are doing Pompey a good turn'. Cicero's 'authority' is diminished because people say, 'He is only doing this because he owes such a debt of gratitude to Spinther'; his 'influence' is nullified by the greater influence of Pompey, who is suspected of wanting the job for himself, and thus of being likely to view opposition to Cicero's proposal of Spinther with some warmth and favour.

45. rebus, 'an affair'.

47. domesticis, 'cronies', 'satellites'.

clam exulceratis, 'secretly aggravated', 'inflamed', 'poisoned'.

48. invidiam, 'disgust'.

ita answers the *ut* at the opening of the sentence: 'As you would expect . . . so it is'. Translate: 'We are coping as best we can with an affair. . . .'

49–50. praesentes tui, 'your people who are on the spot'.
51. laboraremus. See above, section 3, under *laboratur*.

LETTER 11

1. 3. superiora, 'what happened earlier'. The two preceding letters in the collection (*ad Q. fr.* ii. 1 and 2) are concerned with the events of December 57 and January 56.

4–5. Kal. Febr. legationes . . . non est, 'On 1 February an attempt was made to postpone the embassies to the 13th; but the matter was not settled that day.' On the *legationes* see Letter 4, section 5, note. The imperfect tense of *reiciebantur* indicates that the action was not completed. *Eo die* is 1 February, not 13 February.

5. A. d. IIII Non. Febr. 2 February.

Milo. See Letter 8, section 3, note.

adfuit, 'entered an appearance'. Milo was accused by Clodius, who was aedile in 56, on a charge *de vi* (roughly = 'riot') before the *comitia tributa*.

This appearance was at the first in a series of preliminary public hearings (which took the form of *contiones*) before the trial proper began. The trial was eventually abandoned.

6. advocatus. Not 'as an advocate' (the word for which was *patronus*) but 'as a supporter'. By his presence in court an *advocatus* lent his *auctoritas* and *gratia* to the accused.

dixit, 'spoke' on Milo's behalf.

M. Marcellus. Marcus Claudius Marcellus, a solid optimate and as consul in 51 a violent opponent of Caesar, trying to secure his recall from Gaul. He was perhaps like Clodius an aedile in this year (56). His cousin Gaius Claudius Marcellus, consul in 50, married Augustus' sister Octavia and was the father of the Marcellus who was destined to be Augustus' son-in-law, but died prematurely in 23 ('Tu Marcellus eris': Virgil, *Aeneid* vi. 883).

6–7. honeste discessimus, 'we quitted the field with honour'—had the best of the fight.

7. prodicta dies est . . ., 'the next hearing was fixed for 7 February'.

8–9. referebatur . . . praetoribus, 'the question was raised (in the senate) about assigning the quaestors their provinces and about the supply-vote for the praetors'. *Referre* is the regular verb for placing business before the senate. The quaestors had to be assigned provinces since each provincial governor was assisted by a quaestor or pro-quaestor (the governor of Sicily had two). *Ornatio, ornare provinciam* was the technical term for voting the necessary money-grant, supplies, administrative assistance, etc., to a governor before he left to take up his province. Although allotted their provinces and armed with their *ornatio* early in the year praetors did not normally leave Rome until the very end of the year, after the completion of their duties there.

9. res, 'business'.

9–10. querelis . . . interponendis. The gerundive serves to indicate *method*; an absolute participle would have indicated *fact*.

10. C. Cato. See Letter 7, section 15, note.

11. de imperio . . . abrogando, 'to remove Lentulus from his command' (as governor of Cilicia). *Abrogare imperium* = 'to take away *imperium*'; *prorogare imperium* = 'to extend *imperium*'. Abrogation was highly unusual. In recent history (excluding the period of Civil War in the eighties) there had been only one instance, when the proconsul Q. Servilius Caepio (consul in 106) was stripped of his *imperium* after the disastrous defeat at Arausio (Orange) in Provence in 105. (*Lentulo* is the dative of disadvantage, the normal construction after *abrogare*.)

vestitum filius mutavit, 'Spinther's son has assumed mourning'. *Vestitum, vestem mutare* means 'to put on mourning clothes'. Young Spinther did this to indicate publicly his sorrow for his threatened father and to excite public sympathy: a quite usual practice at Rome.

2. 12. sive voluit, 'or rather, that was what he wanted to do'.

13. **surrexit,** 'got up' to speak.

14. **idque ei . . . contigit,** 'and this went on all through his speech'.

non modo ut, 'with the result that not only . . .'.

acclamatione. Not 'acclamation' but quite the reverse: 'shouts of disapproval'.

17. **auctoritate** 'by sheer force of personality'. **peroravit,** normally means 'to close a speech', and *peroratio* is the closing passage of a speech. Here *peroravit* means rather 'succeeded in completing his speech'.

19. **placuerat . . . referre gratiam,** 'for they had decided to return the compliment'.

20. **consisteret,** 'keep firm control of': *consistere* = 'to stand fast', 'hold one's ground'.

hora sexta. The Romans divided the day between sunrise and sunset into twelve *horae*, the length of which varied with the season of the year as days lengthened and shortened. Thus *hora septima* always means the hour after noon (noon itself was *meridies*). In February the period from the beginning of the sixth hour to the beginning of the eighth hour would be from about ten past eleven to ten to two. Since the fun was still going on into the ninth hour the siesta period was being sadly interrupted.

21–3. cum . . . dicerentur. The imperfect tense shows that the scurrilities went on all through the time Clodius was speaking.

23. Clodiam. Sister of Appius Claudius Pulcher and Publius Clodius, and one of the most notorious women in Rome, the Lesbia of Catullus' poems. Among her many lovers was Cicero's young friend Caelius Rufus; and Cicero's defence of him against a charge inspired by Clodia (the *pro Caelio*) is perhaps his most brilliant speech and gave him the chance to paint a vivid picture of this remarkable woman. She was even alleged to have had incestuous relations with her brother Publius; but Roman politicians had a weakness for accusing each other of incestuous practices, so one ought not to place too much credence in the allegation, though no doubt it featured large in the *versus obscenissimi* chanted by Milo's supporters—as perhaps did Catullus' scathing 'Caeli, Lesbia nostra . . .': *Carmen* 58.

23–4. Ille furens et exsanguis . . . necaret, 'Clodius, white with anger, kept on asking his supporters in the midst of all this uproar Who was starving the commons to death?'. A criticism of Pompey's conduct as Commissioner of the Corn Supply.

25. Alexandriam ire. To restore Ptolemy: see Letter 10.

27. 'Crassum'. See Letters 4, section 5, note and 10, section 3, note. This was surely no more than a spur-of-the-moment compliment to Crassus (who was present) and need not mean that he had any serious hopes of the appointment.

Miloni animo non amico, 'in no friendly spirit towards Milo'.

29. exarsit dolor, 'this inflamed their grievances'.

Vrgere, 'applied pressure', 'shoved'.

30. rostris. See Letter 4, section 5, note.

31. nos, 'I'.

ne quid in turba. Some such verb as *accideret* or *fieret* or *detrimenti caperem* must be supplied. This, and the other ellipses—'fuga operarum (fuit)', 'Pompeius domum (rediit)', 'neque ego in senatum (veni)'—add pace and immediacy. But they are not deliberate stylistic artifice, only part of the uncontrived and colloquial and conversational pattern of the whole letter.

32. curiam. The *curia* was the Senate House in the Forum. Meetings of the senate could, however, be held elsewhere, if desired: see note on *ad Apollinis*, below, l. 37.

34. Bibulo. See Letter 5, sections 2 and 6 and Letter 6, section 3, notes. On (the older) Curio, another reliable optimate, see Letter 4, section 5, notes. On Favonius, Letter 4, section 5 and Letter 9, section 7, notes. Servilius was the son of P. Servilius Vatia Isauricus (Letter 10, section 3, note) and himself held the consulship in 48 as colleague of Caesar.

35. animos . . . offenderem, 'to avoid upsetting the conservatives'.

36. in posterum, sc. *diem*.

Quirinalia. The festival of Quirinus (the deified Romulus), celebrated on 17 February each year.

prodixit diem. That is, fixed the day for the next hearing of the charge against Milo.

3. 37. A. d. VI Id. Febr. 8 February.

ad Apollinis, 'at the Temple of Apollo'. *Templum* was customarily omitted in such phrases (rather as we say 'at St. Mary's (Church)'). Since this temple was outside the city limits Pompey, a proconsul in virtue of his *cura annonae*, could attend the meeting. See Letter 4, section 1, note.

41. contra rem publicam esse facta. The standard formula of public censure of activity held to be against the best interests of the state: 'that what had occurred on 7 February had constituted a threat to public order'.

Cato. Gaius Cato. He has already been mentioned earlier with his *praenomen*, and in any case Marcus Cato was out of Rome.

41–3. vehementer . . . accusavit, 'launched a violent attack on Pompey and accused him in a formal speech just as if he were on trial'. *Reus* means the defendant, accused, in a legal case.

44. cum . . . increparet, 'while upbraiding Pompey for hist reachery towards myself'. The *perfidia* lay in having stood by and done nothing to save Cicero from Clodius early in 58, despite earlier professions of support: cf. Letter 7, section 16: 'Pompeius omnia pollicetur' and Letter 8, section 4: 'subita defectio Pompei'.

45. malevolorum. Probably Pompey's ill-wishers, not Cicero's, are meant; but one cannot be sure: it may be both.

46. Crassumque . . . descripsit, 'referred obliquely to Crassus'. Pompey did not actually name Crassus, but made it quite clear whom he meant. *Describere* is used quite regularly with this overtone of maligning somebody: see Lewis and Short for examples.

46–7. munitiorem . . . fore, 'would take more precautions'.

47. Africanus. On Africanus, see Letter 3, section 3, note. It was alleged by some that because of his dogged opposition to the activities of the agrarian commission established by his late brother-in-law, Tiberius Gracchus, his sudden death in 129 should be ascribed to poison administered by the Gracchan supporter Gaius Papirius Carbo, one of the agrarian commissioners. There is no real evidence to support this. Cicero gives it no backing, for the subjunctive mood of *interemisset* shows that he is simply recording what Pompey said. Hence, be careful to translate: 'who (so Pompey said) had been done away with by Gaius Carbo'. Had Cicero written *interemit* it would have been another matter.

4. 48–9. Itaque . . . videbantur. Epistolary imperfect: 'So it seems to me that something big is in the wind.'

49. **haec** looks forward to what follows: *insidias fieri*, etc.

50. **fieri,** 'are being hatched', 'planned'.

51. **sustentari,** 'is being backed'.

51–3. **Clodio . . . confirmari,** 'that money is being made available to Clodius, and both he and Cato are being encouraged by Crassus and Curio, by Bibulus and all his other rivals'.

53. **ne opprimatur,** 'to ensure against being overwhelmed'.

54. **contionario.** *Contionarius* means 'frequenting *contiones*'. Translate: 'The rabble that always crowds to public meetings'. The adjective is derogatory and meant to exclude the sounder section of the citizen body. The ablatives are all descriptive of attendant circumstances.

nobilitate. See Letter 2, section 2, note.

55. **non aequo,** 'biased'.

iuventute improba, 'with the young bloods in an irresponsible mood'. On the *iuventus*, see Letter 4, section 5, notes.

56. **ex agris,** 'from the country'.

57. **manus,** 'bands' of men.

ad Quirinalia. When the next hearing of the charge against Milo was due.

In ea. *Ea* is accusative plural: 'For that occasion' (the Quirinalia).

58–9. **ex Piceno et Gallia.** *Gallia* here means the so-called *ager Gallicus*, the region of Italy lying between Ancona and the River Rubicon. It was neighbour to Picenum, the stronghold of Pompeian power in Italy, which might almost be termed the Pompeian 'barony'.

59. **rogationibus.** On *rogatio* see Letter 4, section 2, note. On the specific *rogatio* about Lentulus Spinther, see above, section 1 and note. What the *rogatio* about Milo was is uncertain, but very likely it concerned his employment and use of hired ruffians.

5. 61. A. d. IIII Id. Febr. 10 February.

Sestius. See Letter 8, section 1, note.

indice . . . Pupinia, 'the common informer Gnaeus Nerius of the

Pupinian tribe'. *Pupinia* stands for *Pupinia tribu*. The addition of the name of the tribe in which Nerius was enrolled indicates that he is a person of no social consequence, otherwise the identification would not be needed.

62. **de ambitu est postulatus,** 'was indicted on a charge of electoral corruption'.

M. Tullio. Otherwise unknown.

63. **ut debuimus.** That is, in view of Sestius' services to Cicero as tribune in 57.

64. **nos totos tradidimus.** 'I have placed myself entirely at his disposal'. Cicero successfully led for the defence in the trial *de vi*, and his speech is extant, the *pro Sestio*.

64–5. **praeter . . . opinionem,** 'contrary to general expectation'.

65. **nos ei . . . iure suscensere,** 'that I was justifiably a little annoyed with him'. Clearly there had been some quarrel between the two, though what about we do not know.

66. **ut,** 'so that . . .'.

67. **itaque faciemus.** Literally 'and so I shall act'; that is 'I shall be as good as my word'. [I have omitted the following sentence in the manuscripts from the text since it is badly corrupted and restoration is very dubious; in any case nothing of any importance is lost.]

68. **sodalitates decuriatique discederent,** 'that the guilds and decurial clubs should disband'. The *sodalitates* had originally been clubs or societies formed for religious or social activities, but in Cicero's day they were all too often used as a 'front' or 'cover' for purposes of gang-warfare and intimidation. The *decuriati* were employed in a similar role with the emphasis on bribery and corruption at elections. (Their name derives from the old *decuriae* of the earlier Roman electoral system, sub-divisions of the *curiae*.) The verb *decuriare*, originally meaning to divide into tens, comes regularly to mean 'to bribe'. Attempts were made more than once to suppress these organizations. Clodius as tribune in 58 specifically moved to legalize them.

69. **ea poena . . . tenerentur,** 'should be subject to the same legal penalties as for riot'.

6. 70. **A. d. III Id. Febr.** 11 February.

Bestia. Lucius Calpurnius Bestia had stood as a candidate in the prae-torian elections the preceding year (57) but without success. Charged now with electoral malpractices, he was convicted despite Cicero's advocacy.

apud, 'before', 'in the presence of'.

71. **Cn. Domitium.** Gnaeus Domitius Calvinus. Consul in 53, after a campaign disfigured by bribery of colossal proportions even by Roman standards, he commanded Caesar's centre at the Battle of Pharsalus in 48 when Pompey was decisively defeated and fled to Egypt and death.

71–2. **incidique . . . in dicendo,** 'and in the course of my speech I happened to come to the occasion when . . .'.

73. **Castoris.** The Temple of Castor and Pollux, usually referred to simply as the Temple of Castor. The three surviving columns of this Temple are the most prominent features in the Forum as it is today.

74–5. προῳκονομησάμην **quiddam** εὐκαίρως . . . **crimina,** 'I seized the opportunity to kill two birds with one stone and say something in advance relevant to the charges being preferred against Sestius'. εὐκαίρως means 'opportunely'. προῳκονομησάμην means literally 'I got things arranged beforehand'. The point is that this incident involved Sestius, and so gave Cicero the chance to work in some advance remarks relevant to the forthcoming trial of Sestius, though it was also relevant to the defence of Bestia.

76. **homini.** Sestius.

77. **eo . . . quod,** 'for this reason, that . . .'; that is, 'especially because'.

gratia, 'goodwill'. No doubt Quintus had been concerned about the recent coolness between his brother and Sestius (above, *iure suscensere*) and had said so in his letters to his brother.

7. 79. **Prid. Id. Febr.** 12 February.

79–80. **apud Pomponium,** 'with Pomponius', 'at Pomponius' house'. Pomponius is, of course, Atticus (Titus Pomponius Atticus was his full name)—whose sister was Quintus' wife.

80. **in eius nuptiis,** 'to celebrate his wedding'. He married a woman called Pilia, and from their union was born a daughter, Pomponia, who married Augustus' marshal and right-hand-man, Marcus Vipsanius Agrippa. *Their* daughter, Atticus' grand-daughter, was Vipsania Agrippina who became the first wife of the future Emperor Tiberius, and mother of his only son, Drusus.

81. **cuius modi tu . . . praedicabas,** 'just as you used to assure me they would be though I could scarcely believe you'—a reference to the period when Cicero was in exile and despaired of the future.

82. **gratiae,** 'influence': see Letter 1, section 4, note.

83. **pietate.** See Letter 10, section 1, note.

suavitate etiam, 'and by your tact, even'. Cicero writes *etiam* because Quintus was usually noted for his tactlessness and hasty temper.

84. **Domus tibi . . . conducta est,** 'the Licinian house by Piso's Pond has been rented for you'. *Liciniana* shows that the house belonged to a Licinius or Licinia, perhaps of the family of the Licinii Luculli or Licinii Crassi.

85. **paucis mensibus . . . ,** 'within a few months after 1 July'. It is not clear to us whether this means that Quintus will be back in his own house on 1 July in a few months' time, or within a few months after 1 July. Quintus of course would know which was meant. 1 July is thus either the beginning or end date of a half-year lease. Probably it is the former.

85–6. **in tuam commigrabis,** 'you will be able to get back into your own place'—Quintus' town house on the Palatine, at present being rebuilt.

86. **tuam in Carinis,** 'your house on the Carinae'. The *Carinae* ('Keels') lay on a spur between the Esquiline and Coelian Hills at Rome. This house was the old family house which had previously belonged to Marcus' and Quintus' father. Pompey had a house on the Carinae too.

86–7. **mundi . . . conduxerunt,** 'has been rented by some charming tenants, the Lamiae'.

87. **Vlbiensem,** 'from Olbia', the principal port on the east coast of Sardinia, where Quintus was now posted as legate of Pompey as Commissioner of the Corn Supply (Letter 9, section 6).

88. **ut te oblectes,** 'how you amuse yourself'. Cf. Letter 6, section 6.

90. **tamen . . . cogites,** 'all the same, remember that that island of yours *is* Sardinia'. Sardinia had a very bad name as an unhealthy and pestilential place. Even in winter—usually the healthier season—it was dangerous.

91. **xv Kal. Mart.** 15 February. The first six sections of this letter had been written early on 13 February (above). This last paragraph was added two days later.

LETTER 12

I. 3. Ain tandem? A colloquial expression, found in Plautus and Terence: see Lewis and Short, under *tandem* B. 'What's all this about, then?' *Ain* is abbreviated from *ais-ne* ('Do you say so?'). *Tandem* is used in its interrogative sense of 'Pray now', 'now then'.

mea, 'my compositions'. Atticus has complained that Cicero had not shown him a copy of his 'palinode' (see below).

4. cuiquam, 'to anyone else'. *Quisquam* is used for 'anyone' in a negative or interrogative sentence. For Atticus as a critic of Cicero's writings, cf. Letter 4, section 3, note.

Vrgebar, 'I was pressed'.

5. ab eo . . . misi. Possibly Pompey, but probably Caesar. See below on the 'palinode'.

exemplar, 'a (spare) copy'.

Quin etiam, 'and besides' ('not but what also').

6. circumrodo . . . , 'for I keep on nibbling at what has to be swallowed at a gulp'.

subturpicula. The minimizing prefix *sub-* (cf. *suscensere*, Letter 11, section 5) and the diminutive ending *-cula* combine to produce a double meiosis: 'a tiny bit shameful'. Shackleton Bailey very happily translates: 'I was not exactly proud of my palinode'.

7. παλινῳδία. A 'palinode' or 'recantation'. It consisted in an apology for his earlier conduct. It may just possibly have been addressed to Pompey, but most probably it was sent to Caesar. If so, the 'palinode' could have been the speech *de provinciis consularibus* which urged Caesar's claims to stay on in Gaul and was generous in its praise of him (sections 18–40); but more likely, in view of the '*non etiam ut scriberem*' (below), it was a formal letter to Caesar.

valeant, 'good-bye to . . .'.

9–10. istis principibus . . . fidei, 'those political leaders of yours—that's what they want to be, and could be, if they had one particle of honesty.' Influential politicians who aspired to leadership in politics were termed *principes viri* or *principes civitatis*. Cicero is being scornful about them; he calls them *isti* because Atticus had many friends among the nobility; see Letter 2, section 2, and note.

10–11. **Senseram . . . ab iis,** 'I had felt it, I knew it: they led me on, they deserted me, they threw me to the wolves'. (The object of *senseram* and *noram* is *perfidiam*, to be supplied from the preceding sentence.) Cicero goes too far. True, many of the nobles caved in when confronted with the re-cementing of the 'Triumvirate'; but, even had they backed him, Cicero could not himself have withstood the pressure to capitulate. His conscience is uneasy, and he is looking for a scapegoat.

11–12. **tamen hoc . . . ,** 'yet I was inclined to see eye to eye with them on political issues'.

12–13. **vix aliquando . . . resipivi,** 'now at long last I have recovered my senses'.

2. 13. **Dices . . . tacerem,** 'you will say that you only urged me to keep my mouth shut'. *Eatenus* means 'thus far', and is answered by *qua*.

14–15. **necessitatem . . . coniunctionis,** 'to bind myself inescapably to this new association'.

15. **ne qua,** 'so that it should not by any means . . .'.

labi, 'to backslide'.

17. **modici,** 'restrained'.

'ἀποθεώσει' ut scripsisti, 'in my "apotheosis", as you put it in your letter'. Atticus had pulled Cicero's leg by suggesting that the 'palinode' was so fulsome in its praise of the addressee as to amount to a 'deification' (*apotheosis*).

18. **erimus uberiores,** 'I shall let myself go more'.

subringentur, 'pull a wry face'—'they' (*ii*) are the nobles.

19. **moleste ferunt,** 'take it amiss', 'are indignant'.

Catuli. Either Quintus Lutatius Catulus, consul in 78, and for some years before his death in 60 the leading personality among the *optimates* (he was brother-in-law to Hortensius), or his father of the same name, the consul of 102. The point is that the Lutatii Catuli were great patrician nobles, Cicero an upstart parvenu from the 'provinces'. This villa, at Tusculum, had also once been owned by Sulla.

20. **Vettio.** Possibly the notorious informer of 59, but it may well be some other Vettius: either way, a person of no social consequence.

domum. Cicero's town house, destroyed by Clodius and now being rebuilt.

21. **'sed quid ad hos?'**, 'but what business is it of theirs?'.

21–2. **et quibus sententiis ... dixisse.** The construction here is difficult to unravel formally, although the sense is perfectly clear. Cicero changes horses in mid stream, starting out with one construction as if *quibus sententiis* is to be governed by *laetati sunt* and then switching to an infinitive object-clause after *laetati sunt*. This is a letter to a close friend, not a carefully constructed speech. It is best to treat *quibus sententiis* as hanging in the air, and translate: 'And as to my contributions to senatorial debates (*sententiae*) in which I said what they themselves agreed with, what really made them happy about them was that what I said offended Pompey.'

23. **Finis sit,** 'Let this be the end', 'I have done with them'.

24. **qui nihil possunt,** 'those who are powerless'—the nobles.

demus operam ut, 'I must see to it that ...'.

3. 25. **'vellem iam pridem'**, 'I could wish you had done it long ago'.

26. **asinum germanum,** 'a complete ass', 'a proper ass'. *Germanus* is literally a full brother (as opposed to a half-brother) and is a favourite word of Cicero's to mean 'genuine' or 'complete'.

28. **Domum ... invisis,** 'your keeping an eye on my house so regularly'—the house on the Palatine which is in course of rebuilding. Cicero is writing from Antium (Anzio), Atticus is at Rome.

29. **Viaticam Crassipes praeripit,** 'Crassipes is robbing you of your welcome-home dinner'. 'Viaticam' = 'cenam viaticam'. Atticus had planned a dinner party for Cicero on his return to Rome, but Crassipes had got in first with an invitation. Tullia's first husband Piso had died in 57; she is now betrothed to young Furius Crassipes, and they were married not long afterwards. The marriage broke up in 53. In 50 Tullia married again, this time Publius Cornelius Dolabella, but again divorce soon followed (in 47).

Tu 'de via recta in hortos?', ' "Straight from your journey to the suburbs?", you say'. Cicero imagines Atticus protesting against his plan to go straight to Crassipes' suburban villa. *Horti* is the Latin term for a comfortable house standing in its own grounds on the outskirts of Rome; it can sometimes have a slightly 'racy' connotation as the sort of place where wild parties might be held. So Shackleton Bailey suggests there may be this edge of raillery in the remark Cicero puts into Atticus' mouth: 'Off to a party as soon as you arrive?'

30. **Videtur commodius,** 'it seems more convenient'.

ad te. *Veniam* is to be understood.

quid enim tua?, sc. *interest.* 'For what difference does it make to you?' A colloquial expression: cf. Plautus, *Amphitryon* 1003, 'Quid id mea?' A single day, says Cicero, can't matter all that much.

31. **tui,** 'your people'. Some servants or employees of Atticus who was amongst other things a publisher and so able to command the services of a specialized staff for such purposes.

31–2. **cum . . . sillybis,** 'along with the shelving and the book-labels'. The *structio* was the arrangement of racks or shelves on which the papyrus rolls were stacked; the *sillybi*—a Greek word Latinized—were the strips attached to the rolls bearing the names of the works and their authors.

LETTER 13

1. 3. **Puteolis,** 'at Puteoli', which lay between Naples and Cicero's villa at Cumae, from which he writes this letter. Puteoli was a busy port, much used by the fast grain-ships from Egypt—hence the source of the rumour.

Ptolemaeum esse in regno, 'that Ptolemy is back on his throne'. The rumour was correct: Gabinius, governor of Syria, had restored him on his own initiative. (See Letter 10 for the fuss about this issue in 57–56.)

5. **pascor bibliotheca Fausti,** 'down here I am making a good meal off Faustus' library'. In English we use similar metaphors, talking of 'browsing' through books or 'devouring' them. Faustus Sulla is the son of the Dictator, and the library will have been of books brought back by his father from Greece and Greek Asia. It seems that Cicero had bought it from Faustus.

6. **his rebus.** Supply *me pasci* from the preceding sentence. *Res* is clearly used here in the sense of 'good things' or 'fare': the Naples area was famous for its sea-food. (*ostreis* = 'oysters' has been suggested as a reading instead of *his rebus*.)

Lucrinensibus. The lake Lucrinus was on the coast near Puteoli (the modern lago Lucrino).

ista, 'those things' (the sea-food), referred to as *ista* because Atticus is imagined to have introduced them into the discussion: 'But I have them too'.

7-9. sed ... ut ceteris ... sed *Ut* is answered by *sic* in the following line: 'But upon my soul, while the present condition of public affairs deprives me of all other diversions, and takes away my appetite for everyday pleasures, so do I find sustenance and refreshment in literature'. For *oblectationibus* compare 'quem ad modum te oblectes' (Letter 6, section 6), 'ut te oblectes' (Letter 11, section 7).

9. sedecula. A diminutive form of *sedes* = 'a little seat'. This seat, and the bust (*imago*) of Aristotle beneath which it stood, were situated in a covered walk at Atticus' house.

10. istorum, 'those consuls of yours': Pompey and Crassus, who held the consulship together in 55 (both for the second time). *Istorum* because Atticus is at Rome, the seat of government.

sella curuli. The curule chair of state, used by consuls, praetors, and curule aediles, who were collectively the 'curule magistrates'. It was inlaid with ivory, and was Etruscan in origin.

11. cum eo. This is Pompey, on whom Cicero will very shortly be paying a courtesy call (below). There is certainly a *double entendre* here: Cicero will be taking a stroll with Pompey quite soon, but politically he is also going to have to walk in Pompey's ways for some time to come.

12. illa ambulatione, '*that* walk' (with Pompey).

viderit. The colloquial use of the future perfect indicative in a hortative sense: 'Chance will have to see (have seen) to that'. Cf. *videro* in Letter 18, section 2.

aut si quis ... deus, 'or the gods, if any god there is to care'. (*Curet* is a generic subjunctive: 'such that he cares', 'of a nature to care'.) Atticus was something of an Epicurean, a philosophy which allowed that divine powers existed but questioned whether they took any interest in human affairs. It is the Epicurean philosophy that Lucretius expounds in his *de rerum natura*.

2. 13. nostram ambulationem. Cicero here switches from the abstract sense of *ambulatio* = 'the act of walking' to the concrete sense of 'a walk' = 'a place where walking is done'. (The same double sense exists in English: cf. the Broad Walk through Christ Church Meadow in Oxford.) '*My* walk' is a colonnaded or cloistered walk being constructed for Cicero at his house in Rome.

Laconicum. A kind of steam or Turkish bath, supposedly originating from Sparta (Laconia).

13–14. **eaque quae Cyrea sint.** Literally: 'those things which are such as to be Cyrean' (generic subjunctive again)—that is to say: 'those things which fall within Cyrus' province'. Cyrus was an architect, a friend of both Cicero and Atticus.

14. **velim quod poteris invisas,** 'please keep an eye on them as much as you can'. *Quod* in its limiting sense, as often in these letters.

Philotimum. Philotimus was a freedman of Cicero's wife Terentia, and acted as her steward. A few years later Cicero had cause to suspect him of mismanagement and dishonesty.

15–16. **ut possim tibi . . . respondere,** 'so that I may be able to pay you back something in *that* regard'. Philotimus was to be prodded into producing some money to set against Cicero's debts to Atticus, who had advanced money to him freely after his return from exile. Cicero was chronically in debt to his friend.

16. **respondere.** Quite commonly used in the sense of making a repayment.

17. **Cumanum,** 'his villa at Cumae'.

Parilibus, 'on the feast of Parilia'. Pales was originally the tutelary deity of shepherds. The Parilia (a form deriving from Palilia) were celebrated on 21 April of each year.

17–18. **misit . . . nuntiaret,** 'he promptly sent someone over to me to pay his respects'.

18–19. **Ad eum . . . scripsi.** Literally: 'When I wrote this, I was on my way over to see him early the following day'. Translate: 'That happened yesterday. I am off to see him early this morning as I write this letter'.

LETTER 14

1. 4. **ludos.** The games (*ludi* was a generic term for public entertainments) were those presented in autumn 55 at his own expense by Pompey to celebrate the opening of his new public theatre and the dedication of the temple of Venus Victrix. They included wild-beast hunts, athletic contests, and dramatic performances; and they were on a scale so lavish as to be long remembered—over a century later the Elder Pliny tells the story (*Natural History* viii. 7) of how the pitiable torments of the elephants moved the usually callous Roman audience to rise as one man and shower curses on Pompey.

4–5. fortunae magis . . . tuae, 'I put it down to your good luck rather than your good sense'. From the way in which Cicero writes, it looks as if Marius' ill health was something of a joke among his friends.

6. cum per valetudinem posses, 'although your health would have allowed you to come'. *Per valetudinem* = 'on the score of health', 'so far as health allowed': cf. *per omnis homines*, below.

7. utrumque looks forward to (i) *et fuisse*, and (ii) *et valuisse*. 'I rejoice on both counts, that . . .'.

8. animo valuisse, 'that you were of sound mind'.

9. modo ut . . . oti tui, 'always provided that you showed a good profit on your leisure'. *Constare* is here used in its book-keeping sense of 'standing' in a set of accounts.

10. in ista amoenitate, 'in those delightful surroundings of yours'. Marius spent most of his time in his villa near Pompeii.

12–13. ex quo tibi Stabianum . . . sinum, 'where you have had a window made for yourself (*perforasti*) and opened up a view of the bay at Stabiae'.*Perforasti et patefecisti* is a sort of hendiadys construction, and is virtually equivalent to *perforando patefecisti*. Stabiae was on the coast south of Pompeii.

13. lectiunculis. A diminutive formed from *lectio*: 'a little light reading'.

15. communis mimos. The adjective *communis* points a somewhat strained contrast between Marius' solitary state at Pompeii and the crowds at Rome: ' while they were sitting half-asleep (through boredom and the heat) among the crowds watching the mimes.' The *mimi* were broad farces, topical, and (frequently grossly) indecent: very popular with the mass of the people, they were not calculated to appeal to a sophisticated taste.

16–17. ad arbitrium tuum, 'of your own choosing'.

18. Sp. Maecius. Spurius Maecius Tarpa was appointed by Pompey as a sort of Lord Chamberlain, that is, a public licenser of plays. He is found performing the same office for Octavian (Augustus): see Horace, *Satires* i. 10. 38: 'quae neque in aede sonant certantia iudice Tarpa', and *ars poetica* 386–7: 'si quid tamen olim / scripseris, in Maeci descendat iudicis auris'.

probavisset. The subjunctive is generic: 'the sort of entertainment that Maecius had approved'.

2. 19. apparatissimi, sed non tui stomachi, 'most lavishly produced, but not to your taste'. *Tui stomachi* is an example of the qualitative or descriptive use of the genitive.

20. **de meo,** sc. 'stomacho': 'Or so I judge from my own (taste)'.

honoris causa. Cicero puns on the two possible meanings of this phrase. The famous retired actors now making a return appearance at the opening of the new theatre *honoris causa* (as a mark of honour or respect to themselves or to the occasion) are said to have originally retired to save their reputations (for the sake of their own honour). The pun can be preserved (following Tyrrell) by translating: 'For, to begin with, there were those who out of respect for the occasion had come back to tread the boards which I always supposed they had quitted out of respect for their own reputations.'

22. **Deliciae vero tuae** 'your particular favourite,'. For *deliciae* = 'pet', 'darling', compare Catullus iii. 4 ('passer, deliciae meae puellae') and vi. 1 (where *delicias tuas* = 'your sweetheart').

23. **ut ei desinere . . . liceret,** 'that nobody would be sorry to see *him* retire'.

24–5. **'Si sciens fallo',** 'if wittingly I fail': part of an oath formula. The character played by Aesopus was taking an oath at the point in the play where unhappily Aesopus' voice failed, thus underlining his failure as an actor.

26. **id . . . leporis.** A partitive genitive: 'that amount of charm'.

27. **Apparatus . . . spectatio,** 'the spectacle of all that lavish display quite took away any gaiety'. The *apparatus* was what we might term the 'trimmings', the stage-equipment and such like that went with the plays. What Cicero means is that the sort of ostentatious display to which he goes on to refer was top-heavy, and crushed the light cheerfulness of the occasion like a butterfly under a steam-roller.

28–9. **animo aequissimo,** 'with perfect equanimity'.

29. **Quid . . . delectationis.** Compare *id leporis* (above).

sescenti. Literally 'six hundred', but in common Latin idiomatic usage it simply meant a very large number, much as in English we may say 'a hundred' or 'a thousand' without meaning that precise figure or indeed anything like it. Hence translate: 'hundreds of mules' or 'a thousand mules'. *Clytaemestra* (the original Greek form of the name Clytaemnestra) and *The Trojan Horse* are of course the titles of plays.

31. **creterrarum.** *Creterra* is a variant form of *cratera* and *crater*, the last

being the Greek word for a bowl in which wine was mixed with water. (The crater of a volcano is so called because of its similarity in shape to a mixing-bowl.)

31–2. armatura varia . . . equitatus, 'a gaudy display of armoured horse and foot'. With *varia* compare *varie* in Letter 4, section 3.

3. 34. operam dedisti . . . tuo, 'you gave your attention to Protogenes' —a servant of Marius' whose job it was to read aloud to him. Such a servant was called an *anagnostes*, a Greek word meaning 'one who reads out loud'.

35. ne tu . . . habuisti. This is *not* the conjunction *ne* (as found introducing negative final clauses, etc.) but the interjection *ne* (cf. Greek ναί, νή). It means 'verily', 'truly', and occurs with *ego, tu, ille, iste, hic* (and their adjectival or adverbial forms). Translate: 'Then you indeed have had a great deal more (literally: not a little more) amusement than any of us.'

37. Graecos aut Oscos. Cicero here refers to *ludi* in the sense of the dramatic performances (*ludi scaenici*). The Greek were those plays which were based on Greek originals or followed the Greek pattern (like the *Clytemnestra* and *The Trojan Horse*). The Oscan were the broad farces (see above). The *Osci* were the native inhabitants of Campania, and Oscan was a dialect of the Sabellian or Sabine group of peoples of Central Italy. The Atellan Farces (*fabulae Atellanae*) were Oscan in origin. The Oscan language survived despite pressure from Latin and Greek, and was still being spoken in Pompeii at the time of its destruction in A.D. 79.

38. in senatu vestro. The word *senatus* was not confined to the senate at Rome, but was also the title of a number of town or municipal councils in Italy. 'Your own senate' is the municipal council of Pompeii (of which Marius was pretty certainly a member)—hence *vestro* not *tuo*, since it is the council of Marius and his fellow Pompeians. Since Pompeii is an Oscan town, Cicero can suggest that Marius can see 'Oscan farces' at its council meetings any day.

40. via Graeca. Location unknown, as is the reason for Marius' supposed aversion to using it. Campania was heavily Grecized—Cumae was the oldest Greek colony in Italy, and Naples (Neapolis) was also colonized from Greece—and there may well have been a number of 'Greek Streets' in the area.

41. gladiatores contempseris. Causal subjunctive: 'Seeing that you had (you who had) nothing but contempt for gladiators'. There must here be an allusion to some incident (lost to us) connected with the

Catilinarian troubles in 63, when the insurrectionaries were alleged to have planned to use gladiators raised in Campania and when there was certainly a threat of serious civil trouble at Pompeii itself (see Cicero, *pro Sulla* 54–5, 60–2).

42–3. et operam et oleum perdidisse, 'that he has wasted time and money'. A proverbial phrase: *opera* is the work or exertion that has been spent for nothing, *oleum* the oil consumed in a lamp used to work by. (There is perhaps a pun here on the use of oil by athletes to oil their bodies.)

43. venationes binae, 'wild-beast hunts twice daily'. These were fights between wild beasts and hunters, or beast-baitings.

45. polito, 'polished', hence 'a man of refinement'.

50. quin etiam, 'rather the contrary'. Cicero's account that there had been 'a certain feeling of pity' and 'a sort of feeling that there was something in common between elephants and human beings' is distinctly mild when compared with that of Pliny the Elder, whose high colouring suggests that the story had often been retold 'with advantages': 'But when Pompey's elephants had lost all hope of escape, they entreated the pity of the crowd by an indescribable sort of behaviour, trumpeting their sorrow at their fate, and so upsetting the crowd that oblivious of General Pompey and the magnificent spectacle he had devised for their honour they rose as one man with tears in their eyes and showered awful curses on Pompey's head, curses for which soon afterwards he paid the penalty' (*Nat. Hist.* viii. 7. 21).

4. 54. non modo . . . liber, 'not only fortunate but also quite idle', viz. free from serious occupation.

54–5. dirupi me . . . tui, 'I almost ruptured myself (with my earnest pleading) at the trial of your friend Caninius Gallus'. Gallus as tribune in 56 was on Pompey's side, and proposed an abortive bill to appoint Pompey to restore Ptolemy. Hence he was on the other side to Cicero, who was backing Spinther (see Letter 10). Pretty certainly Pompey put pressure on Cicero to appear at Gallus' trial: cf. Cicero's remarks in the last sentence of this section.

55. facilem, 'accommodating', that is, as ready to let Cicero retire as Aesopus' audience or following was to let him go.

58. cum antea taedebat cum, 'for in any case (*cum*, answered by *tum* below, in the 'both . . . and' sense) I was already beginning to tire of it (my profession as an advocate) before, at a time when . . .'.

59. **denique,** 'and on top of that'.

62. **homines . . . meritos,** 'men who had not deserved very well of me'. Probably Caninius Gallus fell into this category. There were to be others: the next year (54) Cicero was called on to appear for the defence at the trials of Gaius Messius (tribune 57), Publius Vatinius (tribune 59), and Aulus Gabinius (consul 58) at the insistence of Pompey and Caesar, all of them men with whom he had clashed in the past, sometimes bitterly.

5. 63–4. **Itaque quaero . . . meo.** 'So I am looking for every excuse for at last living my life to suit myself'.

64–5. **istam rationem oti tui,** 'that retired way of life that you have chosen'.

66. **intervisis.** *Intervisere* = 'to visit from time to time'.

67. **lepore tuo,** 'your delightful company'.

68. **propter . . . meas,** 'thanks to the very burdensome calls on my time'.

69–70. **Quibus si me . . . postulo,** 'if ever I win some respite from them (for I do not demand that I be entirely quit of them)'.

70. **commentaris.** *Commentari* = 'to make a study of'.

71. **humaniter vivere,** 'to live as a man ought to live'.

73–4. **lecticula concursare,** 'and join me in an outing in a litter'. Marius' poor health would rule out a walk. (We know that nine years later he was complaining of gout—*ad famm.* vii. 4—and he may have had it already.)

6. 76–7. **quadam epistula subinvitaras,** 'because you had half-invited me in one of your letters'. The prefix *sub-* shows that Marius had not asked outright for such a letter but had hinted or suggested that Cicero write something along these lines. It is often used in this softening and apologizing sense: cf. *subturpicula* in Letter 12, section 1, note.

80–1. **neque in epistulis . . .,** 'and you will not leave any hope you may have of enjoying yourself at the mercy of (being satisfied by) a letter of mine'.

LETTER 15

2. CICERO CAESARI IMP(ERATORI) S(ALUTEM) D(AT)
On *imperator*, see the note on the heading of Letter 3.

1. 3. Vide quam. 'Look how . . .'.

te me esse alterum, 'that you are my second self'. Compare 'alterum se', Letter 9, section 7.

5–6. quocumque exirem, 'to whatever country I might go'. Cicero had been a *legatus* to Pompey since 57 (Letter 9, section 7, note); and in addition to his *cura annonae* Pompey had in 55 been appointed governor of Spain for five years with the right to govern *per legatos*, that is to say, using deputy governors while himself staying in Italy. It seems that Cicero had believed that his own legateship might cease to be merely honorific, and that he might be given an appointment outside Italy. In fact, this did not happen.

6–7. ut eum . . . reducerem, 'so that I might bring him back home loaded down with everything that my devotion and favour could bestow'.

8. commoratio. Pompey in fact lingered in Italy until he was driven out by Caesar in 49.

9. mea quaedam . . . dubitatio, 'and a certain hesitation on my part of which you are not unaware'. What this careful periphrasis conceals is unclear (which was, of course, the object of the periphrasis). It may be (as How suggests) that Cicero wanted to stay and keep an eye on Publius Clodius, but this is only a guess. (Some of the letters from Cicero to his brother Quintus at this period suggest that Cicero may just possibly have had hopes of a consulship for his brother or a second consulship for himself before very long: certainly he was looking to the possibility of some very considerable favour from Caesar.)

10–11. vide quid mihi sumpserim. Literally: 'see what I have presumed for myself', that is: 'See how presumptuous I have been'. The presumption lay in what follows, the promises Cicero had made to Trebatius of future favours from Caesar.

12–13. neque me hercule minus . . . promisi, and, by Heaven, I was no less free in the promises I made him of your favour . . .'. *Promitto* = 'to hold out the hope of'; *polliceor* = 'to promise oneself'.

2. 14. Casus. A chance happening, 'an accident'.

14–15. quasi vel testis . . .tuae, 'as if to bear witness to my judgement and stand surety for your kindness'.

16. Balbo. A most remarkable man. Lucius Cornelius Balbus was born a native of Cadiz (Gades) in Spain, and had had Roman citizenship bestowed on him in the late seventies, becoming attached to Pompey. Later he served as *praefectus fabrum* (roughly, Quartermaster-General) under Caesar when Caesar was governor of Spain in 61–60; and he was now holding the same appointment under Caesar in Gaul, though in fact he spent much of his time at Rome acting as Caesar's confidential agent. In 56 his title to Roman citizenship had been challenged in the courts, and he was successfully defended by Cicero (the extant *pro Balbo* was delivered on this occasion). In the Civil War he was active as Caesar's trusted agent, and later he joined Octavian. In 40 he was appointed to a consulship, becoming the first consul of provincial extraction.

loquerer accuratius, 'while I was having a really serious conversation . . .'. *Accurate* means 'in a detailed, careful, non-casual manner': compare 'accurate sententiam dixi' in Letter 9, section 6.

18. M. Titinium. The manuscripts read (unintelligibly) 'M. itfivium'. The best suggestions for putting them right are 'M. Titinium' or 'M. Fufitium': it is impossible to choose between them. Titinius was the son of Q. Titinius, a banker friend of Atticus. Fufitius occurs as a name in Catullus liv. 5.

19. vel hunc Leptae delega. Again the manuscripts' text is very suspect. If correct (which I doubt) it must be taken to mean: 'Or hand him over to Lepta, if you like, and send me someone else to advance'. Quintus Lepta served as *praefectus fabrum* (see above, note on Balbus) under Cicero himself in Cilicia in 51–50; he may well have transferred to Cilicia from Gaul, as Cicero's brother Quintus did.

21–2. Tanta fuit opportunitas . . . videretur, 'it was such a striking coincidence that it seemed somehow or other the work not of chance but of Providence'.

23. atque ita mitto ut . . . duxerim. Note again the delicate use Cicero makes of this construction which he favours so much. The meaning is crystal clear, but is not easy to convey in English without drastic rephrasing. 'So I send you Trebatius, a man I judged worth sending from the beginning on my own initiative, and now in response to your specific invitation.'

3. 25. velim . . . comitate complectare, 'please treat him with all that kindness for which you are noted'.

27–8. non illo vetere verbo meo, 'not in that hackneyed (trite) phraseology of mine . . .'. Caesar had made fun of the insincerity and triteness of an appeal by Cicero to effect a reconciliation of some sort between Caesar and Milo (on whom see Letter 8, section 3, note).

28. iure, 'rightly', 'with justice'.

29. more Romano, 'in the good old Roman way'—that is, simply and straightforwardly.

non inepti, 'sensible men'.

30. pudentiorem, 'more modest, unassuming'.

31. familiam ducit, 'he is at the head of his profession,' 'at the top of the class'. The phrase comes from the use of the word *familia* to mean a 'company' of gladiators, or such-like.

33. tribunatum . . . praefecturam. The *tribuni militum* were the senior ranking officers of the Roman legions, six to a legion. They were frequently and freely employed as staff officers on general administrative duties. *Praefecti* were officers in command of allied or auxiliary units, especially cavalry, but they too were used for general duties. Both categories of appointment were within the commander-in-chief's gift, and men were often appointed for reasons other than military experience. Compare Caesar, *Bellum Gallicum* i. 39. 2: 'Hic ⟨timor⟩ primum ortus est a tribunis militum, praefectis, reliquisque qui ex urbe amicitiae causa Caesarem secuti non magnum in re militari usum habebant.'

33–4. ullius benefici certum nomen, 'any specific preferment'.

36. gloriolae insignibus. The diminutive has a depreciating effect: 'These little marks of distinction'.

37. 'de manu . . . in manum', 'from my hand to yours'. Cicero was playing with legal phraseology (Trebatius *was* a jurisconsult, and *testis* and *sponsor* in section 2, above, are likewise legal terms). *Manus* had the technical meaning of 'possession' or 'ownership' (the origin of this use is obvious enough). Cicero thus says playfully that he is 'conveying' Trebatius to Caesar, 'making him over' to Caesar.

38. Simus enim putidiusculi, 'allow me to be a little tiresome' (*simus* is a jussive subjunctive). A deprecatory diminutive. For the epithet, compare 'putidum' (Letter 4, section 1, note).

39. **quamquam per te . . .licibit,** 'though I know it is scarcely proper where you are concerned; still, I think, you will permit it'.

40. **me, ut amas, ama,** 'and continue to be my friend'.

1. 4–5. **legitima quaedam . . . tuae,** 'there is a sort of statutory addendum which consists in a recommendation of you'. *Legitimus* means consistent with, as laid down by, a *lex*: compare the phrase *inter legitimos dies* = 'within the statutory period', 'the period laid down by law'.

5. **vulgaris,** 'commonplace', 'run of the mill'.

6–7. **ineptias . . . desideria.** Best treated as hendiadys: 'That silly homesickness you feel for Rome and city life'.

7–8. **et quo consilio . . . consequere,** 'and carry through the plan you set out with with unremitting strength of character'.

9. **tam . . . quam.** Virtually equivalent to *tantum . . . quantum*. Trebatius' friends will show the same forgiveness towards him as the Corinthian dames did towards Medea.

10–11. **'Quae Corinthum . . .'.** This line, and the three quoted later, are from Ennius' *Medea*, a play somewhat loosely based on that of Euripides. Medea had fled from her native land of Colchis and come to Corinth. The quotation is not really all that apt, but it serves Cicero's purpose by helping him to work in a joke about how necessary it was to stir Trebatius out of his metropolitan rut.

11. **optimates,** 'high-born', 'aristocratic'.

12. **gypsatissimis,** 'snow-white'. Gypsum was used by male actors who played women's parts to whiten the hands and arms.

12–13. **ne sibi . . . verterent,** 'that they should not turn it to her discredit that . . .'. *Vitio* is a predicative dative.

14–16. **'Multi . . . improbati'.**
> For many have served self and country well
> In foreign lands; and many who spent their lives
> At home have furthermore won ill renown.

2. 18. **alias,** 'at another time' (whence the English legal expression 'alias': compare 'alibi' = 'elsewhere').

qui ceteris cavere didicisti . . . caveto. A legal pun—Trebatius was a lawyer—compare such phrases as *'caveat emptor'*, 'entering a *caveat'*. We can try to keep the flavour by translating: 'You who are so learned on the subject of escape-clauses will have to take good care to escape those British charioteers.' *Caveto* is an old jussive form (the so-called 'future imperative') = *cave*, such forms lingering longest in legal and constitutional phraseology. The *essedum* was the British war-chariot: Caesar describes its use in battle in *Bellum Gallicum* iv. 33. Caesar had first invaded Britain in the late summer of 55. He sailed again for Britain at the end of July 54.

19–20. **(quoniam Medeam coepi agere),** 'since I have started to stage the *Medea*'. *Agere* (cf. 'act') has this meaning of staging a play.

21–2. **'Qui ipse . . .'.** Literally: 'He who being wise cannot advantage himself is wise to no avail'. 'What use is learning that no profit brings?'

LETTER 17

1. 3. **quid proficiam,** 'with what success' ('what progress I am making').

4. Balbo. See Letter 15, section 2, note.

6–7. **Quinto . . . fratre.** Quintus Cicero had joined Caesar's staff in Gaul as a legate in the early summer. For his dogged defence of his winter-camp against the Nervii, see *Bellum Gallicum* v. 38–41.

7–8. **nihil . . . auri . . . argenti.** An officer on the staff of a general or a provincial governor expected to do well out of his appointment, especially if there was a war being fought. Compare the delightful vignette in Catullus, *Carmen* 10, where Catullus recently back from Bithynia falls to chatting with his friend Varus and his new girl-friend: 'incidere nobis | sermones varii, in quibus, quid esset | iam Bithynia, quo modo se haberet, | et quonam mihi profuisset aere.' Cicero is suggesting that if Trebatius cannot find any better loot he had best loot a chariot to bring him back home.

2. 10. **adsequi quod volumus.** That is, profit and advancement and Caesar's favour.

12–13. **sed . . . plurimum,** 'but, believe me, your own modesty and hard work will help you most of all'.

13–14. **aetatem opportunissimam,** 'just the right age'.

14. **ut,** 'so that' ('with the result that').

LETTER 18

1. 3-6. A. d. IIII Non. Iun. . . . suavitate, 'on 2 June . . . I received your letter from Placentia, and then the next day a second letter from Blandeno along with a letter from Caesar which was all respect and attentiveness and charm'. Placentia (the modern Piacenza) was a town on the Po in the province of Cisalpine Gaul, governed by Caesar conjointly with Transalpine Gaul. Blandeno is not elsewhere mentioned: if the manuscripts' reading is reliable, it must have been a small place not far from Placentia.

6. ista. The *officium*, *diligentia*, and *suavitas* shown towards Cicero by Caesar in his letter. Translate: 'these marks of goodwill'.

7-8. habent enim . . . dignitatem, 'for they are a very potent force for renown and the highest distinction'. What Cicero means is that if he can rely on Caesar's goodwill and political support he and Quintus may look forward to *gloria* and *summa dignitas* for themselves. Whether Cicero had any specific appointment in mind we cannot say: in 53 he became an augur, an appointment in which he took enormous pride and one which he must have owed at least in part to Caesar. His own services to Caesar (whence Caesar's 'indebtedness' or *officium*) included, apart from his speech *de provinciis consularibus* in 56, his speeches in 54 in defence of Caesar's legate Gaius Messius and Caesar's old henchman of 59, Publius Vatinius.

9. plurimi. Genitive of value: 'most precious'.

9-10. tam inservientem communi dignitati, 'working so well to win ('dedicated to winning') distinction for both of us'.

12-16. Litterae vero . . . delectarunt. A rather difficult sentence to disentangle: 'The letter he sent with yours begins by saying how delightful he found your arrival and the renewing of old affection. Then he says he is going to see to it that, in the midst of my sadness and heartsickness for you, I shall be glad that though you are separated from me you are with him rather than anyone else. Believe me, it has given me incredible pleasure.' The *vetus amor* dates from many years back. Caesar was six years younger than Cicero. His mother Aurelia belonged to the family of the Aurelii Cottae, and as a young man Cicero (and no doubt his brother too) had been a great friend of Gaius Cotta and Marcus Cotta (consuls in 75 and 74) and much in their company. No doubt he had got to know the young Caesar well at the time. And both had Marian connections.

2. 16–17. **facis tu quidem . . . hortaris,** 'you certainly act as a brother should in urging me . . .'.

17–18. **currentem nunc quidem.** According to Marcus, Quintus is flogging a willing horse, for Marcus needs no urging but is now himself making all haste to do what his brother urges.

18–19. **Ego vero . . . studio,** 'yes I shall, and with the greatest enthusiasm'. The verb *conferam* is to be supplied from the preceding sentence. *Ego* put emphatically in answer to a question or request virtually means 'Yes'.

21–2. **quam si de nocte vigilassent,** 'than if they had got up at the crack of dawn'.

22–6. **sic ego . . . poeticis.** Cicero carries on with the simile of the late-rising traveller. 'In the same way, since I have been a sluggard in my attentions to your friend for so long, I too will make up for my tardiness by journeying swiftly, with horses or even with the chariots of poetry.'

25. **poema . . . probari,** 'that he likes the idea of my poem', 'of my writing a poem'. The poem would be addressed to Caesar and treat of his exploits in Gaul and Britain. It is part of Cicero's misfortune that he is remembered as a writer of indifferent verse, and laughed at for it. He was not the only one. Julius Caesar and Marcus Brutus (so Tacitus informs us: *Dialogus* 21) 'also wrote poetry and presented their poems to libraries; they were not any better than Cicero, only luckier, in that fewer people are aware that they wrote poetry'. In fact the fragments of Cicero's poetry that survive show that he was not at all a bad poet, although sometimes led astray by vanity into pomposity.

26. **modo mihi date Britanniam quam pingam,** 'just you give me Britain to paint'.

27. **penicillo.** *Penicillum* (literally 'a little tail') means an artist's brush or pencil. (The name of the modern drug 'penicillin' is derived from this.)

29. **videro,** 'I shall have to see'. The colloquial use of the hortative future perfect: cf. *viderit* in Letter 13, section 1.

unus amor, 'love alone', 'love by itself'.

3. 31. persalse, 'very wittily'. *Sal* (= 'salt') is regularly used to mean 'wit'; compare the phrase *sal Atticum*.

humaniter, 'courteously', 'kindlily'.

33. vadimonium concipere, 'to draw up a form of recognizance'. *Vadimonium* was the technical term for 'bail' or 'security' or 'recognizance' to appear on a fixed day before a court or tribunal. Caesar is saying that before Trebatius arrived none of those around him were capable of even the simplest legal expertise, so that a skilled lawyer like Trebatius will be invaluable.

34. M. Curtio. Marcus Curtius Postumus. In the Civil War he chose Caesar's side, and became praetor in 47 or 46. Cicero (who chose to follow Pompey) regarded this as an act of treachery towards himself, since he regarded himself as Curtius' *patronus* (*ad Att.* ix. 6. 2).

Domitius. On L. Domitius Ahenobarbus see Letter 1, section 3, note. He was consul this year (54) along with Appius Claudius Pulcher. The point of the story is that the consuls were quite without power and all hopes of advancement lay in the gift of the 'Big Three', Caesar and Pompey and Crassus. Hence Domitius would have thought that he was being made fun of if Cicero had asked him for the gift of a military tribuneship for Curtius; for it was a regular quip (*cottidianum*) of Domitius' that he possessed not even that small amount of patronage, and he had openly pulled his colleague Appius' leg by suggesting that the reason for his visit to Caesar had been to solicit some such petty office from him. This may be a reference to Appius' visit to Caesar at Lucca in 56; but it makes better sense if Appius had been to see him more recently, perhaps in 55 to solicit support for the consulship or even earlier in 54 as consul. Caesar regularly wintered south of the Alps at some town like Lucca or Ravenna, and was readily available to be visited from Rome.

38. in alterum annum, 'for next year'.

4. 40–2. Tu quem ad modum . . . molliorem, 'rest assured (*scito*) that I am behaving just as you say I should both in matters of state and so far as concerns my personal enemies, and I shall be as gentle as gentle can be'. 'Softer than the lobe of the ear' seems to have been a proverbial expression for supreme gentleness: cf. Catullus, *Carmen* 25 where (among other less delicate expressions) he uses the same image: 'mollior . . . imula oricilla'—possibly Cicero was actually thinking of the Catullus poem.

5. 42. habebant: erat. Epistolary imperfects; translate as present tenses.

43. non nulla spes comitiorum ... incerta, 'there is some hope of elections but nothing to rely on'. What had particularly characterized Roman political life in the last few years, attaining indeed to the status of a crying scandal, had been the conduct of elections. Bribery and corruption and violence at elections (and legislative assemblies) had long been endemic at Rome, and from time to time efforts were made to deal with this by laws and resolutions. Things got no better, only worse; and produced a rich crop of political prosecutions. In 56 the struggle to keep Domitius Ahenobarbus out of the consulship of 55 had resulted in no elections being held that year, thanks to the persistent obstruction of the tribune Gaius Cato; Pompey and Crassus at last won election in January 55 after Ahenobarbus had been driven away from the election-field by armed force. In 55 there was riot and bloodshed at the election of the aediles for 54, and it was said (Plutarch, *Pompey* 53) that it was the return home of Pompey from these elections spattered with blood that gave his wife Julia (Caesar's daughter) the shock which led to her death the next year, for she was pregnant at the time. Again now in June 54 it is clear that there is likely to be trouble over the elections for 53. On 15 July bribery touched new heights, and the rate of interest doubled, so great was the demand for money (*ad Q. fr.* ii. 15. 4). The confusion continued well into 53, the first half of which saw a consul-less Rome, and it was only in July 53—just twelve months late—that Domitius Calvinus and Valerius Messalla were elected consuls for 53 and at once assumed office. Again in 53 the elections for 52 were postponed, thanks to the Milo–Clodius riots (Milo was standing for a consulship in 52, Clodius for a praetorship), and the year 52 opened without consuls or praetors or even *interreges*, so that there was no one at Rome with *imperium*. Only when Pompey was called in after the murder of Clodius was order restored.

43–4. aliqua suspicio dictaturae . . . certa, 'there is some talk of a dictatorship, not that that is reliable either'. By the end of October Cicero wrote to Atticus (*ad Att.* iv. 18. 3): 'Res fluit ad interregnum et est non nullus odor dictaturae, sermo quidem multus.' By November Pompey's hanger-on Lucilius Hirrus came out into the open and began to advocate that Pompey be appointed dictator; but Pompey as usual was keeping his cards well concealed: 'Whether he wants it or not (writes Cicero: below, Letter 20, section 4) it is hard to know, but so long as Hirrus is active he will never convince anyone that he doesn't.'

44–5. **summum otium . . . adquiescentis,** 'calm reigns in the Forum, but it is the calm of decrepitude and not of political harmony'.

45–6. **sententia . . . nostra,** 'my contributions to senatorial debates' On *sententia* see Letter 9, section 6, note. The point of Cicero's remark is that he has now to behave himself, and is not free to say in public what he really thinks.

48. **Τοιαῦθ' ὁ τλήμων . . .** Spoken by Theseus in Euripides' play *The Suppliant Women* (*Supplices* 119): 'Such things does wretched war bring to pass.'

LETTER 19

1. 3. **librari.** A *librarius* was a 'scribe' or 'copyist', or (as here) a 'secretary'.

5. **sic enim habeto,** 'I would have you know'. *Habeto* is, like *iudicato* in the preceding clause, an old form of the imperative: Letter 16, section 2, note.

districtiorem. *Districtus* (from the verb *distringere*) means 'preoccupied', 'busy': the idea is of being at full stretch.

6–7. **atque id . . . maximis,** 'and that too at the most exhausting season of the year and in the middle of a heat-wave'.

8–9. **neque committendum . . . defuisse,** 'and I must avoid doing anything that might give the impression that I have not lived up to the hope and high opinion you and Caesar have of me'. *Vestrae* shows that Cicero has Caesar in mind as well as Quintus, otherwise he would have written *tuae*.

10. **magnam gratiam.** See note on *consulere*, Letter 1, section 4. The men Cicero defended in the courts (and their friends and backers) would be placed in Cicero's debt; and his appearance in these important cases would enhance his *dignitas*, especially if he were successful.

13. **aequis,** 'neutrals', those not committed either way.

14. **propensis in hanc partem,** 'Caesar's partisans'.

2. 15–16. **cum atrocissime ageretur . . .,** 'during the many days when the senate was engaged in a terribly violent debate about electoral corruption'. On this, see Letter 18, section 5, note. Writing to Atticus a little later, Cicero reports that 'all the candidates for the consulship are going to be charged with *ambitus*': *ad Att.* iv. 18. 3.

17–18. nullam medicinam rei publicae. Cicero is mixing his metaphors. *Medicina* means 'remedy' or 'physicking'. But at least he shows he has learnt his lesson, and will not try to set the Republic on its feet without the assurance first of powerful support (such as Caesar and Pompey could provide): so he is keeping well clear of this business.

3. 19. Drusus. This is probably Marcus Livius Drusus Claudianus, who was perhaps praetor in 50 when he is found as president of a court. He was the father of the Empress Livia, wife of Augustus and mother of Tiberius.

de praevaricatione. See Letter 2, section 1, note on 'iudices'.

19–20. tribunis aerariis. The standing courts (*quaestiones perpetuae*) were manned by a panel of *iudices* chosen in equal proportions from senators, knights, and 'treasury tribunes' (or 'paymasters'). Who these last were exactly is uncertain, but most, and perhaps all, of them were of the same standing as the knights: Cicero in a number of passages lumps them in with the *equites*. See Hill, *The Roman Middle Class* 213–14.

20. in summa quattuor sententiis, 'by four votes in all'. The *lex Fufia* carried in 59 by the praetor Q. Fufius Calenus required that the votes of the three classes that made up the juries be reported separately. Clearly some of the senators and knights on this jury must have voted for acquittal, otherwise there would have been a majority for condemnation; what Cicero means is that it was the heavy vote of the 'tribuni aerarii' in his favour that barely saved Drusus. The number of *iudices* empanelled for any given trial varied, though it was large by modern standards; in cases where the number of votes is recorded they range from 50 to 75.

21. damnassent, 'would have condemned him'.

22. Vatinium. Cicero had attacked him savagely when he appeared as a prosecution witness at the trial of Sestius in March 56. It is a measure of his political captivity that he now has to appear for Vatinius' defence two and a half years later at the urgent prompting of Caesar and Pompey. Cicero did manage to get some consolation out of the affair by reflecting that at least it would annoy those false friends of his among the nobility who had flaunted their friendship for the aristocratic Clodius before his eyes: 'Since they had their Publius, they should allow me another Publius (Vatinius) of my own, through whom I might get something of my own back on them' (*ad famm.* i. 9. 19). Vatinius is an oddly engaging character: brash, uncouth, violent, hated by the nobility, yet undoubtedly efficient, the uncouth and violent last years of the Republic suited him admirably. Everyone hated him: 'odissem te odio Vatiniano' wrote Catullus (*Carmen* 14. 3). Yet this grandson of a poor farmer from Reate (birthplace of that other uncouth and engaging Sabine, the Emperor Vespasian) who was in the habit of perjuring himself on the oath of the consulship he would one day have —'per consulatum peierat Vatinius': Catullus, *Carmen* 52. 3—won through to a consulship at the end of 47 and a triumph in 42. There are plenty of good stories about him. One of the best tells how when he gave a gladiatorial show and was pelted with stones by the crowd the aediles declared that he might be pelted only with fruit; one spectator asked if a pine-cone counted as a fruit, and the eminent jurisconsult Cascellius ruled that it could be deemed to be a fruit provided that it was to be thrown at Vatinius. Vatinius' saving grace was a sense of humour; like Vespasian he could laugh at himself. Everyone used to say that he was the greatest ruffian at Rome save for Clodius—everyone except Vatinius, who refused to concede first place to Clodius (Cicero, *in Vatinium* 41). Later, at Brundisium in 49, he treated Cicero with every kindness, and the two letters he wrote to Cicero which now survive are pleasant and easy in tone (*ad famm.* v. 9 and 10).

22–3. Comitia . . . reiecta sunt. On the continual postponement of elections, see Letter 18, section 4, note.

23–4. Scauri iudicium...non deerimus, 'the trial of Scaurus will come on at once, and I shall not fail him'. Cicero's speech *pro Scauro* has not survived, but we are lucky to have part of the commentary on it by Asconius (*in Scaurianam*). Marcus Aemilius Scaurus was the son of the great *princeps senatus* of the time of Marius, and the stepson of Sulla. He was charged with malpractices as governor of Sicily. He was defended by the astonishing total of six counsel, a measure of his inherited family influence: apart from his connections through his father and step-father, he was a Caecilius Metellus on his mother's side, his own son was the half-brother of Pompey's sons (he had married Pompey's wife Tertia after her divorce from Pompey), and his half-sister Fausta was married to Milo. Not only did Cicero and Hortensius lead for the defence, Publius Clodius was also one of his counsel. The case itself was of no political consequence, so that the wide network of connections which Scaurus possessed could operate without trammels and bring together on the same side men usually so hostile to each other as Pompey, Cicero, Hortensius, Milo, Clodius, and Gaius Cato. *Gratia* and *officium* and *necessitudo* are revealed in all their majesty and power as the call goes out to rally to Scaurus' defence. He was acquitted by a handsome margin: out of the 70 *iudices* only eight voted for condemnation.

24–6. Συνδείπνους Σοφοκλέους . . . **probavi,** 'I did not at all like your version of Sophocles' *The Dinner Party*, although I see that you wrote the piece in a light-hearted mood'. There was a satyr-play by Sophocles of this name, and if with Buecheler we read *factam* here (MSS. *actam*) we may suppose that Quintus had sent a version he had made of it to his brother. A little later Quintus wrote that he 'had polished off four tragedies in a fortnight' (*ad Q. fr.* iii. 5. 6). Quintus was particularly fond of Sophocles: cf. *de finibus* v. 3, where Quintus, a participant in the dialogue, is found saying 'Sophocles . . . quem scis quam admirer quamque eo delecter'.

4. 29. **reliqua.** 'what lies ahead', that is, what still remains to be gone through after the landing. Caesar's dispatches of the previous year will have given Cicero a good idea of the difficulties of landing and fighting in Britain: cf. *Bellum Gallicum* iv. 23 ff.

30–1. **magisque sum sollicitus . . .,** 'and I was more worried by having to wait for news than by fear'.

31. ὑπόθεσιν, 'theme' or 'topic': cf. Letter 4, section 4.

34–5. **quibus rebus vis, adiuvabo,** 'I will help you in the ways you wish'.

35–6. γλαῦκ' εἰς Ἀθήνας, 'owls to Athens'. The bird was itself common in Attica, and being the national emblem was stamped on Athenian coins (themselves often called 'owls' as a consequence) which went all over the world. Thus the phrase means 'Coals to Newcastle' —other similar expressions in antiquity were 'Corn to Egypt' or 'Fish to the Hellespont'. To send his own verses to Quintus will be 'coals to Newcastle' because Marcus judged his brother to be the better poet of the two: 'Simul et illud (sine ulla me hercule ironia loquor): tibi istius generis in scribendo priores partis tribuo quam mihi', *ad Q. fr.* iii. 4. 4.

5. 36. **heus tu.** A colloquial expression, very common in Plautus and Terence: 'But hey there! I think you are hiding something from me.'

Quomodonam. Some verb of thinking or saying has to be supplied: 'Exactly what is Caesar's opinion of my verses?'

37. **librum,** 'book' here, in the sense in which we speak of the first 'book' of the *Aeneid* or of *Paradise Lost*.

38–9. **et prima ... legisse,** 'and he liked the early part so much that he says he has never read anything better even in Greek'.

39. ῥαθυμότερα, 'a little careless', 'a bit slipshod'. The Greek word was the one chosen by Caesar himself to describe his feeling about the work.

40–1. **aut res eum aut χαρακτήρ . . .,** 'was it the content or the style he found displeasing?'

42. **ne pilo quidem minus,** 'I shall love myself not a whit less'. *Pilus* (= 'a hair') is often used to denote insignificance: cf. 'nec pili facit uni' (Catullus, *Carmen* 17. 17)—'doesn't care tuppence'.

φιλαληθῶς, 'truthfully', 'frankly' (literally 'in a truth-loving manner').

LETTER 20

1. 4. stomachi. *Stomachus* here means 'annoyance' or 'irritation' (not 'taste' as in Letter 14, section 2).

quo in genere, 'in the same vein', 'of the same type'.

5. Labieno. Titus Labienus was principal legate to Caesar in Gaul and virtually lieutenant-governor, and as such equipped like Caesar with a regular courier service (below, section 2). He was active as a reforming tribune in 63. He came from Picenum, which probably argues early Pompeian connections. On the outbreak of Civil War in 49 he went over to Pompey, and he came very close to beating his old commander Caesar in battle in North Africa in 46. He fell in the final battle of the Civil War at Munda in Spain in March 45.

7–9. ut in istis molestiis . . . profectioni tuae, 'that in the midst of all your irritation and difficulties and homesickness you should remember our original plan behind your going to Gaul'.

9. commoda, 'gains', 'advantages'.

10–11. Quid enim . . . putaremus, 'for what was it that we thought worth the price of our being separated' ('to be bought by our separation')? The subjunctive *putaremus* is generic.

12–13. ad omnem statum nostrae dignitatis, 'for every aspect of our standing in public life'.

13–14. Plura ponuntur...reserventur. Not an easy sentence. The metaphors are taken from the language of commerce. *Ponere* means to 'invest (cf. *pecuniam apud aliquem ponere*): *iactura* has the general sense of 'out-goings', either in the sense of 'loss' or in the sense of 'expenses' or 'costs' which have to be recovered or set against gross profits. What Cicero means is that originally he and Quintus looked to no other profit from Quintus' service with Caesar but security, but there is reason to hope for more than that as things have turned out. Any extra gains (*reliqua*) may be earmarked either (*a*) to cover their original outlay—that is, their separation from each other, the price they had had to pay; or (*b*) to offset any future loss they may suffer. Of the two alternatives, (*a*) gives a much happier sense. So translate: 'There are hopes of bigger profits than we are actually seeking: let any extra gains be earmarked to be set against our original outlay.'

14. **crebro,** 'repeatedly'.

15. **rationem.** See Letter 1, section 1, note.

17–18. **sed eius rei maturitas . . . adpropinquat,** 'but the time is not yet ripe for that, though it will not be long now in coming'.

2. 19–20. **quod si prolatum . . . feramus,** 'which we should not like to see made public knowledge'.

21. **vacuo animo,** 'with a mind free from care'.

22. **Cicero meus.** Cicero's son, now eleven years old.

23. **deinde,** 'after that', 'in future'.

24. **protinus,** 'straight on'.

25. **Nervii.** Quintus went into winter-quarters in the territory of the Nervii, between the rivers Meuse and Scheldt in Belgium, in command of a legion. Later he had to fight resolutely to defend his camp: *Bellum Gallicum* v. 38 ff.

3. 26. **in summo dolore.** Probably because of the death of his daughter Julia, Pompey's wife, who died in late summer 54.

27. **adhibuisset,** 'which you say he showed': the subjunctive is akin to the subjunctive of the alleged reason.

28. **institutum . . . poema.** See Letter 18, section 2, note. The poem was finished by December (*ad Q. fr.* iii. 7. 6).

28–9. **etsi distentus . . . magis,** 'though I am stretched to the limit by work and even more by worry'.

31–2. **his supplicationum otiosis diebus,** 'during these restful days of the solemn thanksgivings'. A *supplicatio* was a solemn thanksgiving to the gods decreed to celebrate national successes. In this instance the 'supplications' were in honour of Caesar's achievements in Gaul.

32. Messallam. Marcus Valerius Messalla was one of the consular candidates. He was eventually elected consul for 53. Along with all the other candidates in this scandalous year, he was threatened with prosecution for electoral corruption: see Letter 18, section 5, note; Letter 19, section 2, note. Public business, including judicial proceedings, was suspended during the period of the *supplicationes*—hence Messalla and the rest were given a breathing-space.

34–5. quod certum consulem . . . dissentitis, 'in reckoning him a certain consul along with Domitius you and Caesar in no way dissent from my own opinion'. The plurals *numeratis* and *dissentitis* show that Quintus was reporting Caesar's opinion as well as his own. They were right: Messalla was eventually elected along with Gnaeus Domitius Calvinus (on whom see Letter 11, section 6, note).

35. Ego . . . praestabo, 'I will vouch for Messalla to Caesar' (that he will find his conduct acceptable).

36. Memmius. See Letter 7, section 5, note. He too was a candidate for the consulship, but he had spoiled his chances by blurting out the details of a deal between himself and Domitius Calvinus to supply the consuls Claudius Pulcher and Domitius Ahenobarbus with a forged law and a forged *senatus consultum* complete with augurs and consulars as false witnesses in return for the support of the consuls in their own electoral campaign.

in adventu Caesaris. Not at Rome but in Cisalpine Gaul. Caesar regularly came south of the Alps into North Italy during the winters he was in Gaul (save in 52/1). From there he could exercise a closer influence on Roman politics; and perhaps Memmius was planning to run up there to see Caesar.

37. hic quidem friget, 'here in Rome, at any rate, he is a non-starter' Compare *refrigescit*, section 4, below; *frigebat*, Letter 4, section 1.

Scaurum. On Scaurus, see Letter 19, section 3, note.

38. abiecit, 'has abandoned', 'thrown overboard'.

4. 38. Res prolatae . . . adducta, 'business has been postponed; the elections have been drawn out to the point of an interregnum'. Cicero means that the continuing delay in holding the consular elections is going to result in an interregnum (and he was right). If no consuls were in office at the opening of a year, a series of *interreges* had to be appointed to fill the gap until consuls could be elected. The name *interrex* goes back to the old regal days of Rome, when he was the man who held office between the death of one king and the accession of another.

39. **Rumor dictatoris.** See Letter 18, section 5, note.

etiam magis, sc. *iniucunda.*

40. **sed tota res . . . refrigescit,** 'but the whole business, while it alarms people, is a damp squib'.

41–2. **Hirrus auctor . . . videtur,** 'it looks as if Hirrus will be the author of the bill' to appoint a dictator. The proposer of a bill or law was commonly called its *auctor*. Gaius Lucilius Hirrus was a tribune designate for 53. He followed Pompey in the Civil War, and was eventually pardoned by Caesar.

42–3. **se ipse amans sine rivali.** Compare Horace, *ars poet.* 444: 'Quin sine rivali teque et tua solus amares.' With the punctuation in the text, fatuity and swollen-headedness are being attributed to Hirrus. But it would be possible to print a full stop after *videtur*; the criticism would then be of Pompey, who is the subject of the following verbs.

43. **Crassum Iunianum.** Like Hirrus, a tribune designate for 53. It seems that Pompey used Cicero to warn Crassus to drop any idea of proposing a dictatorship for Pompey.

44. **velit nolit.** Subjunctives of the indirect question.

46. **loquebantur, agebatur.** Epistolary imperfects.

5. 46. **Serrani Domestici.** Otherwise unknown. The public eulogy which he delivered for his dead son was composed for him by Cicero. For an example of a funeral *laudatio* see the famous *laudatio Turiae* (Dessau, *ILS* 8393 = Ehrenberg and Jones, no. 357); for Caesar's *laudatio* of his aunt Julia see Suetonius, *divus Julius* 6.

47. **a. d. VIII Kal. Dec.** 23 November.

6. 49. **Milone.** See Letter 8, section 3, note. He was planning to stand in 53 for a consulship in 52.

ei nihil tribuit . . ., 'concedes nothing to him and everything to Gutta'. *Guttae* is puzzling, for no Gutta is known who will fit the bill. Hence *Cottae* has been suggested as the right reading, for a M. Aurelius Cotta was probably of praetorian rank at this time; but he is not among the three known candidates for the consulships of 52 (Milo, Plautius Hypsaeus, and Scipio Pius). The answer eludes us.

50. **ut in illum Caesar incumbat,** 'that Caesar will throw his weight behind him'.

51. **nec iniuria,** 'and not without justice'—Milo had worked with Pompey in 57–55.

52. **Intercessorem dictaturae,** 'anyone who vetoes a dictatorship'—there is no particular reference; several tribunes stood ready to veto any proposal to appoint a dictator: 'multi intercessores numerantur' (*ad Q. fr.* iii. 7. 4); but they would need the backing of Milo's gangs ('manu et praesidio') if their legal obstruction were to have any chance of not being overwhelmed by violence.

54. **perferatur,** 'the measure may get through'.

55–6. **stulte bis terque non postulatos,** 'a fool twice, nay three times over, for they are not demanded of him'. (For 'stulte bis terque' compare 'O terque quaterque beati!': Virgil, *Aeneid* i. 94.) A friend of Milo's has died, and as executor Milo proposes to use the occasion to put on some splendid public games in his honour (to win popular favour for his election bid). Cicero thinks this foolish of him on three grounds: (*a*) he has already put on a wonderful show (*munus*) as aedile; (*b*) he cannot afford it; (*c*) his position as executor (*magister*) does not demand it. (Aediles were customarily expected to put on games and shows for the entertainment of the public.)

LETTER 21

1. 3. **Quod tibi discedens . . .,** 'as to the promise I made as I left you . . .'. Caelius had accompanied Cicero part of the way on his outward journey from Rome to Cilicia, as far as the Campanian coast (section 2, below) at least.

4–6. **data opera paravi . . . videatur,** 'I have bestirred myself and got hold of someone to chase up everything so thoroughly that I am afraid you may find his conscientiousness too tiresome'.

5. **arguta.** *Argutus* is a very interesting word. Grammatically it is the past participle of the verb *arguo*, which derives from a root meaning 'bright' 'shining' (ἀργός in Greek). The original meaning of *arguo* was therefore 'to make clear'. The participle was regularly used as an adjective and applied metaphorically in a wide range of contexts. *Manus arguta* is used by Cicero (*de oratore* iii. 20) for 'rapid gestures'. Virgil can

call a horse's head *argutum* = 'clear-cut' 'handsome' (*Georgics* iii. 80). Tongues can be 'piercing' or 'rattling'; voices 'shrill' or 'penetrating'; the Forum 'alive with noise' or 'bustling' (Ovid, *ars am.* i. 80); swallows 'twittering' (*Georgics* i. 377). Here the sense is 'garrulous', 'tiresome'.

6. **curiosus,** 'eager to know everything'.

8–10. **Tamen in hoc te deprecor. . . delegavi.** Literally: 'However, I beg you not to condemn this duty of mine on a charge of arrogance in that (*in hoc... quod*) I have delegated this task to another.' More idiomatically: 'But please, I beg you, do not judge me guilty of being too proud to do you the service you laid on me because I have delegated this task to someone else.'

9–10. **adrogantiae condemnes.** A genitive of the matter involved is used with verbs denoting judicial procedure. The genitive may indicate either the crime (as here) or the penalty (e.g. *capitis*) or the matter concerned in the case (e.g. *repetundarum*).

11–12. **et occupato . . . pigerrimo,** 'busy as I am and, as you well know, the laziest of letter-writers'.

13. **volumen,** 'bundle', 'packet'.

misi. An example of the epistolary perfect. As with the epistolary imperfect, Caelius' action in sending off the packet will be a past event by the time it reaches Cicero. So translate either 'I have sent' or 'I send', *not* 'I sent'.

14–15. **Nescio quoius oti esset . . . animadvertere,** 'I don't know how much free time one would need, not to write out this news, but even to be aware of it at all'. The use of the genitive *oti* here is parallel to such uses as, e.g., *operae est*—'of what leisure it would be a matter'.

14. **quoius.** Caelius is fond of archaic forms like 'quoius' = 'cuius'. Studied archaism was somewhat in vogue in the latter part of the first century, Sallust being the best-known practitioner. The Emperor Augustus, a convinced believer in simplicity and lucidity of style, poked fun at the archaizing style of his stepson Tiberius (Suetonius, *divus Augustus* 86); and Julius Caesar said that the obsolete and rare word was to be shunned as a sailor shuns a reef (Aulus Gellius, i. 10. 4).

16. **fabulae,** 'rumours', 'stories'. **rumores** = 'gossip', 'talk'.

17–18. **ne molestiam . . . exhibeam,** 'to save my wasting money just to cause you annoyance'.

2. 18. **maius,** 'specially important', 'really big': larger, that is, than usual.

19. **quod isti operarii . . . possint,** 'of a kind that these hirelings cannot adequately cope with'—Caelius refers to the hired information-gatherers. An *operarius* is normally a 'labourer' or 'workman', someone who works for hire. *Possint* is a generic subjunctive.

20. **et quae existimatio secuta,** 'and what reaction it produced'. *Existimatio* is the assessment or judgement which will follow such an event.

22. **nulla magno opere exspectatio,** 'no one is expecting anything very much'.

23. **de comitiis Transpadanorum,** 'about the Transpadane elections'. The communities of this part of Italy lacked full Roman citizenship (Letter 1, section 2, note). Caesar had long professed support for their being granted it. Just now there was a crop of rumours that Caesar had ordered them to go ahead and elect local magistrates appropriate to full citizen communities (*quattuorviri*), which would have precipitated a first-class political crisis. As it was, the rumours 'remained warm only as far as Cumae'—or, as we should say, 'cooled off by the time I reached Cumae'. They must have been prevalent in towns to the south of Cumae in Campania, but as Caelius drew closer to Rome they died away to nothing. Caesar did eventually grant the franchise to the Transpadanes in 49.

25. **Marcellus.** See Letter 11, section 1, note. Marcus Marcellus was consul for this year, 51. He took the lead in the movement to recall Caesar from his command in Gaul. Caesar's enemies hoped that if they could get Caesar back in Rome as a *privatus* he could be attacked and condemned in the courts and driven into exile. But Pompey's refusal to co-operate with Marcellus and the extreme *optimates* in 51 made it impossible for them to achieve their end in that year. It was not until January 49 that the senate, with the full backing of Pompey, ordered Caesar to quit his province. Caesar's reply was to cross the Rubicon.

25–6. **adhuc nihil rettulit . . . Galliarum,** 'because so far he has introduced (in the senate) no motion about appointing a successor to the Gallic provinces'.

27–8. **sane quam eos sermones . . . essemus,** 'has wrung from everybody precisely those criticisms which people used to make about him when we were both at Rome'. By putting off positive action (he took none on 1 June either) Marcellus confirmed the general opinion that he was a bumbler: cf. *ad famm.* viii. 10. 3, 'Nosti Marcellum, quam tardus et parum efficax sit'. *Fuerant* is an epistolary pluperfect, to be translated as if it were an imperfect.

3. 29. Tu si . . . offendisti, 'if you have bumped into Pompey'. *Offendere* here simply means 'to come across', 'encounter'. There is no question of 'giving offence'. When Cicero reached Tarentum on his way out to Cilicia, he spent a few days with Pompey on his estate there.

29–30. qui tibi visus sit, 'how you found him', 'how he seemed to you'.

31. voluntatem. The idea is of thinking or planning or reacting to political events, the wishes a man has about them. Translate: 'how his mind is working'.

4. 33. Quod ad Caesarem. Understand some such verb as *attinet*.

33–4. crebri . . . veniunt, 'there is a whole crop of rumours about him, and not pretty ones, but so far they are only whispered'. A *susurrator* is a 'whisperer' or 'tale-bearer'. *Dumtaxat* was originally two words: *dum taxat*—'as far as it extends'.

35. equitem. The singular used collectively: 'his cavalry'. Certainly Caesar's Gallic cavalry was lured into a trap by the Bellovaci and badly mauled: *Bellum Gallicum* viii. 12. All the same, Caelius is probably making a joke by punning on the double meaning of *eques* as both 'a cavalryman' and a member of the equestrian order at Rome. In the late fifties there was widespread hostility to Caesar among the Roman *equites*. The rumours reaching Rome were thin and uncertain, so Caelius cannot have been confident about the truth of the Bellovaci business. But he does know the political situation: 'Lost his *equites*—well *that* he certainly has.'

36. vapulasse. A slang expression: 'has taken a drubbing'. *Vapulare* is an intransitive verb meaning to suffer a cudgelling or whipping.

apud Bellovacos. The Bellovaci lived in the region of the modern Beauvais (which preserves their name). On the fighting against them, see *Bellum Gallicum* viii. 6–23.

38–9. neque . . . vulgo iactantur, 'nor in any case are these unconfirmed reports bandied about in public'.

39. palam secreto, 'as an open secret'.

40. at Domitius, cum manus ad os apposuit. 'but Domitius always covers his lips with his hand'. Domitius Ahenobarbus was the only one of those in the know to make a great mystery about it all by such theatrical gestures. Understand *narrat* after *Domitius*, to be supplied from *narrantur*. Note too that *apposuit* is in the indicative mood. When a temporal *cum*-clause *identifies* the time at which the action of the main verb occurred, the indicative is normal. Perhaps we should regard this as a colloquial usage by Caelius, where the literary usage would have required a pluperfect subjunctive.

40–2. Te a. d. VIIII Kal. Iun. ...perisse, 'as for you, on 24 May the idlers around the Rostra put it about (may they hang for it!) that you were dead'. *Capiti* is the dative of disadvantage, a usage common in comedy.

43. Q. Pompeio. Grandson of Pompeius Rufus, consul in 88 with Sulla, and (through his mother) grandson of Sulla too. He was only a very distant relation of Pompey the Great. As tribune in 52 he was hostile to Milo and to Cicero as Milo's defending counsel and political supporter. Cicero has some nasty things to say about him (Asconius, pp. 37, 42, 49). He was accused by Caelius *de vi* and condemned. It looks as if he was now in hiding. Caelius knows he is in Campania, but the gossipers do not know where he is or what he is doing—otherwise they would not have concocted this story.

43–5. Ego qui . . . esurire, 'knowing as I did that Pompeius was in the boat business at Bauli and so near starving that I was even sorry for him myself'. Bauli was in Campania near the town of Baiae: its modern name is Bacolo. *Embaenetica* is from the Greek word ἐμβαίνειν = 'to embark', and probably means the trade of plying about a harbour between ship and shore in small boats. For the idiom compare 'piraticam facere' (*post red. in sen.* 11), 'naviculariam esse facturum' (*Verrines* II. v. 46). *Scirem* is an example of the generic/causal subjunctive.

45–7. et hoc mendacio . . . optavi, 'and I hope that by this lie we may discharge any dangers that may threaten you'. Caelius hopes superstitiously that this false report of Cicero's murder will so to say discharge any perils that might otherwise have threatened. Normally the ablative after *defungi* is used of the duty or obligation being discharged: e.g. *imperio regis defungi*. Here we must assume *periculis defungeremur* supplying *periculis* from *si qua pericula*. The perfect *optavi* is an epistolary perfect: 'I have formed the hope . . .'.

47. Plancus . . . tuus. The *tuus* is ironical. Titus Munatius Plancus as tribune in 52 supported Clodius and opposed Cicero, Milo, and Caelius. Cicero prosecuted him successfully *de vi* (52 was a violent year!). His brother Lucius was the famous Plancus who was consul in 42, first supported and then deserted Mark Antony, and enjoyed high distinction under Augustus, including the censorship in 22.

congiario. A *congiarium* was a gift or largess of money, normally from a superior to an inferior. Hence its use here is sarcastic: 'a bonus', 'a hand-out'.

48. nec beatus nec bene instructus est. Tyrrell and How both simply render 'neither rich nor even well-to-do'. There seems little sense in this: Plancus has just been given a lot of money by Caesar. Knowing Caelius, one suspects a pun. Certainly *beatus* means 'rich' and *bene instructus* means 'well provided for'. But *beatus* also means 'happy' or 'lucky', and *instructus* means 'versed in' or 'instructed'. The pun cannot readily be conveyed in English, but roughly the idea is: Caesar has presented him with a lot of money, but he is still the old unlucky Plancus, and no better off when it comes to common sense.

49. Tui politici libri . . . vigent, 'your political books are a universal success'. These are the six volumes *de re publica* begun in 54 and published in 51. See introduction to Letter 13.

LETTER 22

1. 4. compositiones. These are matchings of contestants, especially in gladiatorial combats: so 'gladiatorial pairings', 'the draws for gladiators'.

vadimonia dilata, 'adjournments of appearances'. On *vadimonium* see Letter 18, section 3, note.

4–5. Chresti compilationem. *Compilare* means to 'rob' or 'plunder'. It is disputed whether the noun here means 'burglary' or 'robbery', or whether *compilatio* has the sense of our word 'compilation' in the sense of a collection of documents plundered from other sources. Chrestus is unknown, but the name was common among slaves and freedmen.

5–6. quae nobis . . . audeat. Generic subjunctive: 'the sort of things no one dares tell me'.

6–7. Vide, quantum tibi . . . tribuam, 'see how highly I rate you in my judgement'.

7. iniuria, 'without justice', 'without good reason'.

πολιτικώτερον, 'with more flair for politics', 'a more political animal'. The comparative of the Greek word πολιτικός = 'political' or 'politically minded': it is constructed with the ablative of comparison *te*.

8. **curo mihi scribas.** *Ut* is omitted after *curo*, as often.

12–13. **ab homine longe in posterum . . . exspecto,** 'I look to hear what is going to happen, as from a man who gazes well ahead into the future'.

14. **formam,** 'plan', 'blueprint'.

2. 17. **nostrum,** 'of us here': Cicero includes his travelling companions and acquaintances at Athens in the plural.

cum Pompeio. See Letter 21, section 3.

18. **sermonibus,** 'conversations'.

19. **quae nec possunt scribi.** The neuter plural *quae* does not agree formally with the antecedent *sermonibus*: it is the sort of things that were said, rather than the actual *sermones* during which they were said, that are in question. The logical connection is clear enough.

20. **tantum habeto,** 'be content with this much', 'count on this much'. On the form *habeto*, see Letter 16, section 2, note.

20–1. **civem egregium . . . paratum,** 'that Pompey is a great patriot and stands ready in heart and mind to take whatever steps are needed to safeguard our country's interests'.

22. **complectetur,** 'he will take you to his bosom'.

23–4. **Iam idem illi . . . solent,** 'these days he sees eye to eye with us on the question of who are the good men and who the bad'. (Literally:'the same people seem good and bad citizens to him (*illi*) as usually seem so to us'.) It had not always been so. In 52 Pompey had been against Milo whom Caelius and Cicero supported, and for men like Pompeius Rufus and Munatius Plancus whom Cicero and Caelius opposed.

3. 25–7. **Ego cum Athenis . . . dedi.** Note the epistolary tenses here:'As for myself (the word *ego* is resumptive and emphatic), having spent exactly ten days at Athens with our friend Caninius Gallus much in my company, I am now leaving here on 6 July as I send you this letter, such as it is.'

26. **Gallus . . . Caninius.** When he omits the *praenomen*, Cicero quite regularly inverts the order of *nomen* and *cognomen*. As tribune in 56 Caninius Gallus had backed Pompey for the job of restoring Ptolemy Auletes to Egypt.

27. hoc . . . litterarum. Clearly depreciatory: the idea is 'this much of a letter'.

27–9. Tibi cum . . . prorogetur, 'while I am anxious for you to take the greatest care in looking after all my interests, there is nothing more vital than to ensure that my provincial command is not extended'. Cicero was very much afraid that the political manœuvres by Caesar's enemies to secure Caesar's recall from Gaul might so affect normal provincial allocations that his own one-year governorship of Cilicia might be extended. He bombarded his friends at home with constant appeals to see to it that this did not happen—almost every letter he wrote from Cilicia harped on the same theme.

30–1. Quod quando . . . constitues. '*Quod* is the connecting relative, referring to what has gone before. 'But as to this (i.e. preventing an extension of my term as governor), when and how and through whom action should be taken you yourself will best decide.'

LETTER 23

1. 3–5. Etsi . . . putares, 'although I am in the middle of my journey and actually on the road as the publicans' letter-carriers are leaving, and I am continuing my march, still I have decided to snatch a moment so that you will not think me unmindful of your directive'.

3–4. publicanorum tabellarii. On the 'publicans' see Letter 5, section 4, note. Their messengers formed a useful addition to the governor's own postal service.

5. mandati tui. Atticus had told Cicero to write as often as he could.

6–7. dum haec . . . perscriberem. The final use of the subjunctive after *dum*, indicating design. The clause gives the limit which it is the aim of the writer or speaker to reach.

7. orationem. A formal or set discourse as opposed to a casual conversation (*sermo*): translate 'a longer and more careful exposition'.

2. 8. Maxima exspectatione, 'amidst the greatest expectation' on the part of the provincials. Cicero's reputation as a champion of honest and just administration in the provinces was of course responsible for these hopes.

9. prid. Kal. Sext. 31 July.

10. moratos triduum Laodiceae. Laodicea, Apamea, and Synnada were the administrative centres of three districts in Phrygia which had originally formed part of the province of Asia, but had since 56 been part of Cilicia. Cicero spent three days at each town holding assizes. We must understand *moratos* (*esse*) and an asyndeton between *venisse* and *moratos*: 'I arrived . . . and spent three days, etc.' *Synnade* is the Greek locative form of *Synnas*: but the town is more usually called *Synnada* (a neuter plural form) as in *ad Att.* v. 20. 1, where Cicero uses the locative form *Synnadis*.

11–12. **imperata ἐπικεφάλια solvere non posse,** 'that people could not pay the poll-taxes which had been demanded of them'. Ἐπικεφάλια means levies or taxes imposed 'on heads' as opposed to crops or goods sold or in transit, etc. Whether these poll-taxes represented extortionate demands made by Cicero's predecessor Appius Claudius to line his own pockets, or were local taxes imposed by the local authorities to raise the money needed to pay the taxes demanded by the Roman government, we do not know.

12. **ὠνὰς omnium venditas,** 'everybody's tax-liabilities have been sold'. The ὠναί were the proceeds of taxes. Again it is not clear to us whether these were local taxes which the local authorities had sold the right to collect to speculators, or whether the taxes due to Rome had been sold by Appius Claudius to *publicani* in return for discharging the tax-debt due to Rome. Either way it comes to the same thing: either the governor or the local authorities have sold the taxation rights to contractors who will bear down hard to get their money back with a good profit on top.

12–13. **civitatum gemitus ploratus,** 'weeping and wailing from the cities'. Cicero switches from the accusative and infinitive construction after *audivimus* to the use of the ordinary accusative. A province was divided up into its constituent *civitates*, each of which comprised an urban centre and an area of surrounding country for which the centre was responsible. The magistrates of the *civitates* were responsible for the routine administration of their own areas.

13. **monstra quaedam. . . .** The accusative plural is in apposition to all the facts just mentioned: 'dreadful things, the work not of a human being but of some horrible wild animal'. In writing to the 'horrible wild animal' himself, however, Cicero is always careful to be not merely polite but even unctuous in his praise. The truth about Appius Claudius was reserved for Atticus' and Caelius' private ears.

3. 15. **sumptus,** 'expenditure'.

16. **legatos.** See Letter 9, section 7, note.

quaestorem. Each governor had his quaestor, who acted as a sort of financial secretary of the province. See Letter 11, section 1, note.

17–18. **scito . . . ne ligna quidem,** 'understand that I am declining to accept not only fodder or what is customarily given in accordance with the Julian Law but even firewood'. In 59 Caesar had carried a *Lex Julia de repetundis* which scrupulously regulated not merely a governor's financial conduct in the matter of public accounts, etc., but also defined carefully what supplies he could properly exact for his official use. Cicero is being careful not even to requisition these supplies, like fodder and firewood or a house to stay in, although he could have done so perfectly legally.

19. **quattuor lectos et tectum quemquam,** 'somewhere to sleep and a roof of sorts over my head'. I am not clear why Cicero specifies 'four' beds. Perhaps for himself and the three senior members of his staff.

20–1. **et in tabernaculo . . . plerumque,** 'but I stay in my tent for the most part'. When *et* follows a negative, as here, it has the force of 'but'.

21–2. **concursus fiunt . . . ,** 'people come crowding in from the country-side and all the villages and towns'.

23. **adventu nostro,** 'at my mere arrival'.

23–4. **iustitia . . . cognita.** Ablative absolute. *Abstinentia* is not 'abstinence' but rather 'self-restraint' or freedom from covetousness: simply translate it as 'honesty'.

4. 26. **Appius.** Caesar's predecessor as governor. See Letter 9, section 6, note, for his hostility to Cicero in 57. He was the elder brother of Publius Clodius, and consul in 54. He was ironically enough elected censor in 50, and was given command of Greece by Pompey in 49.

26–7. **in ultimam provinciam . . . usque,** 'he took himself off to the other end of the province, as far as Tarsus'. Tarsus was close to the Syrian border. This was very rude of Appius. Cicero expands on this matter in another letter written to Atticus a day or two later (*ad Att.* v. 17. 6): 'When our friend Appius saw that I was just about to arrive, he left Laodicea and went off to Tarsus. There he is holding an assize, although I am now in the province. This is quite wrong of him, but I do not pursue the matter, for I have quite enough on my hands in healing the wounds which have been inflicted on the province. And I take care to do this with as little disgrace as possible to him. But please tell our friend Brutus this, that it was not the act of a gentleman ("illum fecisse non belle") for Appius to put the greatest possible distance between us on my arrival.'

27. **forum agit,** 'is holding an assize'. As Cicero had now arrived, this was improper: see preceding note.

de Partho. Singular for plural: 'the Parthians'. They had overwhelmed Crassus and his legions at Carrhae only two years earlier. Before leaving Italy Cicero had had disturbing reports of trouble from them. In Cilicia he had only two legions to call on, both seriously under strength. In the end, although at one time there was even talk of sending out Caesar or Pompey to take command in the east, the scare blew over.

28. **concisos,** 'cut to pieces'.

nuntiabant. This and the other imperfects in this section are epistolary tenses.

29. **Bibulus.** Marcus Calpurnius Bibulus had been Caesar's colleague as consul and his bitter opponent in 59 (see Letter 5 and notes). He was married to Porcia, daughter of Marcus Cato—after his death in 48 she married Marcus Brutus. In 49–48 he commanded Pompey's naval forces against Caesar in the Adriatic with commendable tenacity. Like Cicero, he had declined to go to a province after his consulship; hence he was now caught along with Cicero by Pompey's new law (see introduction to Letter 21) and the two of them were assigned the consular provinces of Cilicia and Syria respectively for 51–50.

30. **id autem facere,** sc. *eum*—though the omission of 'eum' here is most unusual. Perhaps we should correct to '*id autem eum* facere', assuming that 'eum' has dropped out after '—em'.

31. **quod tardius vellet decedere,** 'because he wants to delay his departure' from the province. (Note that *vellet* is the subjunctive of the alleged reason, as is clear from the preceding *dicebant*.) Cicero and Bibulus had been assigned their provinces for one year with effect from the day they arrived there. Thus by delaying his arrival Bibulus would postpone his departure date as well. As to the reason for his action, this is no place to go into the complicated details of a very vexed issue. Briefly, it was part of the complex manœuvring to supersede Caesar in his Gallic provinces: by ensuring that the consular province of Syria would have a tenant and not be free for allocation when the next allocation of provinces was discussed, Bibulus would help to increase the

pressure to name one or both of the Gauls as a consular province available for assignment to someone other than Caesar.

32. bidui, 'two days' journey': understand *bidui iter* or *bidui spatium*.

1. 3–6. Quod et res p. . . . gaudeam, 'I am happy to do what I am prompted to do both as a loyal citizen and as a personal friend—that is, rejoice that your courage and honesty and application, recognized here at home in your civil career at the hour of crisis, are being employed with no less conscientiousness in command of our armies abroad'. The time of crisis at home refers to Cicero's handling of the Catilinarian insurrection a sconsul in 63.

5. domi togati, armati foris. Literally 'of you wearing a toga at home and armed abroad'. The genitives *togati* and *armati* agree with a substantive *tui* to be supplied from the preceding *tuam*: as *tuus* = *tui* 'of you', it is common to attach to it a qualifying adjective in the genitive case (cf. 'solius meum peccatum', Letter 30, section 2). The locatives *domi* and *foris* are regularly contrasted in Latin in the sense of 'at home' and 'abroad' (*foris* meant originally 'out of doors', 'away from home'). The toga was pre-eminently the garb of peace and civil life. The chiasmus of (*a*) *domi* (*b*) *togati* (*b*) *armati* (*a*) *foris* is very studied.

6. administrare. Here used in an intransitive sense.

pro meo iudicio, 'in accordance with my judgement', 'conscientiously'.

7. innocentia, 'incorruptibility', hence 'honesty'.

7–8. defensam provinciam . . . Faced with the threat of a Parthian invasion, Cicero had relied on the natural strength of Cilicia's mountain frontier to secure it against immediate danger, and concentrated on the defence of the exposed client kingdom of Cappadocia to the north and the stabilization on his throne of its king Ariobarzanes. At a critical moment he had moved up in support of Gaius Cassius (the future tyrannicide) at Antioch in Syria, and the news of his approach at the head of his troops had contributed to Cassius' success in beating off a Parthian attack.

9. sociorum revocatam . . . voluntatem, 'and the loyalty of our allies won back to enthusiastic support for our rule'.

10. **sententia mea et decreto**, 'by my speech and support for a decree'. On *sententia* see Letter 9, section 6, note. Cato means that he spoke in favour of the senate's passing a decree to congratulate Cicero on his energetic action; he did not, however, support the suggestion that a *supplicatio* be decreed in recognition of this action.

2. 10–13. **Supplicationem decretam...gaudeo,** 'as to the decreeing of a public thanksgiving, if you prefer that in a matter where our country was well served not by luck but by your own good sense and discretion we should give thanks to the immortal gods rather than put it down to your own credit, I am happy that the decree was passed'. (This translation is rather cumbersome, but so is Cato's Latin.) On *supplicatio* see Letter 20, section 3, note. *Referre acceptum* is a metaphor from accounting. Cato comes dangerously close to being downright offensive to Cicero here (observe how neatly Cicero replies to this point in Letter 23) in suggesting that Cicero is being rather silly if he prefers credit to be given to heaven (that is, mere luck) rather than to his own exertions and sense.

14. **triumphi praerogativam**, 'the first step to a triumph', 'a guarantee of a triumph'. The adjective *praerogativus* (from *praerogare* = 'to ask beforehand') was normally applied to the century or tribe to which it fell by lot to cast the first vote at an assembly. In the consular elections in particular the vote of the *centuria praerogativa* was regarded as establishing a trend which would be reflected in the subsequent voting: Cicero even went so far as to say in the *pro Murena* (38) that it had invariably forecast the eventual result—'tanta illis comitiis religio est ut adhuc semper omen valuerit praerogativum'. Here the adjective is used in a metaphorical sense by Cato (so too by Cicero, *Verrines* I. 26: 'praerogativam suae voluntatis'). Cato says he hopes Cicero is not being misled by the unfounded expectation that the voting of a *supplicatio* is an earnest that the greater honour of a triumph will follow.

15–16. **neque supplicationem . . . et triumpho.** *Neque . . . et* joins or contrasts two propositions of which the first is negative and the second positive: cf. Letter 31, section 1, 'neque tibi . . . coramque' (in Greek we find οὔτε . . . τε).

19–20. **quod ego mea sententia censebam**, 'and this was what I was arguing for in my speech'.

3. 22. **pluribus.** Understand *verbis*.

23–5. **et voluisse . . . gaudere.** A rather laboured piece of writing totally lacking in any hint of sincerity: 'to convince you that while I advocated (*voluisse*) what I personally believed would add the greatest lustre to your renown I am at the same time delighted that you have got what you yourself preferred'. In the two *et . . . et* clauses understand *id* as the object of *voluisse* and *id* as the subject of *factum esse* as antecedents to the two *quods*.

25–6. instituto itinere . . . praesta, 'and continue on the path you have taken, and demonstrate your strictness and conscientiousness to our allies and our country'.

LETTER 25

1. 3–4. opinor, apud Naevium, 'in Naevius' play, I think it is'. Cicero affects a modest vagueness. The line is a trochaic trimeter from the play *Hector proficiscens*. Gnaeus Naevius was one of the founders of Latin poetry, his active writing life stretching from about 235 to 200. As well as tragedies and comedies derived from Greek models he also wrote an epic poem, the *Bellum Poenicum*. He was free in his attacks on the leading politicians of his time, and eventually so exasperated the leading Metellus of his day that he was imprisoned. He had no false modesty, witness the epitaph he composed for himself: 'Inmortales mortales si foret fas flere, / Flerent divae Camenae Naevium poetam. / Itaque postquam est Orchi traditus thesauro, / Obliti sunt Romai loquier lingua latina.'

4. profecto, 'truly'.

6–10. Ego vero . . . dares. Very emphatic—answered by the section beginning *Sed . . .* a few lines further on. 'Speaking personally, what with the congratulations contained in your letter and the honour you did me in your speech in the senate, I cannot feel that there is anything still remaining for me to achieve; and I find it most flattering and gratifying that you willingly granted to friendship what you could grant unhesitatingly (*liquido*) to truth.' The language is stiltedly correct, the sarcasm evident but unprovable.

10–11. Et si non modo . . . nostra, 'and if—I will not say everybody —but even a good number of our fellow countrymen were Catos . . .'.

12. currum . . . lauream. The chariot and the laurel wreath were the prerogatives of a man celebrating a triumph.

13–14. Nam ad meum sensum . . . iudicium, 'for to my way of thinking and in conformity with that pure and scrupulous judgement of yours . . .'. *Ad* here has the sense of 'in relation to', 'in accordance with'.

15–16. **quae est ad me . . . necessariis,** 'a full version of which has been sent me by my friends'. Cicero is letting Cato know that he knows precisely what Cato did say in his speech to the senate.

2. 17. **superioribus litteris.** Two earlier letters from Cicero in Cilicia to Cato survive as *ad famm.* xv. 3 and 4. Cicero had specifically asked Cato for his support in the senate for the public recognition of his (Cicero's) achievements in the military sphere. In section 11 of the latter letter he explicitly says that he wants Cato to back any such move that may be made in the senate, and in section 14 that he sees such public honour as some sort of salve for the wounds his public dignity had suffered in the past.

17–20. **quae etiam si . . . videatur,** 'and even if this wish of mine seems to you ill-founded, it does still have this sound basis—not that the honour seems one too eagerly to be craved, but one which, none the less, if it is offered by the senate, ought very much not to be spurned'.

21. **illum ordinem,** 'that order', viz. the senate.

22. **usitato praesertim,** 'an honour which is moreover customary'. In Cicero's day the strict conditions previously necessary for the grant of a triumph seem to have been considerably relaxed. Neither of his predecessors had achieved any striking military successes, yet Lentulus Spinther had celebrated a triumph and Appius Claudius was hoping for one.

23. **tantum ex te peto, quod amicissime scribis,** 'and all I ask of you, to use your own most friendly words . . .'. Cicero picks up the penultimate sentence of Cato's letter (Letter 24, section 3).

26–8. **resque ipsa . . . quod scribendo adfuisti,** 'and the very fact that you were a witness to the decree'. On *scribendo adesse* see Letter 9, section 6, note.

30. **propediem,** 'very soon'.

31. **atque utinam . . . ,** 'and I pray with our country in a happier state than I fear it will be'. The struggle between Pompey and Caesar was approaching the crisis, and threatened to erupt (as it did less than six months later) in civil war.

LETTER 26

1. 3–4. **Tanti non fuit . . . careres,** 'it wasn't worth capturing the King of Parthia and storming Seleuceia if it meant missing the spectacle of the things that have been going on here at Rome'. Caelius is fancifully exaggerating Cicero's military successes in the east. Arsaces was the founder of the Parthian ruling house, and his name was used as a title by his successors (as the name 'Caesar' was to be at Rome). Seleuceia was the Greek city on the Tigris founded by Seleucus, one of the successor kings who had divided up Alexander the Great's empire after his death: it was opposite the Parthian royal residence at Ctesiphon.

3. **Tanti non fuit.** *Tanti* is a genitive of price or value followed by a restrictive *ut*-clause: 'not worth enough to justify'. One might have expected the potential subjunctive *fuisset* ('it would not have been') rather than the indicative *fuit*: this is probably a colloquial usage, similar to such phrases as *satius fuit* or *melius fuit* also used with a potential sense of 'it would have been better'.

5. **numquam tibi oculi doluissent.** As we should say in English: 'It would have been a sight for sore eyes.'

repulsa. Regularly used to mean a 'defeat' in an election. Lucius Domitius Ahenobarbus (on whom see Letter 1, section 3, note) had been beaten by Mark Antony in the election to the augurship which had become vacant on the recent death of the orator Quintus Hortensius. Antony had been strongly backed by Julius Caesar.

6–8. **Magna illa comitia . . . praestiterunt,** 'it was a big election, and it was very plain to see that people's voting followed party loyalties; only a handful did their duty by honouring personal friendships'. Normally one would have expected that in such an election all the usual personal ties of *officia* and *gratia* and *amicitia* (Letter 1, section 4, note) would have had free play; but the critical political situation at Rome turned it into a trial of party strength between Caesar and his opponents.

9–10. **ut ne familiarem quidem suum . . . ,** 'that even among his own close friends there is no one he hates as much as me'. Caelius had been active and prominent in supporting Antony.

10. **per iniuriam,** 'unfairly', 'unjustly'. The point is that as an ex-consul and a great *nobilis* Ahenobarbus thought it downright scandalous that he should lose the augurship to so young a competitor as Antony, who was only of quaestorian rank. More than that, Ahenobarbus no doubt supposed that he was in some sense *entitled* to the office, since it had been his own father who had just over fifty years earlier carried the *lex Domitia* which had first opened appointments to the great priestly colleges to popular election. (On these colleges, see Letter 9, section 7, note.)

11. quoius ego auctor fuerim, 'for which he holds me responsible'—such is the force of the subjunctive *fuerim*: see Letter 11, section 3, for a comparable use of *interemisset*. On the form *quoius* for *cuius*, see Letter 21, section 1, note: the antecedent of *quoius* is the clause *sibi ereptum auguratum.*

11–13. Nunc furit . . . Antoni, 'now he is furious that people should be so gleeful at his discomfiture, and he is slapping writs on anyone who was more than usually active in Antony's support'. (The manuscripts' text is corrupt, and reads: 'suum dolorem *unumque move* studiosiorem Antoni'. The text I have printed is the suggestion of Mendelssohn: it certainly gives the sort of sense required better than other suggested corrections which may be palaeographically closer to the manuscripts.) We have here two easy-going constructions in one sentence, typically Caelian syntax: *furere*+accusative and infinitive ('is wild at the fact that . . .') and *gaudere*+accusative ('enjoy', 'rejoice at' something).

13–16. nam Cn. Saturninum ... absolutionem, 'for Gnaeus Domitius has personally indicted young Gnaeus Saturninus, against whom there is certainly a lot of prejudice on account of his conduct hitherto. This trial is now eagerly awaited, and even with confidence now that Sextus Peducaeus has been acquitted'. Gnaeus Domitius is the son of the defeated candidate, Lucius Domitius, his mother being Cato's sister Porcia. Young Saturninus had presumably been very active for Antony. As a member of the family of the famous popular tribune of 103 and 100 he may well have had traditional ties of *amicitia* with the Ahenobarbus family, since the tribune of 104 and author of the *lex Domitia* (above) may well have been a political ally of the tribune Saturninus. Hence young Saturninus will probably have been one of those whose personal ties of support to Ahenobarbus had been overridden by party loyalties. His apparently scandalous private life made him an early target for attempted revenge. All the same, the recent acquittal of Peducaeus (on what charge we do not know) makes Caelius think Saturninus has a good chance of getting off too. This Peducaeus was the brother of Manius Peducaeus (Letter 8, section 3).

2. 17–18. me in annum pacem non videre, 'that I do not see peace lasting another year': a colloquial ellipse.

19–21. Propositum . . . dimicaturi, 'the issue over which the men in power are going to do battle is this'. In these few lines Caelius pinpoints the issue which led to the armed clash between Pompey and Caesar with admirable succinctness. Caesar was convinced (and with justice) that if he surrendered his provincial command and his loyal legions and returned to Rome as a *privatus* his political and personal enemies, assisted by Pompey's military strength, would attack him in the courts and drive him into exile and political oblivion. On their side, Pompey and the extreme *optimates* were appalled at the prospect of what might happen if Caesar should hang on to his command until elected to a second consulship, when with his *imperium* protecting him from prosecution he could be expected to achieve political dominance at Rome. Hence Caesar, if he was to be flushed into the open and prosecuted in the courts, had to be extruded from the cover of his proconsular command and his legions before the consular elections in summer 49—for Caesar would be legally eligible to stand for a second consulship then. When in January 49 the senate took the fateful decision and ordered Caesar to quit his province, he had no choice but to surrender or fight. Inspecting the field after the decisive battle of Pharsalus, Caesar himself declared (Suetonius, *divus Julius* 30): 'Hoc voluerunt. Tantis rebus gestis Gaius Caesar condemnatus essem nisi ab exercitu auxilium petissem.'

21–2. quod Cn. Pompeius constituit . . . tradiderit, 'that Gnaeus Pompeius has resolved not to put up with Gaius Caesar's being elected consul in any circumstances unless he first surrenders his army and his provinces'.

24. fert illam tamen condicionem, 'however he offers the following condition'. Caelius here makes the first mention of the proposal, later formally moved in the senate by the tribune Curio, and persistently advanced by Caesar, that both Pompey and Caesar should simultaneously resign their military commands to ease the tension. (Pompey's command in Spain had been renewed for a further five years in 52.)

25. Sic illi amores. The *amores* and *coniunctio* refer of course to the original alliance of Pompey and Caesar in 60 which had led to the 'First Triumvirate', and which had been cemented by the marriage of Pompey to Caesar's daughter Julia.

26. obtrectationem, 'bickering', 'sniping'.

27. neque mearum rerum . . . capiam. *Mearum rerum* is an objective genitive depending on *consili*, itself a partitive genitive depending on *quid*: 'What decision about my own course of action'.

28. quod non dubito. It is probably best to take *quod* here as hanging very much in the air syntactically: 'As to which, I do not doubt . . .'.

29–31. **Nam mihi cum hominibus his ... odi.** The text I have printed
was suggested by Madvig, and it has won wide acceptance as the best
cure for a corrupt text in the manuscripts. 'For on the one side I have
both influence and close personal ties with the individuals concerned;
while on the other I love the cause but detest its supporters.' The first
people mentioned (*hominibus his*) are Caesar's adherents, personal friends
of Caelius like Curio and Dolabella and Antony; the *causam illam* is the
cause of Republican government, many of whose prominent advocates
like Appius Claudius and Domitius Ahenobarbus were men for whom
Caelius felt a deep personal distaste. Cicero found himself in a somewhat
similar quandary (as Caelius supposed he would). As Cicero himself
put it: 'Ego vero quem fugiam habeo, quem sequar non habeo.'

3. 31. **Illud te non arbitror fugere,** 'I am sure that you are not blind
to the fact that . . .'.

32. **civiliter,** 'by constitutional means'.

33. **honestiorem,** 'more honourable'.

34. **firmiorem.** Understand *partem*: 'the stronger party'.

et id melius statuere ... sit, 'and to equate virtue with security' (literally: 'and to hold that that which is safer is better').

35–6. **quique res iudicant.** That is, *et eos qui res iudicant* = 'those who
control the courts'. Caelius means the *equites* and *tribuni aerarii* who along
with the senators constituted the *iudices* of the Roman courts.

37. **timore.** The fear is no doubt fear of prosecution.

37–8. **exercitum conferendum non esse,** 'there is no comparison
between the two armies'. Clearly it is Caesar's victorious veteran legions
that Caelius regards as incomparably superior, for he judges that
Caesar's will be the stronger side should it come to war.

38. **Omnino,** 'in any case', 'all in all'.

4. 40–2. **Scis Appium censorem ... agere,** 'do you know that our censor Appius is doing the most amazing things here, and conducting the
most searching inquiry into plate and pictures, land-holdings and debt?'
Censors were properly and traditionally concerned to prune extravagance in personal expenditure on luxuries, to castigate debt, and of
course to deal with real property in general. The amusing thing was that
Appius was himself anything but a paragon of virtuous and moderate
living. The famous and dour Cato the Elder had as censor delivered a
well-known speech *de signis et tabulis*: no doubt Caelius expected Cicero

to catch the allusion, and the strangeness of Appius' aping the great Cato.

42–3. persuasum est ei . . . esse, 'he has convinced himself that the censorship is a matter of soap and soda'. *Lomentum* (*lavamentum*) was a preparation of bean-meal and rice favoured by Roman ladies as a skin-conditioner. *Nitrum* was washing-soda: cf. Jeremiah 2: 22, 'For though thou wash thee with nitre, and take thee much soap, yet thine iniquity is marked before me.'

44–5. nam sordis eluere vult . . .aperit, 'for in wanting to wash the dirty linen he is exposing his own nakedness (literally: his own veins and flesh)'. That is, Appius is inviting caustic comment on his own moral shortcomings.

46–7. haec risum veni. . . agere, 'come and have a good laugh at all this: a trial under the Scantine law under the presidency of Drusus, Appius investigating pictures and plate!' *Risum* is an example of the use of the supine to express end or aim or purpose: like the infinitive and the gerund, it governs an accusative object, *haec* (with the following accusative and infinitive clauses as complex nouns in apposition to *haec*). The *lex Scantinia* was a law which dealt with sexual perversions and unnatural practices. Clearly Drusus' own reputation was not lily-white. (He was probably Marcus Livius Drusus Claudianus, the father of the Empress Livia, wife of Augustus.)

48–9. Curio noster . . . existimatur, 'our friend Curio is reckoned to have acted with good sense in withdrawing his opposition to the supply-vote for Pompey'. The question was one of voting money to pay Pompey's troops. As tribune Curio could use his veto against such a supply-bill. His *sapientia* lay either in not precipitating a crisis by persisting in his opposition, or in seeing that it would be unwise to make enemies of Pompey's troops, or in both.

50. alter uter eorum, 'one or other of them'—the two in question being Pompey and Caesar.

53. summo periculo. A good example of a routine type of scribal error one finds in manuscripts. The manuscripts here read *suo*, which makes no sense. Older editors realized this and altered *suo* to *tuo*. But it is as good as certain that the error arose because an original *summo* had been abbreviated to *su̅o̅* and then miswritten as *suo*.

54. parabat. Epistolary imperfect.

LETTER 27

2–3. **TVLLIVS TIRONI SVO...,** 'Tullius sends his very best wishes to his dear Tiro, and so do my son Cicero and my brother and my brother's son'. Cicero's brother Quintus had accompanied him to Cilicia as his legate. The two boys joined their fathers on the trip home. *S. P. D.* is the standard abbreviation for *salutem plurimam dat (dant)*.

1. 4. **Paulo facilius . . .,** 'I did think that I could bear missing you a little more easily'.

6.**magni ad honorem nostrum interest,** 'although it is vital to my public position'. By *honos* here Cicero probably refers to his hopes of being granted a triumph. (For this use of *ad*, see Letter 25, section 1, note.)

7. **discesserim.** The subjunctive is causal: 'because I have left you behind', 'in leaving you behind'. But one can see how it merges into the generic use of the subjunctive.

8. **prorsus.** To be taken with *navigare*: 'to continue the voyage'.

9. **muto.** Tyrrell and Purser take this as a rare example of *muto* used intransitively: but it is also possible to assume *consilium* as the object of *muto* here—'I approved your decision nor do I now seek to alter it'.

10–11. **sin autem . . . est.** Note that the verbs are in the indicative mood and the present and perfect tenses: 'But if, now that you have begun to take nourishment, you think that you can catch me up, the decision is yours.'

12. **Marionem ad te eo misi,** 'my object in sending Mario to you was . . .'. (Mario was a slave of Cicero's.) '*eo*' looks forward to '*ut*'.

2. 14. **commodo valetudinis tuae,** 'without damage to your health'. This use of the ablative of *commodum* is common in phrases like *commodo meo (tuo) (suo)* and so on. Cf. Letter 10, section 3: 'quod commodo reip. facere possis'.

16. **Patris,** 'at Patrae': locative case.

18. **Leucade,** 'at Leucas': again a locative, formed from the Greek stem which gives *Leucas, -cadis* in Latin. Leucas was the chief port of the island of Leucas which lies off the north-west coast of Greece south of Corcyra (Corfu).

18–20. **et comites . . . idebus.** The adjective *idoneam* qualifies all three nouns while agreeing grammatically with the last of them: 'You are to be careful to see that your entourage, the weather, and the ship are all as they should be.' *Comites* here means not just 'companions' but people to accompany and look after Tiro (cf. the splendid entourage of Musicus referred to in the introduction).

20. **videto.** The jussive form of *videre*: cf. Letter 16, section 2, note.

21–3. **Quod valetudini . . . meae,** 'you will be most obedient to my wishes if you do what contributes most to your own health', 'you will serve my wishes best by doing what best serves your own recovery'.

3. 23. Haec pro tuo ingenio considera, 'make up your mind about this in the light of your own good sense'.

23–4. **ita te desideramus, ut amemus,** 'as for myself, my longing to have you with me is balanced by my concern for you'. The subjunctive *amemus* after *ita . . . ut* here gives a limiting force, which would be lost by the simple indicative *amamus*—which would mean 'My longing for you is as great as my love for you'.

25. **illud igitur potius,** 'so the former (love) must prevail'. *Illud* regularly refers to the more distant of two alternatives, *hoc* to the nearer.

26–7. **De tuis . . . gratissimum,** 'out of all your countless services to me this will be the most welcome'.

LETTER 28

1. 3. a. d. XIII Kal. Mart. 17 February. It is to be presumed that Pompey is replying at once.

5–9. **Quod putavi . . . dubitamus,** 'what I thought would happen and warned you about in advance is happening: he is avoiding battle with you for the time being, and trapping you in a net by concentrating his forces so as to cut your communications with me and prevent your uniting your own reliable forces with the legions here whose loyalty is uncertain'. The *ut velit* clause is an example of the explanatory use of the subjunctive with *ut*, which is really just a form of the consecutive clause of fact which states an actual result. The two legions with Pompey, the Sixth and Fifteenth, had previously served under Caesar and had only been released to Pompey in 50; hence their loyalty was not above suspicion, whereas the major part of Domitius' forces had been levied in Pompey's own 'barony' of Picenum.

11. **voluntate . . . confido.** Both the ablative and the dative are found after *confido*.

11–12. **ut de omnibus fortunis r. p. dimicem,** 'to risk our country's fate on a battle'.

12–13. **neque etiam . . . convenerunt,** 'nor have the conscripts levied for the consuls been concentrated yet'. *Dilectus* or *delectus* was the regular term for a levy of troops. Though from Marius' consulship onwards compulsory conscription into the Roman army had normally given way to voluntary recruitment, conscription had never been abolished and was always available as a recourse in emergencies. The consuls of 49, Gaius Claudius Marcellus and Lucius Cornelius Lentulus Crus, were of course the official leaders of the constitutionalist forces.

2. 15. **ut te explices,** 'to slip out of the net', 'extricate yourself'. Cf. *ut te implicet*, above.

17–19. **et, si convenirent, . . . praeterit,** 'and even if a concentration were effected, just how little we can trust them to do—why they do not even know each other by sight!—against veteran legions, cannot escape you'. Note that by his use of the indicative *noti sunt* Pompey makes an objective statement of fact about these fresh levies; the use of the subjunctive would have given a different nuance—'how little we can rely on men who do not even know each other'.

LETTER 29

2. CICERONI IMP. Since Cicero had not yet crossed the city boundary (*pomerium*) into Rome since his return from Cilicia, he was still *cum imperio* as a proconsul and hence properly addressed as 'Imperator': see Letter 3, note on 'Imperatori' (*ad init.*) and Letter 4, section 1, note on 'circo Flaminio'. In fact, as proconsul Cicero had been commissioned to supervise the government levy in Campania; but by the end of January he had retired to his estate at Formiae.

1. 3. **Furnium nostrum.** Gaius Furnius was tribune in 50, and had supported the vote of a *supplicatio* to Cicero, to whom he was therefore persona grata.

tantum, 'only just', 'scarcely', 'barely'.

4. **meo commodo,** 'without upsetting my plans': cf. Letter 27, section 2, note.

5. **essem in itinere.** Caesar was marching on Brundisium, which he reached on 9 March.

5–6. **praeterire . . . quin.** An unusual construction, but one also used by Sallust in *Catiline* 53. 6: 'silentio praeterire non fuit consilium quin utriusque naturam et mores . . . aperirem.'

8. **ita de me mereris,** 'so well do you deserve it of me', 'so deep is my debt to you'.

9. **ad urbem,** 'outside Rome'. *Ad* is used here in the sense of 'near', 'in the neighbourhood of'. Like Cicero, the proconsul Caesar could not cross the *pomerium* and enter the city without automatically divesting himself of *imperium*.

10. **ope omnium rerum,** 'assistance in all matters'.

11. **Ad propositum revertar.** Either (*a*) 'I will now return to what I began with'—that is an apology for the briefness of this letter; or (*b*) 'I will return to this subject later'—the subject of Cicero's co-operation. I prefer (*a*) since one would expect some adverb like *alias* or an adverbial phrase like 'as soon as I have the time' to complete the sense of (*b*).

LETTER 30

1. 3. **iustas causas adfers,** 'you advance good reasons'.

4. **Ille.** Caesar.

5. **Alexandria teneri,** 'cooped up in Alexandria'. Caesar had pursued Pompey to Egypt, where Pompey had been treacherously murdered on landing. But Caesar's attempts to settle the dynastic affairs of the country led before long to his being attacked in overwhelming force by the royal army and penned up in a corner of Alexandria. The fighting throughout the winter was bitter and desperate, but finally Mithridates of Pergamum and other eastern rulers arrived with relieving forces, and on 26 March 47 Caesar broke out of Alexandria and joined Mithridates. Next day he shattered the Egyptian army and that same evening received the surrender of Alexandria. Even after this six months delay, however, Caesar did not hurry back to Italy: he stayed on in Egypt till the beginning of June.

5–6. **de illis rebus,** 'about affairs there'.

6–7. **hi autem . . . commoraturi,** 'while these people from Africa look like arriving at any moment, and the Achaean contingent and those in

Asia look like rejoining them or staying on in some free locality'. Cicero
is referring to the various Pompeians who scattered to Africa, Greece, and
Asia after the defeat at Pharsalus, and who he now thinks will be back in
Italy before long. By *libero aliquo loco* Cicero means a community which,
though *de facto* subject to Roman control, was technically independent
and in formal treaty relations with Rome, in other words a *civitas libera*.

9–10. Sum enim solus . . .ostendatur, 'for I am quite alone, or alone
but for one other, in having no avenue of return to them [the Pom-
peians] nor any glimmer of hope held out to me by these people here
[the Caesarians in Italy]'. The 'one other' (*aut cum altero*) was Laelius
(section 2, below). The subjunctives *sit* and *ostendatur* are, of course,
generic subjunctives. The antecedent to *cui* is Cicero himself.

11. idque erat cum aliis. Epistolary imperfect: 'And that is along with
other reasons why . . .'.

2. 13. Minucium X̄Ī̄Ī sola curasse, 'that Minucius has only managed
twelve thousand (sesterces)'. On the expression of money sums in Latin,
see Appendix 2. Minucius was a banker at Tarentum; Atticus had
arranged that he should advance Cicero 30,000 sesterces.

Quod superest, 'The balance'.

14–16. Quintus non modo non . . . urgear, 'so far from sending me an
earnest appeal, Quintus has written me a most hurtful letter; and as for
his son, he has written with astonishing hatred. I am weighed down by
every misfortune you could conceive of.' Cicero's relations with his
brother and his nephew were going through a very bad patch just now.
They had gone to Caesar after Pharsalus to seek pardon, and they were
apparently hoping that they would gain it by blackening Cicero's
character and putting all the blame on him; yet Cicero himself had
written most generously to Caesar absolving his brother from all responsibility or approval for his own political hostility to Caesar. (See especially *ad Att.* xi. 9, 10, and 12.) Happily Quintus made amends before long,
and the two brothers were reconciled by June (*ad Att.* xi. 23. 2). Other
troubles also afflicted Cicero at this time. He was quarrelling with his
wife, Terentia; and the scandalous behaviour of Dolabella, husband of
his beloved Tullia, made a divorce unavoidable.

17. faciliora, 'easier to bear'.

peccati dolor, 'my grievous sense of guilt', 'my bad conscience'.

18. socios . . . quos putavi. That is, Cicero had expected that other
Pompeians would follow his example after Pharsalus and return to

Italy: but even had they done so, he would have had small consolation in the thought that others were in the same boat as himself.

19–22. **Sed habet aliorum omnium ratio . . . coeperint,** 'but everybody else's situation offers a way of escape, mine none. Some were taken prisoner, some trapped. They come under no suspicion about their loyalty, and of course this will be even more true once they have got clear and begun to join the others.' On *ratio*, see Letter 1, section 1, note. Tyrrell and Purser take *expedierint* and *coeperint* as perfect subjunctives ('now that they have got clear and joined the others'); I prefer to take them (as does Shackleton Bailey) as future perfect indicatives.

22. **Ii autem ipsi,** 'even those'.

23. **ad Fufium venerunt.** Quintus Fufius Calenus (Letter 4, section 1, note) had been put in charge of Achaea (Greece) by Caesar. These people here mentioned are the *Achaici* (section 1, above). They had surrendered to Calenus, which was rather different from Cicero's case, since he had voluntarily returned to Italy.

24–5. **ad illos se recipere volent.** *Illos* here are the Pompeians.

26. **Solius enim meum peccatum,** 'my crime, and mine alone'. The genitive *solius* agrees with a *mei* understood; cf. Letter 24, section 1, note.

27. **et fortasse Laeli,** 'and perhaps Laelius' too'. This is Decimus Laelius, who had held command of the Asiatic ships in Pompey's fleet in 48 and blockaded Brundisium during the campaign that led up to Pharsalus. Cicero and Laelius had been specifically exempted by name in an edict issued by Mark Antony (in charge of Italy in Caesar's absence) which on Caesar's order banned from Italy any former Pompeians whose cases Caesar had not examined personally: *ad Att.* xi. 7. 2.

27–8. **Nam C. quidem Cassium.** The *nam* picks up the argument of *Solius enim meum peccatum . . .* after the interruption of *Sed quid me id levat?* Cassius had, like Cicero, originally intended to make his peace with Caesar after Pharsalus, but is now said to have changed his mind about going to Alexandria. He is Gaius Cassius Longinus, the future tyrannicide, who as proquaestor in Syria in 51 had repelled the Parthian attack on Antioch. Along with Brutus, he commanded the Republican army at the battle of Philippi.

3. 29–30. **non ut queas . . . conficiunt,** 'not supposing that you can rid me of my worries but to discover whether you have anything to contribute on these matters which are wearing me out'. The expression *non ut* *queas* seems to mean 'not with the intention that you should be able'—i.e. that was not in my mind as the object or consequence of my writing to you.

31. **ad quae gener accedit,** 'on top of which there is the matter of my son-in-law . . .'. On Dolabella's conduct, and the *cetera* which Cicero could not bring himself to write about, see the note on Quintus Cicero, above, section 2.

32. **Quin etiam Aesopi filius . . .,** 'and then again Aesopus' son is a terrible trial to me'. This was Marcus Clodius Aesopus, son of the actor Aesopus, a personal friend of Cicero's who had enjoyed a reputation as a tragic actor equalling that of the famous Roscius in comedy. The son had inherited a considerable fortune from his father and was squandering it in profligacy and extravagance. Horace, who pillories him in *Satires* ii. 3. 239 ff., suggests an affair with Metella, a notorious adulteress, who was also engaging the attentions of Cicero's son-in-law Dolabella.

Prorsus nihil, 'absolutely nothing'.

34. **aliquo propius,** 'somewhere closer'—to Rome, where Atticus is.

4. 36. **De Fufidianis . . .,** 'as to the estate of Fufidius, why was it that nothing could be settled?' The family of the Fufidii was prominent in Arpinum, Cicero's own native town. Cicero had inherited under the will of this Fufidius along with other co-heirs.

36–7. **Genus enim condicionis,** 'the form of settlement'.

38. **licitatione expleri posset,** 'could be made good by auction'. If heirs failed to reach a satisfactory agreement among themselves about the division of an estate, especially if the estate could not conveniently be divided into the prescribed shares, it was possible to put the estate up for auction, and divide the sum realized, perhaps with one of the heirs buying out the others on the valuation (as Quintus Cicero bought out his co-heirs of the Argiletum building (Letter 4, section 7, note)).

39–41. **suspicor . . . malle,** 'for I suspect that my co-heirs think that I am in a parlous situation, and so prefer to leave the business unsettled'. Cicero's prospects might be thought doubtful should the Pompeian cause triumph, and Cicero suffer punishment for his defection.

41. **Prid. Id. Mai.** 14 May.

LETTER 31

I. 3. de obitu Tulliae. The date of Tullia's death is not certain, but it must have been about the middle of February 45.

4. sane quam pro eo ac debui, 'as I was clearly in duty bound to do'. Cf. Letter 21, section 2: 'sane quam eos sermones expressit. *Atque* (*ac*) is used to express comparisons ranging from exact identity to complete difference: e.g. *idem atque, alius atque*. Here *pro eo ac* = 'in exact proportion to'. Compare *in Cat.* iv. 3: 'debeo sperare deos pro eo mihi ac mereor relaturos esse gratiam.'

5. istic, 'there with you'.

6. coramque, 'in person', 'to your face'. On *neque* followed by *-que*, cf. Letter 24, section 2, note.

7. Etsi. Answered in due course by *tamen*.

genus hoc consolationis, 'this sort of consolation'—though Tyrrell and How prefer to render 'Condolence in general'.

8. acerbum, 'bitter'. The basic meaning was 'sour', 'unripe'; then it was transferred to describe anything premature or before its time, especially bereavement.

confieri. The use of *fio* as the passive form of *facio* is rare in compounds.

13. brevi. Often used without a noun almost as an adverb = 'briefly'.

14. non quo . . . existimem. *Non quo* followed by the subjunctive is regular usage for expressing a cause or reason which is not true; it is natural for the rejected ('unreal') reason to have a subjunctive verb. Here the real reason also has a subjunctive because of *forsitan*, which introduces a note of uncertainty.

2. 17. intestinus, 'private' or 'domestic'.

20. dignitatem, honores omnis. This, despite the fact that Sulpicius had been appointed governor of Achaea by Caesar.

21–3. aut qui non in illis rebus . . . existimare, 'or how must any heart steeled by these experiences not by now be callous and treat everything as of lesser worth?'—lesser, that is, than the liberty and dignity that have been lost. The order of words makes it preferable to treat *qui* as the adverb = 'how?'

3. 23. An illius vicem, cedo, doles? 'Or is it on her account, may I ask, that you are grieving?' *Cedo* is the second person singular imperative of a defective verb probably compounded from the roots *-ce* and *da-*: 'give it here'. It is common in Latin comedy. Tacitus (*Annals* i. 23) tells how the mutinous legionaries in Pannonia murdered a brutal centurion whose habit of breaking his centurion's stick while beating soldiers and then calling for a new one had won him the nickname of 'cedo alteram'—'old give-us-another-one'.

24–5. et tu veneris et nos saepe incidimus. The meaning is quite clear, but the syntax is not strictly correct, since *incidimus* is correlate with *necesse est* while *veneris* is subordinate to *necesse est*. For a similar carelessness, see Letter 34, section 8, note.

25–6. non pessime cum iis esse actum, 'that they have not suffered the worst fate'; that is, they have been much luckier than others who are still alive to see the sad things that are going on.

26. licitum est. The older-fashioned form of *licuit*, appropriate in a lawyer like Sulpicius.

29. primario, 'of the first rank'. Tullia must have been about thirty when she died, but *adulescens* is very loosely employed in Latin. On her three marriages, see below, section 5, note.

30–2. Licitum est tibi, credo . . . putares. The *credo* underlines the irony of this suggestion: 'It was open to you, I imagine, to choose as befits your dignity from among the young men of today a son-in-law to whose honour you would think you could safely entrust a child of yours.' The plural *liberos* is used in the same way as for instance *Catones* = 'a Cato', 'a man like Cato'.

33. florentis, 'grown to manhood'.

34. rem. Here in the sense of 'wealth', 'inheritance'.

per se, 'in their own right'—that is to say, not under the stifling domination of an autocratic ruler.

34–5. honores ordinatim petituri essent, 'who could seek election to public office in due progression'. The reference is, of course, to the *cursus honorum* stretching by legally regulated stages from minor magistracies up to consulship. Under Caesar, such offices were at the dictator's own disposal.

35–6. in amicorum negotiis libertate sua usuri, 'who could freely help their friends in their need'. No doubt Sulpicius is thinking principally of legal assistance, which would come most naturally to his mind and Cicero's. The same idea is brought out in Horace's famous

Regulus Ode: 'Quam si clientum longa negotia | diiudicata lite re-
linqueret' (iii. 5. 49–50). *Negotium* means generally 'business', 'affair',
often (but not always) with the idea of some difficulty or trouble-
someness being involved.

37. At vero, 'but of course': a regular formula when some objection is
being contemplated.

38–9. haec sufferre et perpeti. 'to bear and put up with these present
ills'.

4. 39–41. Quae res mihi . . . possit, 'and this experience which brought
me no little comfort I should like to recall to you, in case perhaps the same
thought may lighten your own sorrow'. *Quae res* looks forward to the
story Sulpicius goes on to tell in the following paragraph.

42. Ex Asia rediens. After Pharsalus Sulpicius had withdrawn to
Rhodes (which was reckoned as part of the province of Asia) until his
appointment to Achaea. This whole passage has been greatly admired
for its style and its content, and imitated by St. Ambrose (*Letters* i. 39. 3)
and Byron (*Childe Harold* 4. 44): it is perhaps rather too mannered to
appeal to modern tastes so much.

Megaram versus, 'towards Megara'—on the isthmus north of Corinth.

43. circumcirca, 'round about', apparently a colloquial usage.

46. prostrata et diruta, 'lifeless and ruined'. No doubt there is some
literary exaggeration here, but all the towns named had indeed suffered
horribly. Megara was stormed and sacked by Fufius Calenus after
Pharsalus; Aegina, its inhabitants sold into slavery by the Romans in
210, had more recently suffered badly from the pirates before Pompey
cleared them from the seas; the Piraeus had been burned to the ground
by Sulla in 86; and Corinth had never revived after its destruction by
Mummius in 146—though Caesar did later give it new life by planting
a colony there.

47. egomet. An emphatic form of *ego* (cf. *nosmet*), here naturally employed with *mecum*.

Hem! A Roman way of representing a sigh in the form of a word: in
English we should write 'Ah!'.

homunculi, 'little men'.

49. brevior, 'only too brief', 'all too brief'.

oppidum. An abbreviated form of *oppidorum*.

50. **te . . . cohibere**, 'pull yourself together'.

53. **fac . . . proponas**, 'I recommend you to meditate on this'.

Modo, 'but a little while ago'.

54–5. **de imperio populi Romani . . .facta est**, 'there has been such a grievous weakening of the power of the Roman people'. Rome had not *lost* any of her empire, but her stability and reputation had suffered because of the civil war.

55. **conquassatae**, 'shaken to their foundations'.

56. **in unius mulierculae animula . . . facta est**, 'if we suffer loss in the fragile life of one frail woman': the diminutives are both an expression of pity and a plea for a sense of proportion.

57–8. **diem suum obisset.** A euphemistic way of saying *mortem obisset*: the idea is of appearing on the day appointed for one's death.

58. **moriendum fuit.** Compare 'quod certe *fuit* aptissimum': Letter 8, section 4, note. The indicative imparts a greater certainty and inevitability than the potential *fuisset* could give; and the fact that Tullia would have had to die one day was in no way hypothetical.

59. **homo**, 'mortal', 'a human being'.

5. 59. **Etiam tu**, 'do you likewise . . .'.

61. **tua persona.** *Persona* originally meant 'a mask' through which an actor spoke (*per-sono*), and hence a character in a play (*dramatis personae*). Then by metaphor the word was transferred from its theatrical background to mean in general the part or character one plays in life. Translate: 'Which befit the person that you are'; 'your position in the world'.

62. **una cum re publica fuisse**, 'that she lived as long as our country lived'.

64. **adulescentibus primariis.** Tullia had three husbands: Gaius Piso, Furius Crassipes, and Cornelius Dolabella, all of noble family.

64–5. **omnibus bonis prope perfunctam esse**, 'she enjoyed pretty well every blessing life can offer'.

66–7. **hoc nomine.** A metaphor from book-keeping, but so well worn that it has almost ceased to be a metaphor, like its English equivalent: 'on this account'.

69. **imitare.** Though normally a deponent verb (*imitor, -ari*) in the Latin of Cicero's day, this verb (like a number of other deponents) retained an active form in archaic and colloquial Latin. This form, like

other archaisms in this letter, is the product not so much of a deliberately archaizing style as of Sulpicius' legal background (legal language in any society always tends to hang on to older forms), and perhaps too of a deliberate injection of a gently colloquial tone into a rather formal letter. Note that in strict logic *noli* cannot qualify the infinitive *neque imitare*: the sense requires something like *neve velis imitare* to be supplied, but the meaning is quite clear all the same.

alienis, 'other people's'.

72. **ea tute tibi subiace ... propone,** 'bring them to your own attention and set them before your mind'. *Tute* (like *egomet*, above) is an emphatic form, occasioned by the juxtaposition of the two second-person pronouns.

6. 73–4. **minuat ac molliat.** Generic subjunctives.

74–5. **Hoc te exspectare tempus ... occurrere,** 'for you merely to wait for this time to arrive is a shame on you: rather of your wisdom you should go to meet (anticipate) this result'. That is, Cicero has enough sense to know that all sorrow abates with the passage of time, so he ought not tamely to give way to misery but to pull himself together now in the knowledge of this truth.

75–6. **Quod si etiam inferis sensus est.** This delicate agnosticism was typical of many members of the Roman upper classes of Cicero's day; and sometimes in those who favoured the Epicurean philosophy it extended to outright scepticism (cf. Lucretius: *de rerum natura*, Book iii). Cicero himself normally shared this agnosticism; but the pain and grief of Tullia's death would not allow him to persist in it, and led him to argue that the human spirit was immortal. Tacitus, *Agricola* 46 affords an obvious parallel to this passage: 'Si quis piorum manibus locus, si, ut sapientibus placet, non cum corpore extinguuntur magnae animae, placide quiescas.'

76. **qui illius in te amor fuit,** 'such was her love for you'. (On *pietas*, see Letter 10, section 1, note.) Such parenthetic relative clauses are commonly used to account for something as arising from a characteristic trait in the person concerned. Another form of the idiom is exemplified by 'qua prudentia fuit' (ablative of description): Tacitus, *Hist.* ii. 37.

77. **hoc te facere.** That is, to give way to grief: 'to behave like that'.

80–3. **quoniam in eam fortunam devenimus ... lugere,** 'since we have fallen so low that we must bow even to such a consideration, do not so act as to lead anyone to suppose that you are mourning not so much a daughter as the sorry plight of your country and the victory of your opponents'.

85. prudentiae tuae, 'your own common sense'.

88. apisci. The form *adipisci* is much commoner: again, Sulpicius is using an old-fashioned language.

aliquando. The word parallels the preceding *aliquotiens* ('on other occasions'); though it usually means 'at some time' or 'at another time', it can often mean (as here) simply 'now', or 'at long last'.

89. aeque, 'just as handsomely'.

90. haec una. That is to say, the virtue of being able to bear adversity bravely.

LETTER 32

1. 3. Ego vero, 'for my part I . . .'. Cicero is picking up a point made by Curius in an earlier letter.

4–5. quin hinc ipse . . . audiam, 'on the contrary, I long to fly away from here myself and reach some place "Far from the madding crowd" '. The line 'Where I shall hear neither the name nor the deeds of the Pelopidae' is a favourite of Cicero's and is quoted by him on a number of occasions (Letter 33, section 2). The Pelopidae were the family whose eponymous founder Pelops gave his name to the Peloponnesus, its most famous members being Agamemnon and Menelaus, the Homeric Kings of Argos and Laconia. The idea is therefore of some remote place where nothing ever happens and no news of great events disturbs the tranquillity of life. Cicero's words are reminiscent of Psalm 139, verse 9: 'If I take the wings of the morning, and dwell in the uttermost parts of the sea'. The idea of taking wing like a bird and flying away is common enough in antiquity: cf. Alcman's beautiful poem 'The Halcyons' (*OBGV* 115); and Euripides, *Hippolytus* 732 ff.

6. qui his rebus intersim. A good example of how the generic and causal uses of the subjunctive merge into each other: 'in being party to these happenings'.

7. Ne tu. Not the conjunction *ne*, but the interjection *ne*: see Letter 14, section 3, note. 'Certainly *you* seem . . .'.

8–9. etiam auditu acerba sunt, 'are bitter even to hear' ('in the hearing').

9–12. In campo . . . posita esset, 'at any rate you were not in the Campus [Martius] when at eight o'clock in the morning the chair of Quintus Maximus (whom *they* called "consul") was set up ready to hold the quaestorian elections'. On the Roman division of the day, see Letter 11, section 2, note; on *campus* and *comitia*, Letter 1, section 1; on the *sella* (*curulis*), Letter 13, section 1, note. *Illi* denotes the Caesarians, as *ille* in the next sentence is Caesar himself: Cicero chooses not to regard the mere nominee and creature of Caesar as a true Roman consul. Quintus Fabius Maximus, the undistinguished bearer of a famous name, had served as a *legatus* to Caesar in the Munda campaign. Caesar himself had been sole consul for the first nine months of 45, but on his return to Italy he resigned and had Gaius Trebonius and Maximus appointed for the last three months of the year. His absence from Italy also caused the delay in the quaestorian elections, normally held in the summer.

13–14. qui comitiis tributis esset auspicatus . . . habuit. The subjunctive here has a concessive force: 'though he had taken the auspices for the tribal assembly, he held a centuriate assembly'. On the various assemblies of the Roman people, see Letter 9, section 4, note. The auspices were taken before such an assembly got down to business to secure an assurance that the gods were favourable. Caesar (who was in any case due to preside as dictator at the quaestorian elections) did not bother to retake the auspices for a meeting of the centuriate assembly, as strictly he should have done. The point is that quaestors were elected by the tribal assembly, consuls by the centuriate assembly: the voters were the same, but they were marshalled in different groupings.

14. hora septima, 'just after noon'.

renuntiavit. *Renuntiare* is the regular word for declaring the result of an election.

14–15. qui usque ad K. Ian. . . . postridie, 'to hold office until 1 January, that is until the following morning'.

15–16. Ita Caninio consule . . . prandisse, 'know then that in the consulship of Caninius nobody ate lunch'. The point of the joke is that normally 'in the consulship of X' denoted a whole year: see Letter 2, section 1, note. Gaius Caninius Rebilus had served under Caesar in Gaul: for his energy at Uxellodunum in 51 see *Bell. Gall.* viii. 26 ff. He governed Africa in 46, where he accepted the surrender of Thapsus: *Bell. Afr.* 93.

17. mirifica vigilantia. Ablative of description.

17–18. qui . . . somnum non viderit, 'seeing that he didn't get a wink of sleep throughout his entire term of office' (such is the force of the sub-junctive *viderit*). The official year ended at midnight on the day of Rebilus' election. Macrobius (2. 3. 6) gives a selection of the numerous jokes Cicero made in addition to the two here. Caninius' consulship (Cicero said) was like the atoms of Epicurus, too small to be seen by the naked eye; the result was that Rebilus could not be sure in whose con-sulship he had been consul. When Rebilus reproached him for not having paid a formal courtesy call, Cicero replied: 'I was on my way, but night arrived before I did'. And punning on *dialis*, he declared: 'We are used to *flamines diales* (Priests of Jupiter), but now we have *consules diales* (one-day consuls).'

2. 21–2. nisi me in philosophiae portum contulissem, 'had I not found a safe haven in philosophy'. Cicero was extraordinarily productive in this field at this time. In 45 and 44 he wrote: the *Consolatio, Hortensius,* the four books of the *Posterior Academics,* the five books *de finibus,* the *Tusculan Disputations, de natura deorum, de divinatione, de fato, de senectute, de amicitia, de gloria,* and *de officiis.*

23–6. Cuius quoniam proprium . . . utitur. Cicero and Curius are playing with legal terms. *Mancipium* and *nexum* in Roman law denoted full ownership of property on watertight legal title. *Usus et fructus* is rendered in English legal language by 'usufruct', that is 'use and enjoyment' of something of which you are not the legal owner. Translate: 'And since you write that you belong to him lock, stock, and barrel, while the rights I have over you are only of use and enjoyment, I will settle for what you offer. For a man only truly owns what he uses and enjoys.'

26. Sed haec alias pluribus, sc. *verbis scribam*: 'but more of this anon'.

3. 27. Acilius. There is some disagreement about whether this is Marcus (or Manius) Acilius Glabrio, son of the praetor who presided at the trial of Verres, or Marcus Acilius Caninus. Whichever he was, he had now been sent to govern Achaea in succession to Servius Sulpicius.

28. maximo meo beneficiost. The manuscripts preserve the elision (for *beneficio est*) and Cicero may well so have written the words. The meaning is: 'is very greatly in my debt'. The ablative of quality here is most unusual, but can be paralleled in *Philippics* 8. 18. Acilius' indebted-ness to Cicero would make him responsive to Cicero's commendatory letter to Curius, who had business interests centred on Patrae in Achaea. On this system of reciprocal favours, see Letter 1, section 4, note.

iudicio capitis, 'on a capital charge'.

29. **rebus salvis,** 'successfully', that is, without loss. In Cicero's day the sentence of death was not carried out (at any rate on prominent citizens); if convicted on a capital charge a man lost his citizen rights and possibly also his property, or such of it as he had not salted away safely.

LETTER 33

1. 3. **Idus Martiae.** The Ides of March 44 was of course the day of Caesar's assassination.

4. **odi poenam ac doloris,** 'revenge for our hatred and misery'. It is unusual, but not unparalleled, to find *poena* used thus; cf. *ad Att.* i. 16. 7: 'poenas peteret sui doloris'.

istim. If the reading is retained, and not replaced by *istinc*, *istim* must here mean 'from Rome' ('from where you are'). [*Istinc* is in fact a shortened form of *istim-ce*.]

5. ᾿Ὦ πράξεως καλῆς μέν, ἀτελοῦς δέ, 'O what a fine deed, but only half-done'. This may be a quotation from a Greek play, otherwise unknown; but it may simply be that Cicero breaks into Greek at this point. (The genitives are genitives of exclamation, common in Greek drama with exclamatory particles.) Cicero more than once regrets that Antony had not been murdered along with Caesar. Writing to Cassius in February 43 (*ad famm.* xii. 4. 1), he echoes his wistful words to Trebonius in Letter 35, section 1.

6–7. **et quam illam clientelam honestam iudicem,** 'and what a great honour I hold it to be their patron'. On *clientela*, see Letter 7, section 16, note. Cicero had been quaestor at Lilybaeum in Sicily in 75, and won a considerable reputation and influence there—see his amusing remarks in *pro Plancio* 64–6. This influence he had of course consolidated and extended by his brilliant prosecution of Verres in 70 on behalf of the Sicilians.

7. **Multa illis Caesar,** sc. *dedit.*

me invito. Ablative of attendant circumstances: 'Nor did this displease me.'

Latinitas. *Latinitas* (Latin status) or *ius Latii* had originally been the condition of the communities of Latium. As Roman control extended over the whole of Italy, 'Latinity' became divorced from Latium (most of whose communities were absorbed into the Roman state after the

Latin revolt of the late fourth century), and was represented by the 'Latin colonies', *coloniae Latinae*, that Rome planted throughout Italy to serve the double purpose of providing land for her own and allied citizens and acting as loyal garrisons at strategic points. As a result of the Social War of 91 to 88 full Roman citizenship had been accorded to all the communities of Italy south of the Po; but in 90 the communities north of that river in Transpadane Gaul had been granted only the *ius Latii*. Thus 'Latinity' finally emerged as a sort of half-way house between non-citizenship and full citizenship, and as such it continued to be employed for nearly three hundred years down to the Emperor Caracalla. The main features of the *ius Latii* were that it conferred on its holders the private (as opposed to political) rights of Roman citizenship—the *ius commercii* and *ius connubii*—and also that the local magistrates of a Latin community became *ex officio* Roman citizens.

8. **Verum tamen—** , 'but be that as it may—'. What Cicero means is that the grant of Latin status to the Sicilians is now water under the bridge.

Ecce autem Antonius, 'but now along comes Antony . . .'.

8. **legem 'a dictatore comitiis latam',** 'a law supposedly carried by the dictator (Caesar) at a citizen assembly'. *Figere legem* means to post a copy of a law in a public place: this might be done on wood or stone or bronze. It was one of Cicero's standard public charges against Antony that he abused his position after Caesar's death to make grants and issue edicts and post laws which were in fact his own but which he claimed were Caesar's. This private letter to Atticus shows that the sort of accusations that Cicero made against Antony in, for example, the *Second Philippic* (esp. 97 ff.) had plenty of substance behind them. (In fact it seems that nothing ever came of this particular law: it must have been treated as of no effect.)

10. **qua Siculi cives Romani.** Understand *fierent* or *facti essent*.

vivo illo, 'while Caesar was alive'.

11. **Deiotari nostri.** King Deiotarus of Galatia in Asia Minor. He fought on Rome's side against Mithridates and was rewarded by Pompey in his reorganization of the East by extension of his territory. Loyal to Pompey in the Civil War, he had been deprived of much of his territory by Caesar. He had now seized most of it back again: according to Cicero (*Philippics* ii. 93–5) he paid Antony ten million sesterces for recognition of his title. Cicero calls him *noster* because he was a friend of his: Cicero had defended him before Caesar in 45.

12. **omni regno,** 'of any kingdom'.

Fulviam. This very remarkable woman was married to three of the most remarkable men of this time: the widow in turn of Publius Clodius and Gaius Scribonius Curio, she was now the wife of Mark Antony. She loathed Cicero, and he loathed her.

sescenta similia, 'there are countless similar cases'. On *sescenta*, see Letter 4, section 2, note.

12–13. **Verum illuc referor.** 'but I am brought back to that other point'—that is, the Buthrotum affair.

13–15. **tam claram tamque testatam rem . . . plura,** 'with a case as clear-cut and well attested and just as that of Buthrotum, surely we shall succeed at least to some extent? And all the more so, the more examples there are of this kind'. The Buthrotum affair is well known to us from a series of letters written by Cicero about this time (*ad Att.* xvi. 16 A–F). As a punishment for its support of Pompey this town in Epirus had been savagely fined by Caesar. When it failed to pay, Caesar confiscated its land for allotments. But Atticus stepped in and paid the fine out of his own pocket, and got Caesar to agree to rescind the confiscation. However, the business was still hanging fire, and it was by no means certain that the confiscation would not be put into effect. (For *rem tenebimus*, cf. *teneri res*, Letter 10, section 3.)

2. 16. **Octavius.** *Agit* must be supplied. Octavius had reached Naples on 19 April, and two days later arrived at the house of Philippus, next door to Cicero. Balbus, Hirtius, and Pansa were with him, and addressing him as 'Caesar' (*salutabant* is an epistolary imperfect). But though adopted by Caesar in his will, Octavius had not yet gone through the necessary legal procedures for ratifying the adoption. So Cicero and Philippus scrupulously went on calling him 'Octavius'.

17. **Philippus.** Lucius Marcius Philippus, consul in 56, was Octavius' step-father.

17–18. **ne nos quidem,** 'neither do I'.

18. **Quem.** That is, Octavius.

19–20. **negant haec ferri posse,** 'and declare that the existing situation is intolerable'. Antony had not so far shown any anxiety to pursue and punish Caesar's assassins, and was in fact trying to find some middle ground. Octavius' friends, all loyal Caesarians (Hirtius wrote the Eighth Book to complete the *bellum Gallicum* and Pansa had been a pro-Caesarian tribune in 51), were all for more vigorous measures: *nostris* (our friends the 'liberators') *mortem minitantur*.

20. **Quid censes,** 'what do you suppose will happen'—understand *eventurum esse* or some such words.

puer. Octavius was born on 23 September 63, so he was still only 18 years old. But to call him *puer* is none the less slighting. Antony meant to be slighting too when he said of Octavius: 'puer qui omnia nomini debes'. Both Cicero and Antony made the (quite understandable) mistake of underestimating the genius and maturity and dogged determination of this extraordinary young man.

22. **conscientia facti sui,** 'in the consciousness of their great deed'— the murder of the tyrant Caesar.

22-3. **sed nos . . . iacebimus,** 'but it will be all up with us'. *Iacere* is regularly used in this sense of lying fallen or prostrate.

23-4. **'ubi nec Pelopidarum'.** See Letter 32, section 1, note.

24. **inquit,** 'as the poet says'.

Haud amo vel hos designatos, 'I am not at all enamoured even of these consuls-designate', viz. Aulus Hirtius and Gaius Vibius Pansa, who were with Octavius. Both died in the Mutina campaign in 43 when as consuls they led the government forces against Antony.

25. **declamare,** 'to give lessons in public speaking'.

apud aquas . . . acquiescere. Cicero loved puns: 'So that even down here by the sea I find myself landed with work.'

26. **Sed hoc meae nimiae facilitatis,** 'but this is what comes from my being too easy-going'. This feature of Cicero's character was remarked on by Caesar: 'Atqui si quisquam est facilis, hic est' (*ad Att.* xiv. 1. 2).

26-8. **Nam id erat quondam . . . item,** 'for once upon a time this was almost obligatory; but now, however things may be, it isn't the same'. Cicero means that while Caesar was still alive he had little option but to indulge Caesar's friends. Shackleton Bailey renders *quoquo modo se res habet* as 'however *bad* things are', but I doubt if Cicero is being so specific: Cicero simply means that he goes on being obliging even though there is no longer any necessity for it.

3. 30. delectem . . . litteris, 'to provide entertainment by my letters'. The verb *delectem* is used absolutely, so that there is no need to understand or supply *te* as an object.

30-1. **Tu si quid erit . . . quicquid,** 'write me about anything that happens, and particularly any news at all about Brutus'. Marcus Junius Brutus, the tyrannicide, was the son of Caesar's lover, Servilia, and successively son-in-law of Appius Claudius Pulcher and Marcus Cato. He had followed Pompey, but was pardoned after Pharsalus: Caesar advanced him to the governorship of Cisalpine Gaul in 46 and the urban praetorship in 44. Along with Cassius, he died leading the last Republican army to defeat at Philippi in 42 against Antony and Octavian.

32. **x Kal.** 22 April—this letter was written after Caesar's revision of the calendar (Appendix 1), so April now had 30 days, not 29 as before.

accubans apud Vestorium, 'while at dinner with Vestorius'.

32-3. **hominem remotum a dialecticis . . . exercitatum,** 'he may not be much of a philosopher, but he is pretty well up in mathematics'. As Shackleton Bailey points out, the science of numbers was an important branch of ancient philosophy: remember Pythagoras, and Plato's insistence on the fundamental role of mathematics in philosophy. Hence Cicero's comment on his friend's skill in figures (Vestorius was a successful banker at Puteoli) is another punning kind of joke of the sort Cicero enjoyed. His own conversations with Atticus frequently were about philosophy, but that could not be expected of Vestorius.

LETTER 34

1. 5. **maximi.** Genitive of price or value.

6. **ut incorrupta maneret laborabam,** 'I was anxious that it should remain unimpaired'.

7-8. **quod . . . offenderet.** Generic subjunctive: 'which could offend'.

8-11. **Eo minus credebam . . . benevolentiam,** 'I was accordingly the less ready to believe that someone as wise and experienced as you are could have been got to believe anything hastily, especially since I have always felt towards you, and still do, an affection which is both spontaneous and enduring'.

12. **criminibus,** 'charges', 'accusations'.

13. **ut par erat . . . nostra,** 'as befitted your exceptional kindness and our friendship'. The ablative with *par* is an unusual construction. Although (unlike Tyrrell and How) I cannot accept that Cicero *de divinatione* ii. 114 'ut constantibus hominibus par erat' is a similar example (*hominibus* is probably a dative), parallels can be found in other writers: 'scalas pares moenium altitudine' (Sallust, *Jugurtha* 44), 'in qua par facies nobilitate sua est' (Ovid, *Fasti* vi. 804).

2. 15. Nota enim mihi. The so-called 'transitional' or 'resumptive' use of *enim*: 'Well, I am aware of . . .', 'Yes, I am aware of . . .'.

16. contulerint. The subject of the verb is indefinite: 'the slurs people have put upon me', 'the charges people have made against me'.

Vitio mihi dant, 'they hold it to my discredit'. The predicative use of the dative; cf. Letter 1, section 3 'fuit et mihi et fratri magno usui'.

18–19. proinde ac si iam vicerint, 'for all the world as if they have proved . . .': *vincere* is used in the sense of prevailing in an argument: cf. 'id dicendo vincere non postulo', section 4, below.

19–20. Sed non agam astute, 'but I shall not play the subtle lawyer'.

22. re offendebar, 'I was upset by what he did'.

23–4. causam dissensionis, 'the grounds of the quarrel'—between Caesar and his political enemies.

25. honoris, 'office', 'advancement'.

27. minus . . . cum possent, 'although they had less influence with him than I'.

28. Atque etiam res . . . deminuta, 'more than that, I suffered personal financial loss through Caesar's law'. It is pretty certainly Caesar's debt law of 49 that Matius refers to. By this enactment Caesar required creditors to accept the real property of their debtors in settlement of debts at its pre-war valuation (property values had fallen dramatically with the outbreak of war); and further any interest already paid was to be counted against the debt. Hence, as a rich man and a creditor, Matius actually was out of pocket by his friend's law.

29. cuius beneficio plerique . . . in civitate. Thanks to Caesar's generous concessions about debt, many of those now so pleased at his death had been saved from bankruptcy and consequent *infamia*, which entailed certain civil disabilities: hence they were enabled to continue in full enjoyment of the citizenship (*remanserunt in civitate*).

31. aeque ac pro mea salute . . . laboravi, 'I worked as hard to secure pardon for my defeated countrymen (i.e. Pompeian supporters) as if it had been for my own salvation'.

3. 33–4. cum . . . illi et invidiae . . . fuerint, 'especially since the very same men were responsible for both his unpopularity and his destruction'. Matius has in mind men like Brutus and Cassius, pardoned Pompeians who were promoted by Caesar and infected his own followers with disaffection. (The datives are predicative.)

34–5. 'Plecteris ergo', 'you shall smart for it, then'.

36. O superbiam inauditam . . . licere, 'what unparalleled effrontery! To think that one side should be free to boast about a crime which the other may not even deplore with impunity!' Two methods of expressing an exclamation: a plain accusative of a noun (cf. *me miserum*), and an accusative and infinitive.

38–9. suo potius quam alterius arbitrio, 'at their own choosing rather than at another's bidding'.

39. ut quidem isti dictitant, 'as those friends of yours themselves keep saying'.

4. 40–1. Sed nihil agunt, 'but they achieve nothing'.

44. si id opto . . . facti, 'if all I hope for is that they should feel regret for what they have done'.

46. At debeo pro civili parte , 'but they say it is my duty as a loyal citizen'. The conjunction *at* introduces a supposed objection.

46–8. Id quidem me cupere . . . non postulo, 'that *is* what I long for; but if neither my life hitherto nor my hopes for the future confirm it without my opening my mouth, I do not look to prove it by argument'.

5. 49. ut rem potiorem oratione ducas, 'to believe that actions speak louder than words'.

50. si sentis expedire recte fieri, 'if you accept that a man ought to be guided by his conscience'.

51–3. An quod adulescens . . . retexam, 'or am I now in my declining years to abandon the principle I set before myself when I was a young man . . . and unpick the pattern of my life?' *Praeceps* ('precipice', 'precipitous') means literally 'falling headlong, headfirst'; hence *praecipitata aetas* is that age which has passed the watershed of life and is sliding down the other side. *Retexere* means to unweave what has been woven.

54–6. neque quod displiceat . . . casum, 'but neither will I do anything to upset anyone, except that I do grieve at the sad fate of a man who was to me a very dear friend as well as a very great statesman'.

56. Quod si aliter essem animatus, 'but even if I were minded otherwise'.

58. in dissimulando timidus . . . existimarer, 'be thought a hypocritical coward in seeking to conceal it'. *Vanus* = 'shallow', 'empty'.

6. 59. Caesaris victoriae, 'in honour of Caesar's victory'. The games were properly in honour of the goddess Venus, to whom Caesar had vowed a temple and a cult in return for victory at the battle of Pharsalus. They were held in the last days of July each year. Octavian (*Caesar adulescens*) presented them, but Matius and other friends supplied the necessary finance (*curavi*).

60. **privatum officium,** 'my duty as a personal friend'.

61. **munus,** 'obligation', 'service'. The word can also mean a public show or entertainment, the idea being that such were given to express gratitude to the people or to the gods.

62. **etiam mortui,** 'even now that he is dead'.

63–4. **optimae spei adulescenti . . . non potui,** 'and I could not refuse the request of a young man of the highest promise and in every way worthy of Caesar'.

7. 65. **salutandi causa,** 'to pay my respects'. The *salutatio* was a formal call, and very appropriate in this case since Antony was consul and hence entitled to such marks of formal respect.

65–7. **ad quem qui . . . reperies,** 'yet you will find those who judge me lacking in love for my country haunting his house in droves to crave or carry away some favour'. *Frequentis* is accusative plural; *ventitare* a frequentative form of *venio* (cf. *dictitant,* above, section 3).

67–71. **Sed quae haec est adrogantia . . . diligam,** 'but what insufferable arrogance this is, that whereas Caesar never interfered to stop me enjoying the company of anyone I chose—not excluding people he himself disliked—these men who have robbed me of my friend are seeking by their malicious slanders to stop me caring for whom I choose'. The syntax is clumsy, but the meaning plain enough. *Eos . . . conari* is an accusative and infinitive noun-clause in apposition to *quae adrogantia*. *Quod* is a cognate accusative governed by *interpellavit* and anticipating the clause *quin . . . uterer,* which is explanatory (or 'epexegetic') of *quod*; the whole being also in apposition to *eos conari ne*.

8. 72–3. **parum valitura sit,** 'will avail me too little', 'will be insufficient armour'. The future subjunctive is unusual after *vereor,* but the phrase *in posterum* here underlines the future sense.

73–4. **aut ne etiam ii.** Strictly *aut ne* is wrong, since it is preceded not by *aut ne* but by *ne aut*. All that is required is *aut*. But there is no point in making a fuss about it, or citing parallels. We all make similar slips in our everyday speech and letters, saying (for example) 'both by scrimping and saving' when we should strictly say 'by both scrimping and saving' or 'both by scrimping and by saving'. Here we have a slip of just this sort; cf. Letter 31, section 3, note, for another.

75. **mei quam sui similis,** 'more like me than themselves'.

76. **si optata contingent,** 'if the things I hope for fall out'—that is, 'If my hopes are realized'.

76–7. **in otio Rhodi,** 'in retirement at Rhodes'. *Rhodi* is a locative case.

77–8. **ita ero Romae . . . cupiam.** Literally: 'I shall live in Rome in such a way as always to desire that things should be done rightly'. Better: 'I shall stay on in Rome and demonstrate my unswerving determination to see right done'.

78. **Trebatio nostro.** On Trebatius, see Letters 15–17. He was a common friend of Cicero and Matius, and had acted as an intermediary between the two men.

79. **simplicem,** 'straightforward'.

80. **aperuit,** 'revealed'.

81. **quo magis iure colere . . . fecit.** Literally: 'and has brought it about that I ought to cherish and cultivate him more rightly'—because of his services in reconciling the two friends. More idiomatically: 'and has given me even greater cause to cherish and respect him'.

82. **Bene vale.** Never used by Cicero himself, but it is used by Curius (*ad famm.* vii. 29. 2.).

LETTER 35

1. 3. Quam vellem . . . haberemus. Cicero uses almost identical words in writing to Gaius Cassius about this time (*ad famm.* xii. 4. 1): 'Vellem Idibus Martiis me ad cenam invitasses; reliquiarum nihil fuisset.' On his regret that Antony had not been murdered along with Caesar, see Letter 33, section 1, note.

epulas, 'feast'.

4. **reliquiarum,** 'left-overs'.

4–6. **At nunc cum iis . . . querelam,** 'but now we are having such trouble with these people that that heavenly service you and your friends (*vestrum*) did for our country occasions some cause for complaint'.

7. **seductus est,** 'lured away'. Antony was deliberately detained when Caesar entered the senate on the Ides. Brutus was determined that the

glory of the assassination of the tyrant should not be marred by other murders, and the conspirators had a very healthy respect for Antony's great physical strength and courage (Plutarch, *Antony* 13—where we are told that it was this same Gaius Trebonius who had advised against inviting Antony to join the conspiracy on the ground that he was too loyal to Caesar).

8. **haec pestis,** 'this scourge'—that is, Antony. Cicero begins the sentence with Antony in his mind, and so writes *seductus*, but later changes to *haec pestis.*

interdum . . . tibi subirascor, 'I occasionally feel mildly annoyed with you'.

10–11. **foedissimum discessum,** 'disgusting departure'—for Cisalpine Gaul at the end of November 44.

11. **senatus haberi libere . . . ,** 'as soon as it was possible to hold a truly free meeting of the senate'. *Habere senatum* is a regular phrase for holding a meeting of the senate.

11–13. **ad illum animum habuisti . . . ,** 'I returned to that spirit which I used to have in the old days, which you and that splendid patriot your father always talked of and loved'. The *animus* is that which Cicero showed in the years before 56, most particularly in his consulship in 63. Cicero described Trebonius senior as 'splendidus eques Romanus': Antony, however, called him a 'clown' (*scurra*)—*Philippics* xiii. 23. (*Reverti*, the perfect tense of *reverto*, is the one tense of this verb regularly used intransitively, that is without a reflexive pronoun).

2. 14. **a. d. XIII K. Ian.** 20 December (44).

deque alia re referrent, 'and sought a discussion on another matter'. We know from the speech Cicero delivered at this meeting of the senate (the *Third Philippic*) that the business put before the house by the tribunes was 'for the provision of an armed guard so that the new consuls might be able to hold a meeting of the senate on 1 January in safety' (section 13). But Cicero ignored the resolution, using it merely as a launching-pad for a speech which dealt with the whole political situation. His final motion (sections 37–9) asked that Decimus Brutus be confirmed as governor of Cisalpine Gaul and Antony's appointment to that province be regarded as invalid; and that Octavian, and the two legions which had mutinied against Antony's authority, be honoured and thanked for their loyalty to constitutional government. As the senior ex-consul present, Cicero spoke first, but the *sententia* (Letter 9, section 6, note) he delivered did not have to be confined to the question (*relatio*) put. On this, cf. Tacitus, *Annals* xiii. 49: 'licere patribus [senators], quoties ius dicendae sententiae accepissent, quae vellent expromere relationemque in ea postulare.' The most famous example of this practice of departing from the original motion (it was termed *egredi relationem*) was of course that of the Elder Cato, who at every meeting of the senate persisted with the demand 'Carthaginem esse delendam' (Pliny, *Nat. Hist.* xv. 74).

15. **totam . . . sum complexus,** 'I embraced the whole condition of public affairs'.

egique acerrime. *Agere* is the regular word for the public presentation of a case.

16–17. **virtutem consuetudinemque,** 'its traditional courage'.

17. **Magis animi quam ingeni viribus,** 'more by moral force than by argument'.

18. **contentio atque actio,** 'and the energy of my delivery': *actio* seems here to refer to the 'delivery' of an orator (cf. *egit*, above). Thus *Brutus* 68: 'Actio eius [Pompeii] habebat et in voce magnum splendorem et in motu summam dignitatem.'

20. **tempus ullum intermisi . . . agendi,** 'I have missed no opportunity not merely for reflection but also for action about our country's affairs'.

3. 22–3. **Quod nisi . . . perscriberem,** 'as to which, did I not suppose that you are being kept informed of the news from Rome and all public business, I should be writing to you fully myself'.

25. **summatim,** 'in summary', 'the main heads'.

consularis. The ex-consuls were the natural leaders of opinion.

26. **male sentientis,** 'ill-disposed'.

26–7. **magnum damnum . . . Servio,** 'we have suffered a great loss in Servius'. This is Servius Sulpicius (Letter 31). On 4 January 43 the senate chose him and Lucius Piso (consul in 58) and Lucius Philippus (consul in 56) to constitute an embassy to Antony to enjoin him to quit Cisalpine Gaul and put himself under the instructions of the senate and people of Rome. But Sulpicius died on the journey.

27. **L. Caesar.** The consul of 64, and uncle of Mark Antony. See Letter 1, section 2, note.

28–9. **consules egregii.** Hirtius and Pansa: Letter 33, section 2, note.

29. **D. Brutus.** Decimus Junius Brutus had been appointed governor of Cisalpine Gaul by Caesar and took over his command there in April 44. Though highly favoured by Caesar, and named by him in his will among the 'second heirs', he had joined the conspiracy to murder him. He vigorously resisted Antony's attempt to take over the province.

Caesar. Contrast Cicero's reluctance to address Octavian thus in Letter 33, section 2, note. Now (at any rate for the time being) Octavian is on the 'right' side.

30. **spero equidem reliqua,** 'I hope that there is more to come'.

31. **legionesque duae.** These were the *Legio Quarta* and the *Legio Martia*, which had switched their allegiance from Antony to Octavian shortly before Antony set off north at the end of November 43. (*Ille* is Octavian.)

32–3. **atque is oppositus esset terror Antonio,** 'and so given Antony this cause for alarm'.

35. **arbitrabar.** Epistolary imperfect.

APPENDIX 1

THE ROMAN CALENDAR

THE twelve months of the Roman year were: Januarius, Februarius, Martius, Aprilis, Maius, Junius, Quintilis (*or* Quinctilis), Sextilis, September, October, November, December. The months after June were named 'fifth', 'sixth', 'seventh', and so on because down to the middle of the second century B.C. the Roman official year had begun on 1 March.

Until Julius Caesar reformed the calendar in 47/46, March, May, July (Quintilis), and October each had thirty-one days; February had twenty-eight; and the remaining months twenty-nine days each. This gave a total of 355 days for the year, just over ten days short of the true length of a solar year. To correct this discrepancy an extra month was inserted or 'intercalated' at regular intervals: it consisted of either 27 or 28 days, and was simply called the 'intercalary' month: *intercalaris* or *intercalarius mensis*. When such a month was intercalated, it was intruded between February and March,[1] with February ending on 23 February.

The calendar, and the duty of intercalating it, since they originally had been very much part of the religious and sacral sphere of life, were the responsibility of the College of *Pontifices* (see Letter 9, section 7, note). Abuse was possible, since the Pontiffs could use their discretion about intercalation, and by electing to intercalate or not to intercalate in given years they could by this device lengthen or shorten the terms of office of particular magistrates and pro-magistrates. In the closing years of the Republic, the calendar became very erratic, largely for reasons of this kind and perhaps too partly because of the prolonged absences of the *Pontifex Maximus* Julius Caesar after 58. After the year 57 intercalation took place only twice before Caesar's reform (in 54 or 55, and in 52). In the years from 65 to 56 the Roman calendar lagged behind the solar year by margins of the order

---

[1] That is, at the end of the old official year, which had begun on 1 March Even after the change to 1 January as the beginning of the official year, this February date was still retained for intercalations.

of ten to twenty days; thereafter the gap increased to a month and more, and got steadily wider as the years passed until Caesar had to inflate the year 46 to the staggering total of 445 days to achieve the required synchronization with the solar year. Only in 45 did the official and solar dates at last coincide.

The new Julian calendar was of course not Caesar's own work. He employed the Alexandrian astronomer Sosigenes to produce the necessary calculations. The Roman year was now extended to 365 days by giving to the twelve months the same number of days they each have in modern calendars. Every fourth (or leap) year an extra day was added between 23 and 24 February. This produced a year about eleven minutes too long, and a further adaptation had to be ordered by Pope Gregory XIII in 1582; but substantially our modern calendar is the work of Caesar and Sosigenes.

The month Quintilis was renamed Julius in honour of Caesar, and later the month Sextilis was called Augustus in honour of his great-nephew and adopted son.

Calculation of dates

The Romans did not number the days of each month consecutively, as we do. They calculated the days in a rather clumsy fashion by counting back from three fixed points in each month: the Kalends, the Ides, and the Nones.[1] The Kalends was always the first day of the month. The Nones and the Ides varied: in the four long months of thirty-one days, March, May, July, October, the Nones was the seventh day of the month and the Ides the fifteenth; in the other eight shorter months they were respectively the fifth and the thirteenth days.[2]

---

[1] *Kalendae, -arum* (compare Greek καλέω, Latin *calare, clamare*) originally meant the day when the order of days and business for the coming month were publicly 'proclaimed'. *Idus, -uum* (fem.) may come from an Etruscan word *iduo* = 'to divide'; or alternatively from a Sanscrit root meaning 'to lighten', hence the day of the full moon—in either case, the mid point of the month is denoted. *Nonae, -arum* was the ninth day by inclusive reckoning before the Ides.

[2] The old doggerel is helpful as a mnemonic:

> In March, July, October, May,
> The Nones fell on the seventh day.

Other dates were got by counting back from the three fixed days. The day before each was 'prid(ie) Kal.', 'prid. Non.', 'prid. Id.'. Otherwise the reckoning was inclusive, that is to say, both days at each end of the count were included in the total. Thus the Ides of March were 15 March, but 13 March was 'a(nte) d(iem) iii Id. Mart.'; 'a.d. v Non. Mai.' was 3 May; 'a.d. xii Kal. Dec.' was 19 December (in the pre-Julian calendar when December had only twenty-nine days), and so on.

APPENDIX 2

ROMAN MONEY

THE basic Roman coin for reckoning prices and values was the *sestertius*, a word formed from *semis-tertius* = two and a half. Its original value was two and a half *asses*. In its abbreviated form, *sestertius* was written HS: H was originally II, and S was short for *semis*—so HS = 2½.

The figure of two and a half *asses* was chosen as a convenient one for a coin at a time when the *denarius* was worth (as its name indicates) ten *asses*. The *sestertius* was thus worth one quarter of a *denarius*. But early in the Hannibalic War the *as* was devalued; the *denarius* was retariffed at sixteen *asses*, and the *sestertius* became worth four *asses*. So, in Cicero's day, the *sestertius* was worth four *asses* and four *sestertii* equalled one *denarius*.

Since the *sestertius* was a coin of small value, it was commonly counted in thousands. It then took the form *sestertium*, an abbreviated genitive plural: *mille* or *milia sestertium* being understood from the simple genitive. Further multiplication was effected by using the distributive adverbs, which served to multiply by a further factor of one hundred: thus *deciens sestertium* = *deciens* (*centena milia*) *sestertium* = 10 × 100 × 1,000 = one million sesterces.

These numerals were commonly abbreviated. Thousands of sesterces were indicated by drawing a line over the figures. Thus $\overline{\text{HS}}$ = 1,000 sesterces; HS DCCXXV = 725 sesterces, but HS $\overline{\text{DCCXXV}}$ = 725,000 sesterces. Hundreds of thousands were shown by enclosing the figures with straight lines on three sides. Thus $\lceil\overline{\text{HS}}\rceil$ = 100,000 sesterces, and HS $\lceil\overline{\text{DCCXXV}}\rceil$ = 72,500,000 sesterces.

It may be convenient here to notice some other numerical abbreviations, even if they do not occur in the present selection of letters. CIƆ = M = 1,000. IƆ (that is, half of CIƆ) = D = 500. CCIƆƆ = 10,000. CCCIƆƆƆ = 100,000. CCCCIƆƆƆƆ = 1,000,000.

It is a waste of time to try to give modern sterling or dollar equivalents for the values of ancient money. Quite apart from the fact that nowadays rapid inflation would make any equivalents out of date almost before the ink was dry on the printing presses, the simple fact has to be faced that our modern societies differ so radically and fundamentally from ancient societies in their structure and resources and technology that such direct comparisons are quite impossible. The average material standard of living of the ordinary man in modern western countries—in clothing, housing, food, material possessions, luxuries even—is infinitely higher than that of the inhabitants of ancient and medieval countries; while the gulf between the rich and the poor is incomparably narrower than it was in the past. The poorest Roman knight owned a capital of at least 400,000 sesterces; the unskilled Roman labourer would be lucky to earn 1,000 sesterces a year. Transpose this into modern terms, when the English unskilled labourer of 1968 earns about £750 p.a., and the equivalent to the minimum knight's capital is £300,000. And on top of this we must remember that the Roman knight was not troubled by the swingeing taxation nowadays levied on the income from such sums.

All we can hope to do is to steer by some reference points, of which I append a few so as to give some idea of the scales involved.

In Cicero's day, a man needed to own property worth at least 400,000 sesterces to rank as an *eques*. Under Augustus, a senator had to own property worth at least one million sesterces. A free unskilled labourer would earn about a *denarius* (four sesterces) a day—say about 1,000 sesterces a year, since he could not count on working all 365 days. Until Julius Caesar put up his pay, a common soldier received two sesterces a day and had to buy his own food: Caesar raised his pay to about 900 sesterces a year plus free food. The price of wheat fluctuated widely, for it was affected by such factors as weather and piratical activities and so on: in Sicily in the late seventies it averaged about three sesterces for a *modius* (= between $\frac{1}{8}$ and $\frac{1}{4}$ bushel). In Cicero's day olive-oil probably averaged two to three sesterces for a litre. A list outside an inn at Pompeii advertised (mid first century A.D.) wine at prices ranging from one to four *asses* a pint. About this same period, cheap dyed wool could be had for between two and four *asses* the pound. Cicero's rich contemporaries would pay anything from 500,000 to 2,500,000 sesterces for a town-house at Rome. Unimproved farmland of lowish quality might be got for upwards of 1,000 sesterces for a *iugerum* (about three-fifths of an acre); but we hear of 11,500,000 sesterces being paid for 1,000 *iugera* near Cicero's country house in the favoured area of Tusculum.

CONCORDANCE OF LETTERS

1	ad Att. i. 1	18	ad Q. F. ii. 14
2	ad Att. i. 2	19	ad Q. F. ii. 16
3	ad famm. v. 7	20	ad Q. F. iii. 6
4	ad Att. i. 14	21	ad famm. viii. 1
5	ad Att. ii. 15	22	ad famm. ii. 8
6	ad Att. ii. 21	23	ad Att. v. 16
7	ad Q. F. i. 2	24	ad famm. xv. 5
8	ad Q. F. i. 4	25	ad famm. xv. 6
9	ad Att. iv. 1	26	ad famm. viii. 14
10	ad famm. i. 1	27	ad famm. xvi. 1
11	ad Q. F. ii. 3	28	ad Att. viii. 12d.
12	ad Att. iv. 5	29	ad Att. ix. 6a.
13	ad Att. iv. 10	30	ad Att. xi. 15
14	ad famm. vii. 1	31	ad famm. iv. 5
15	ad famm. vii. 5	32	ad famm. vii. 30
16	ad famm. vii. 6	33	ad Att. xiv. 12
17	ad famm. vii. 7	34	ad famm. xi. 28
	35 ad famm. x. 28		

VOCABULARY

The figures (1), (2), (3), (4), *denote the conjugations of verbs*

abicio, -icere, -ieci, -iectum (3), abandon, throw away.

ablatus, (past part. of *aufero*).

abrogo (1), abrogate, annul.

absolutio, -onis (f.), acquittal.

absolvo (3), acquit.

abstinentia, -ae (f.), restraint, uprightness.

abstuli (perf. of *aufero*).

absum, -esse, afui, be absent; distant from.

abundantia, -ae (f.), plenty; copiousness.

abutor, -uti, -usus (3), abuse, misuse.

accedo, -cessi, -cessum (3), approach.

accedit ut it also happens that.

acceptum referre, to put to the credit of.

accerso, -ivi, -itum (3) = *arcesso* = summon.

accessio, -onis (f.), addition, accession.

accidit ut, it happens that.

acclamatio, -onis (f.), outcry.

accubo (1), to recline (at table).

accudo (3), to rivet, hammer together.

accurate (adv.), carefully, studiedly.

acer, -cris, -cre (adj.), sharp; energetic; brave.

acerbus, -a, -um (adj.), bitter.

acquiesco, -quievi, -quietum (3), rest, relax; acquiesce.

actio, -onis (f.), speech; delivery.

adduco, -duxi, -ductum (3), bring, draw.

adfero, attuli, allatum (3), advance; contribute.

adficio, -feci, -fectum (3), affect; influence.

adhibeo, -hibui, -hibitum (2), apply; invite; display.

adimo, -emi, -emptum (3), take away, deprive.

adiungo, -iunxi, -iunctum (3), join to, ally.

adiuro (1), swear, promise.

administro (1), (trans.) administer; (intrans.) govern.

admiratio, -onis (f.), wonder, astonishment.

admonitio, -onis (f.), warning.

adparo (1), provide; prepare.

adquiro, -quisivi, -quisitum (3), acquire, get, amass.

adsedeo, -sedi, -sessum (2), sit down; sit down by.

adsensus, -us (m.), agreement, assent.

adsentio, -sensi, -sensum (4), agree, assent to.

adsequor, -secutus (3), follow; gain, achieve.

adsiduitas, -atis (f.), application, constancy.

adsum, -esse, -fui, be present; put in an appearance.

adulescens, -entis (m.), young man.

adversor (1), oppose, resist.

adverto, -verti, -versum (3), notice, perceive.

advocatus, -i (m.) supporter.

advolo (1), fly (to).

aedilis, -is (m.), aedile.

aeger, -ra, -rum (adj.), ill, sick.

aegre (adv.), scarcely, with difficulty.

aequus, -a, -um (adj.), fair, just, reasonable.

aes alienum, aeris alieni (n.), debt.

aestimo (1), reckon; make an estimate of.

aetas, -atis (f.), age.

ager publicus (m.), public (state-owned) land.

ago, egi, actum (3), institute an action at law.

agrarius, -a, -um (adj.), agrarian.

ain? (= *ais-ne?*), what's that you say?

alias (adv.), at another time.

alienatio, -onis (f.), alienation, estrangement.

alieno (1), alienate, estrange; banish.

alienus, -a, -um (adj.), (i) belonging to someone else; (ii) hostile, inimical.

alienus, -i (m.), a stranger, outsider.

aliquando (adv.), at some time; ever; at last.

aliquoties (adv.), several times.

alter, -tera, -terum (adj.), one of two; the other of two.

ambitio, -onis (f.), ambition, desire for advancement.

ambitus, -us, (m.), bribery, electoral corruption.

ambo, -ae, -o (adj.), both.

amitto, -misi, -missum (3), lose; surrender.

amoenitas, -atis (f.), pleasant ation, natural beauty.

amplus, -a, -um (adj.), spacious; great; dignified.

animadverto, -verti, -versum (3), note, attend to; draw attention to.

animatus, -a, -um (adj.), minded; spirited.

animula, -ae (f.), dim. form of *anima* = soul.

animus, -i (m.), spirit, vigour; mind.

annona, -ae (f.), corn, grain.

antepono, -posui, -positum (3), place before; prefer.

antiquo (1), vote against, reject.

aperio, -perui, -pertum (4), open, reveal; open up.

apertus, -a, -um (adj.), open; frank.

apiscor, aptus (3), acquire, attain to.

apparatus, -a, -um (adj.), ready; well-supplied, sumptuous.

apparatus, -us (m.), display, parade; preparation, equipment.

aptus, -a, -um (adj.), fitting, suitable.

apud (prep. w. acc.), near; in the presence of; at the house of.

arbitratus, -us (m.), choice, wish.

arbitrium, -i (n.), judgement, decision, authority.

ardeo, arsi, arsum (2), burn, be on fire.

argutus, -a, -um (adj.), tedious; shrill; cunning.

armatura, -ae (f.), armament.

ars, artis (f.), skill; trade; art.

arx, arcis (f.), citadel, stronghold.

ascendo, -scendi, -scensum (3), mount, ascend.

asinus, -i (m.), ass; blockhead.

aspernor (1), spurn, reject, despise.

astutus, -a, -um (adj.), sly, cunning, adroit.

atrox, -ocis (adj.), terrible, fierce, cruel.

auctor, -oris (m.), originator, mover, author.

auctoritas, -atis (f.), authority, standing.

auctus, -a, -um (adj.), increased, augmented.

auditor, -oris (m.), listener, hearer.

auditus, -us (m.), noise, hearing.

aufero, abstuli, ablatum (3), take away, remove, steal.

augeo, auxi, auctum (2), increase, augment.

augur, -uris (m.), augur.

auspicor (1), take the auspices (for).

aveo (2), be eager, desire.

avoco (1), call away.

avunculus, -i (m.), uncle.

barbatulus, -a, -um (adj.), wearing a small beard.

beatus, -a, -um (adj.), fortunate; well-to-do.

bellus, -a, -um (adj.), handsome, charming; polite.

beneficium, -i (n.), service, kindness, favour.

benevolentia, -ae (f.), goodwill, kindness.

benignitas, -atis (f.), kindness, warmth.

bestia, -ae (f.), wild beast, brute beast.

bibliotheca, -ae (f.), library.

biduum, -i (n.), a period of two days.

bini, -ae, -a (adj.), two apiece; a pair.

bis (adv.), twice.

bona, -orum (n. pl.), goods, property.

cadaver, -eris (n.), dead body, corpse.

caenum, -i (n.), filth, muck.

calamitas, -atis (f.), ruin, loss, misfortune.

caleo, -ui (2), be warm, hot.

calleo (2), become hardened, thick-skinned.

calor, -oris (m.), heat, warmth.

calumnia, -ae (f.), chicanery, malicious craft.

campus, -i (m.), the Campus (Martius).

careo, -ui (2), lack, be deprived of.

caritas, -atis (f.), scarcity, high price.

carpo, carpsi, carptum (3), (i) pluck, (ii) carp at, slander.

casus, -us (m.), chance; misfortune.

causa, -ae (f.), cause; case.

cautus, -a, -um (adj.), cautious, sensible.

cĕdo (arch. imperative), out with it; look here; give it here.

celebro (1), throng; celebrate; honour.

celo (1), hide, conceal.

ceno (1), dine.

censeo, -sui, -sum (2), move; vote; express an opinion.

censura, -ae (f.), censorship.

centuriatus, -a, -um (adj.), divided into hundreds, 'centuriate'.

cesso (1), leave off, stop, cease.

cibus, -i (m.), food.

circumcirca (adv.), round-about.

circumfluo, -fluxi, (3), abound in.

circumrodo, -rodi (3), nibble.

circumsedeo, -sessi, -sessum (2), surround.

circumsto, -steti, stand around.

citius (adv.), sooner, more quickly.

civiliter (adv.), in a lawful fashion; politely.

civitas, -atis (f.), state; citizenship; civil rights.

clamor, -oris (m.), shout, cry, up-roar.

classis, -is (f.), fleet.

clementia, -ae (f.), mercy, clemency.

cliens, -entis (m. or f.), client, dependant.

clientela, -ae (f.), following; dependence.

cogitatio, -onis (f.), reflection, consideration.

coheres, -edis (m. or f.), co-heir.

cohibeo, -ui, -itum (2), hold together, hold back; restrain.

cohortor (1), encourage, exhort.

colo, -ui, cultum (3), cultivate, pay court or respect to.

comes, -itis (m.), companion.

commemoro (1), recollect; remind; recount.

commendo (1), commend, support, back.

commigro (1), move, remove to.

committo, -misi, -missum (3), entrust, commit; venture, engage.

commode (adv.), conveniently.

commodum, -i (n.), advantage, convenience.

commodus, -a, -um (adj.), convenient, suitable.

commoror (1), delay, linger, tarry.

commulcium, -i (n.), a drubbing.

communico (1), share; impart.

communis, -e (adj.), common, shared.

commuto (1), change; exchange.

comparatio, -onis (f.), preparation.

comparo (1), prepare, make ready.

comperio, -peri, -pertum (4), discover, find out.

compilatio, -onis (f.), compilation, pot-pourri.

complector, -plexus (3), embrace, surround.

compleo, -plevi, -pletum (2), fill up; make up; fulfil.

complexus, -us (m.), embrace.

complures, -ia (adj.), numerous, very many.

compositio, -onis (f.), matching, pairing.

comprobo (1), approve fully; establish firmly.

concedo, -cessi, -cessum (3), withdraw, give way, yield.

concilio (1), unite, bring together; procure.

concipio, -cepi, -ceptum (3), express; comprehend, grasp.

concisus, -a, -um (adj.), cut to pieces.

concito (1), urge on, excite.

concordia, -ae (f.), agreement, harmony.

concupisco, -pivi, -pitum (3), covet, seek eagerly.

concurro, -curri, -cursum (3), run together, flock to.

concursatio, -onis (f.), concourse, flocking together.

concutio, -cussi, -cussum (3), shake, shatter; alarm.

condicio, -onis (f.), condition; proviso.

conduco, -duxi, -ductum (3), bring together; hire.

confero, contuli, -latum (3), (i) compare; (ii) confer, grant; (iii) collect.

conficio, -feci, -fectum (3), bring about; complete.

confido, -fisi, -fisum (3), be confident, believe firmly.

confirmo (1), strengthen.

confiteor, -fessus (3), admit.

congiarium, -i (n.), donation, grant, dole.

coniectura, -ae (f.), inference, guess.

coniunctio, -onis (f.), alliance.

coniunctus, -a, -um (adj.), allied.

coniungo, -iunxi, -iunctum (3), ally, join together.

coniuratio, -onis (f.), conspiracy.

conlega, -ae (m.), colleague.

conlego, -legi, -lectum (3), bring together, collect; compose.

conor (1), try, attempt.

conquasso (1), shake down, ruin.

conquiesco, -quievi, -quietum (3), rest, be still.

conscientia, -ae (f.), awareness, consciousness.

conscius, -a, -um (adj.), aware.

conscribo, -scripsi, -scriptum (3), enrol, call up.

consensio, -onis (f.), agreement, harmony.

consentio, -sensi, -sensum (4), agree, assent.

consequor, -secutus (3), achieve, win.

consessor, -oris (m.), one who sits next to another.

considero (1), consider carefully.

consilium, -i (n.), (i) advice, plan, decision; (ii) council, advisory board.

consolatio, -onis (f.), comfort, consolation.

consolor (1), comfort, console.

conspectus, -us (m.), sight, view; appearance.

consputo (1), spit at.

constans, -antis (adj.), reliable, dependable.

constantia, -ae (f.), patience; reliability.

consto, -stiti, consist of.

consuesco, -suevi, -suetum (3), become accustomed to.

consuetudo, -dinis (f.), use, habit, custom; friendship, intimacy.

consulo, -ului, -ultum (3), consult; have regard for the interest of (with dative case).

consulto (adv.), deliberately, designedly.

consultum, -i (n.), decree, decision.

consumo, -sumpsi, -sumptum, use up, waste, consume.

contemno, -tempsi, -temptum (3), despise.

contendo, -tendi, -tentum (3), (i) strive, struggle; (ii) maintain, argue.

contentio, -onis (f.), (i) energy, drive; (ii) quarrel.

continentia, -ae (f.), moderation, restraint.

continuo (adv.), straightaway, at once.

contio, -onis (f.), public-meeting.

contionarius, -a, -um (adj.), go-to-meeting.

contiono (1), to harangue a public meeting.

controversia, -ae (f.), quarrel, dispute.

contumelia, -ae (f.), affront, insult, outrage.

contumeliosus, -a, -um, abusive, insulting.

convalesco, -valui (3), to get better, become strong.

conventus, -us (m.), assembly, meeting.

converto, -verti, -versum (3), turn round; direct towards.

convicium, -i (n.), abuse.

coram (adv.), face to face, in person.

coram (prep. w. abl.), in the presence of.

correctio, -onis (f.), rectification, amendment.

corrigo, -rexi, -rectum (3), correct, set right.

corruo, -rui (3), fall to the ground, collapse.

cotidianum, -i (n.), a commonplace, a regular quip.

cotidianus, -a, -um (adj.), daily, everyday.

cotidie (adv.), every day.

creber, -ra, -rum (adj.), crowded; frequent; numerous.

crebro (adv.), frequently, repeatedly.

creditor, -oris (m. or f.), creditor.

creterra, -ae (f.), a mixing bowl.
crimen, -inis (n.), charge, accusation; crime.
criminor (1), charge, accuse.
cubiculum, -i (n.), bedroom.
cumulo (1), heap up; crown.
cupiditas, -atis (f.), greed.
curia, -ae (f.), the Senate House.
curiosus, -a, -um (adj.), inquisitive; careful.
curo (1), see to; take care; look after.
currus, -us (m.), chariot, carriage.
curulis, -e (adj.), curule.
　(**sella curulis,** the ivory inlaid chair of a senior magistrate).
custodio, -ivi, -itum (4), guard, watch, keep safe.

damno (1), condemn, convict.
damnum, -i (n.), loss, damage.
decedo, -cessi, -cessum (3), depart; yield to.
decerno, -crevi, -cretum (3), decree, decide.
decipio, -cepi, -ceptum (3), deceive.
declamo (1), to speak in public; to teach oratory.
decretum, -i (n.), decree.
decuriati, -orum (m.), bribery-agents.
dedecus, -oris (n.), disgrace.
deditus, -a, -um (adj.), devoted.
defectio, -onis (f.), betrayal, desertion.
defessus, -a, -um (adj.), worn out, wearied.
deficio, -feci, -fectum (3), fail, give up, fall short.
deformatus, -a, -um (adj.), misshapen.
defungor, -functus (3), discharge, fulfil.
dego, degi (3), pass, spend.

delectatio, -onis (f.), amusement, pleasure.
delecto (1), delight, give enjoyment.
deleo, -levi, -letum (2), destroy, annul, obliterate.
deliberatio, -onis (f.), careful thought, deliberation.
deliciae, -arum (f.), pet, favourite, darling.
deminuo, -minui, -minutum (3), lessen, diminish.
demissus, -a, -um (adj.), downcast.
demo, dempsi, demptum (3), take away, subtract.
demolior, demolitus (4), destroy, pull down.
demonstro (1), prove, indicate.
denique (adv.), at last; in short; then.
depono, -posui, -positum (3), put down, renounce, resign.
descisco, -scivi, -scitum (3), depart, desert, revolt from.
describo, -scripsi, -scriptum (3), allude to; describe; mark out.
desero, -serui, -sertum (3), abandon, desert, neglect.
desiderium, -i (n.), longing.
desidero (1), long for, miss.
designatus, -a, -um (adj.), designate, elect.
desino, -sii, -situm (3), stop, cease.
despicio, -spexi, -spectum (3), look down on, despise.
desum, -esse, -fui, be absent, wanting.
detrudo, -trusi, -trusum (3), eject, push away.
deturbo (1), drive away, dislodge.
devoro (1), swallow, gulp down.
dialectica, -ae (f.), the art of dialectic.
dictatura, -ae (f.), dictatorship.
dictito (1), assert frequently.
diem dicere, to prosecute, arraign.
diem obire, to die.

differo, distuli, dilatum (3), (i) put off, postpone; (ii) to differ from, be different.

diffido, -fisus sum (3), to lack confidence, mistrust.

dilatio, -onis (f.), postponement.

dilectus, -us (m.), military levy, conscription.

diligens, -entis (adj.), conscientious, careful.

diligentia, -ae (f.), conscientiousness, attentiveness.

diligo, -lexi, -lectum (3), esteem, love, value highly.

dimico (1), strive, fight.

dimitto, -misi, -missum (3), send away, discharge.

diripio, -ripui, -reptum (3), plunder, pillage, tear away.

dirumpo, -rupi, -ruptum (3), rupture, break in pieces.

diruo, -ui, -utum (3), destroy, pull down.

discedo, -cessi, -cessum (3), depart, come away.

discessus, -us (m.), parting, departure.

discidium, -ii (n.), separation, severing.

disco, didici (3), learn.

discordia, -ae (f.), disagreement, estrangement.

dissimulo (1), dissemble, disguise.

dissipo (1), scatter, rout; squander.

dissuasor, -oris (m.), opposer.

distentus, -a, -um (adj.), distracted, extended.

distineo, -tinui, -tentum (3), keep apart, divide.

districtus, -a, -um (adj.), busy, occupied.

divinitus (adv.), inspiredly, divinely.

dodrans, -antis (m.), three-fourths.

doleo, dolui (2), grieve, suffer.

dolus malus (m.), fraud (legal term).

domi (loc. adv.), at home (as opposed to 'outdoors' or 'abroad').

dulcedo, -inis (f.), sweetness, charm.

dumtaxat (adv.), at any rate, at least.

durus, -a, -um (adj.), hard; cruel; stern; unkind.

ecquis, ecquid (interr. pron.), **ecquisnam, ecquidnam,** whether any, if any.

edictum, -i (n.), edict, decree.

efficio, -feci, -fectum (3), bring about, effect.

effugio, -fugi (3), escape, avoid.

egeo, -ui (2), to be in need, to be without.

egomet (pron.), I myself.

egregius, -a, -um (adj.), outstanding, distinguished.

elicio, -licui, -licitum (3), to induce, entice out, elicit.

eligo, -legi, -lectum (3), pick out, choose.

eluo, -lui, -lutum (3), cleanse, wash away.

embaenetica, -ae (f.), boat-hiring.

emo, emi, emptum (3), buy, purchase.

epulae, -arum (f.), banquet, feast.

eques, -itis (m.), (i) horseman; (ii) a member of the order of '*equites*' or 'knights'.

equestris, -e (adj.), pertaining to an *eques*; equestrian; knightly.

equitatus, -us (m.), cavalry.

erga (prep. w. acc.), towards.

erigo, -rexi, -rectum (3), raise up, exalt; arouse, incite.

eripio, -ripui, -reptum (3), snatch away.

erro (2), wander, stray; be in error.

essedarius, -i (m.), a fighter in a Celtic war-chariot (*essedum*).

esurio (4), starve, be hungry.

etsi (conj.), although.

everto, -verti, -versum (3), overthrow, demolish.

exardesco, -arsi, -arsum (3), to burn, take fire, be inflamed.

exaudio (4), hear plainly.

excedo, -cessi, -cessum (3), go away from; exceed.

excipio, -cepi, -ceptum (3), catch, snatch, receive.

excito (1), arouse, summon.

excrucio (1), torture, torment.

excurro, -curri (-cucurri), -cursum (3), run out, hasten away.

excusatio, -onis (f.), excuse, defence.

exerceo, -ui, -itum (2), occupy; practise, exercise.

exercitatus, -a, -um (adj.), practised, experienced; harassed.

exhaurio, -hausi, -haustum (3), draw out, empty, exhaust.

exhibeo, -hibui, -hibitum (2), produce, display.

exigo, -egi, -actum (3), drive out; exact, demand.

exiguus, -a, -um (adj.), tiny, scanty.

existimatio, -onis (f.), opinion; reputation, good name.

exitium, -ii (n.), ruin, destruction.

exitus, -us (m.), end, outcome; way out.

exopto (1), desire eagerly, pray for.

exorior, -ortus sum (3 and 4), spring up, arise.

expedio, -ivi (-ii), -itum (4), (i) get clear, extricate; (ii) make ready.

expedit (impers.), it is advantageous, expedient.

expeditus, -a, -um (adj.), unimpeded.

expleo, -plevi, -pletum (2), fill up; fulfil, discharge.

explico (1), disentangle.

exprimo, -pressi, -pressum (3), extort, press out; express.

expugno (1), take by storm.

exsanguis, -e (adj.), pale, bloodless.

exsolvo, -solvi, -solutum (3), loosen, untie; pay, discharge.

exspectatio, -onis (f.), expectation, anticipation.

exstinguo, -stinxi, -stinctum (3), quench, blot out.

exsto, -stiti (1), stand out, be visible; remain.

extorqueo, -torsi, -tortum (2), extort, wring out.

extrudo, -trusi, -trusum (3), push out, drive out.

exturbo (1), drive away, displace.

fabella, -ae (f.), a little tale.

fabula, -ae (f.), story; plot or story of a play; play, drama.

facilis, -e (adj.), easy; easy-going, accommodating.

facilitas, -atis (f.), (i) friendliness, good nature; (ii) opportunity, availability.

facinus, -oris (n.), deed; bad deed, crime.

facultates, -ium (f.), resources.

faenus, -oris (n.), interest (on loans); debt.

fallacia, -ae (f.), fraud, deceit.

fallo, fefelli, falsum (3), to make a slip; lead astray.

fames, -is (f.), hunger, starvation.

familiaris, -e (adj.), friendly.

familiaris, -is (m.), friend, acquaintance.

familiaritas, -atis (f.), friendship, intimacy.

fas (indecl. n.), that which is lawful, permitted, right.

faveo, favi, fautum (2), favour, support (with dative).

fere (adv.), almost, nearly; usually.

ferio (4), strike, beat.

festinatio, -onis (f.), hurrying, haste.

festivus, -a, um (adj.), agreeable, pleasant.

fides, -ei (f.), trust; loyalty; credit.

figo, fixi, fictum (3), fix, post.

filiolus, -i (m.), a little son.

fletus, -us (m.), weeping.

floreo, -ui (2), flourish, prosper.

fluxus, -a, -um (adj.), flowing; changeable.

foedus, -a, -um (adj.), disgusting, foul.

forensis, -e (adj.), relating to the forum; judicial.

foris (adv.), out of doors; abroad.

fors, *abl.* **forte** (f.), chance, luck.

fortuito (adv.), by chance, accidentally.

forum agere, to hold an assize.

frango, fregi, fractum (3), break, shatter.

fraternus, -a, -um (adj.), fraternal.

fraudo (1), cheat, defraud.

fremitus, -us (m.), murmuring, growling.

fremo, -ui, -itum (3), murmur, growl.

frequens, -entis (adj.), crowded; frequent.

frequentia, -ae (f.), concourse, crowd.

fretus, -a, -um (adj.), relying on.

frigeo (2), be cold; flag, fall flat.

frons, frontis (f.), forehead.

fructus, -us (m.), enjoyment; proceeds, profit.

fruor, fructus sum (3), delight in, enjoy; gain advantage from.

fucus, -i (m.), dye; deceit, pretence.

funditus (adv.), utterly.

fungor, functus sum (3), perform, accomplish.

funus, -eris (n.), funeral.

furor, -oris (m.), madness, raving.

gaudeo, gavisus sum (2), rejoice, delight in.

gavisus (adj.), past part. of 'gaudeo'.

gemitus, -us (m.), sigh, groaning.

gemo, -ui, -itum (3), sigh, groan.

gener, -eri (m.), son-in-law.

genus, -eris (n.), birth, descent; type, kind.

germanus, -a, -um (adj.), genuine, real.

gero, gessi, gestum (3), conduct, manage.

glorior (1), glory in, boast.

gradus, -us (m.), step, stair.

grandis, -e (adj.), large, important.

gratia, -ae (f.), charm; influence; favour.

gratias agere, to thank.

gratificor (1), oblige, gratify.

gratulatio, -onis (f.), congratulation.

gratulor (1), congratulate (w. dative).

gravis, -e (adj.), serious, weighty, important.

gravitas, -tatis (f.), seriousness, authority.

gypsatus, -a, -um (adj.), whitened with gypsum.

habitator, -oris (m.), dweller, tenant.

hem ! (interj.), ah! oh!

me hercle, hercule ! (interj.), by Hercules! good heavens!

Hermathena, -ae (f.), a double bust of Hermes and Athena.

heus ! (interj.), hey! hallo there!

hilaritas, -atis (f.), cheerfulness gaiety.

homunculus, -i (m.), dimin. form of *homo*.

honestas, -atis (f.), honour, probity.

honestus, -a, -um (adj.), honourable, upright.

honos (honor), -oris (m.), (i) honour, distinction; (ii) public office.

horreo (2), shiver, shudder (at).

hortor (1), encourage, egg on.

humaniter (adv.), politely; with resignation.

humanus, -a, -um (adj.), decent, civilized.

humilis, -e (adj.), low, humble.

iaceo (2), to lie (down); to be done for, dispirited.

iacto (1), throw, throw away; boast, vaunt.

iactura, -ae (f.), loss, sacrifice; expenditure.

iam pridem (adv.), long ago, by now, at last.

idcirco (adv.), on that account.

idoneus, -a, -um (adj.), appropriate, suitable.

ignosco, -novi, -notum (3), forgive, overlook.

imago, -inis (f.), likeness, portrait; shadow, pretence.

imbecillitas, -atis (f.), feebleness.

imbecillus, -a, -um (adj.), feeble.

imitor (1), copy, imitate.

immanis, -e (adj.), huge; monstrous, frightful.

immemor, -oris (adj.), forgetful, unmindful.

immoderatus, -a, -um (adj.), immoderate, unreasonable.

impedio (4), hinder, obstruct.

impello, -puli, -pulsum (3), drive; strike.

impendo, -pendi, -pensum (3), impend; expend.

impensa, -ae (f.), expenditure, outlay.

imperator, -oris (m.), a holder of *imperium*; commander.

imperium, -ii (n.), supreme authority.

impetro (1), obtain, effect.

impetus, -us (m.), force; attack.

implico (1), entangle, implicate, trap.

impressus, -us (m.), impress, imprint.

improbitas, -atis (f.), wickedness, dishonesty.

improbo (1), disapprove, reject.

improbus, -a, -um, wicked, dishonest.

imprudentia, -ae (f.), folly, lack of common sense.

impulsus, -us (m.), pressure, instigation.

impunitus, -a, -um (adj.), unpunished.

inanis, -e (adj.), empty; useless.

incido, -cidi (3), light on, chance on.

inclinatio, -onis (f.), inclination; goodwill, support.

incolumis, -e (adj.), without harm or loss, undamaged.

incommodum, -i (n.), misfortune, setback, loss.

inconstans, -antis (adj.), fickle, unreliable.

incorruptus, -a, -um (adj.), unimpaired, uncorrupted.

increpo, -avi (-ui), -atum (-itum) (1), rebuke, upbraid, reproach.

incumbo, -cubui, -cubitum (3), lean on, press; apply oneself to.

incunabula, -orum (n.), swaddling clothes, *hence* cradle, birth place.

index, -icis (m.), informer, spy.

indicium, -ii (n.), evidence.

indigeo, -ui (2), stand in need of, lack.

indignor (1), hold unworthy, be offended.

indormio (4), sleep, go to sleep.

induco, -duxi, -ductum (3), bring in, lead in, induce, introduce.

ineo, -ii, -itum (irreg.), enter, undertake; inherit.

ineptiae, -arum (f.), foolishness, absurdity.

ineptus, -a, -um (adj.), foolish, awkward, clumsy.

iners, -ertis (adj.), sluggish, lazy.

infamia, -ae (f.), disgrace, ill repute.

inferi, -orum (m.), the dead, spirits of the dead.

infimus, -a, -um (adj.), lowest, humblest, bottommost.

infirmitas, -atis (f.), weakness.

informatus, -a, -um (adj.), sketched in outline.

ingemo, -ui (3), sigh, groan (over).

ingenium, -ii (n.), nature, character; skill, intelligence.

initium, -ii (n.), beginning.

iniuria, -ae (f.), injustice, wrong.

inopia, -ae (f.), want, need, lack.

inops, -opis (adj.), without means, wanting.

inservio (4), serve, be devoted to.

insidiae, -arum (f.), plot, trap.

insignis, -e (adj.), remarkable, distinguished.

insolens, -entis (adj.), unusual, unused to.

instituo, -ui, -utum (3), arrange, prepare, begin, decide.

instructus, -a, -um (adj.), well provided; learned.

insuetus, -a, -um (adj.), unaccustomed; unused.

insulsus, -a, -um (adj.), insipid, tasteless.

integer, -gra, -grum (adj.), whole, undiminished, sound.

intemperantia, -ae (f.), excess, immoderation.

intercessor, -oris (m.), a vetoer.

intercludo, -clusi, -clusum (3), cut off, shut in.

interdum (adv.), from time to time.

intereo, -ii, -itum (3), die, perish.

interest (impers.), it concerns, is of importance.

interimo, -emi, -emptum (3), kill, murder.

intermitto, -misi, -missum (3), leave off, interrupt, neglect.

intermortuus, -a, -um (adj.), moribund.

interpello (1), interrupt, impede, disturb.

interpono, -posui, -positum (3), interpose.

interregnum, -i (n.), interregnum.

intersum, -esse, -fui, to be present, take part in.

interviso, -visi, -visum (3), look after, visit occasionally.

intestinus, -a, -um (adj.), internal, domestic.

intimus, -a, -um (adj.), intimate, confidential.

intimus, -i (m.), a close friend.

inveho, -vexi, -vectum (3), attack, assail.

invenio, -veni, -ventum (4), find, discover.

invideo, -vidi, -visum (2), envy, grudge.

invidia, -ae (f.), envy, ill-will.

invidiosus, -a, -um (adj.), hateful, detested.

inviso (1), visit, go to see.

invitus, -a, -um, unwilling.

iracundia, -ae (f.), rage, irascibility.

iste, -a, istud (adj.), that of yours, your.

istim (adv.), from there, from where you are.

istinc (adv.), from there, from where you are.

iudex, -icis (m.), judge, member of a jury.

iudicialis, -e (adj.), judicial, relating to a court.

iudicium, -ii (n.), (i) trial; (ii) judgement, opinion.

iudico (1), judge, decide.

iure (adv.), rightly, justifiably.

iuro (1), swear, take an oath.

ius, -iuris (n.), law, legal right or authority.

iustus, -a, -um (adj.), upright, fair, proper.

iuventus, -us (f.), youth; (meton.) young men.

labor, lapsus sum (3), slide, slip.

laboro (1), work, toil, be hard-pressed.

laedo, laesi, laesum (3), injure, insult.

laetitia, -ae (f.), joy, delight.

laetor (1), rejoice, be delighted.

languens, -entis (adj.), languid, fainting, helpless.

languidus, -a, -um (adj.), faint, sluggish.

lanio (1), cut to pieces, mangle.

lapsus, -a, -um (adj.), fallen, downcast.

largitio, -onis (f.), generosity; bribe.

laurea, -ae (f.), (crown of) laurel.

laus, laudis (f.), praise; glory.

lecticula, -ae (f.), a small litter or carrying-chair.

lectiuncula, -ae (f.), a short reading, browse.

lectus, -a, -um (adj.), picked, chosen.

lectus, -i (m.), bed, couch.

legatio, -onis (f.), the office of legatus; embassy, delegation.

legatus, -i (m.), legate; lieutenant; staff officer; envoy.

legitimus, -a, -um (adj.), allowed or prescribed by law.

lego, legi, lectum (3), pick, select, collect; read.

lego (1), appoint as a legate; bequeath.

lenio, -ivi, -itum (4), mitigate, soften.

lepus, -oris (m.), charm, wit, grace.

levis, -e (adj.), light, fickle, trivial (opp. to *gravis*).

levitas, -atis (f.), fickleness, irresponsibility.

levo (1), relieve, lighten, raise up.

libens, -entis (adj.), willing, eager.

libenter (adv.), willingly.

liber, -era, -erum (adj.), free, independent.

libertas, -atis (f.), freedom.

libertus, -i (m.), a freedman (manumitted slave).

liberus, -i (m.), child.

librarius, -ii (m.), copyist, secretary.

licet, -cuit, -citum (2, impers.), it is allowed; granted that.

licitatio, -onis (f.), auction, sale.

lignum, -i (n.), (fire)-wood.

liquidus, -a, -um (adj.), clear, pure.

lis, litis (f.), a legal action or suit.

litus, -oris (n.), shore, beach.

lomentum, -i (n.), soap.

longinquitas, -atis (f.), length, duration.

luceo, luxi (2), shine, grow bright.

lucet, it is daylight.

luctus, -us (m.), grief, sorrow.

ludi, -orum (m.), public games or shows.

ludo, lusi, lusum (3), play; make sport; make a joke.

ludus, -i (m.), game, sport.

lugeo, luxi, luctum (2), mourn; bewail.

ux, lucis (f.), light; daylight, dawn.

maereo (2), grieve, be pained.

maledictum, -i (n.), abusive language.

malevolentia, -ae (f.), ill-will, hostility.

malevolus, -a, -um (adj.), hostile, unfriendly.

mancipium, -ii (n.), legal ownership.

mandatum, -i (n.), order, instruction, charge.

mando (1), charge, entrust.

mane (adv.), early in the morning.

mansuetudo, -inis (f.), gentleness, kindness, forgiveness.

manus, -us (f.), hand; band, group.

materia, -ae (f.), subject-matter.

maturitas, -atis (f.), ripeness, readiness; promptness.

maturo (1), make haste.

maturus, -a, -um (adj.), ripe; prompt.

matutinus, -a, -um (adj.), morning.

medicina, -ae (f.), treatment, remedy.

mediocris, -e (adj.), ordinary; moderate; unremarkable.

mendacium, -ii (n.), lie, falsehood.

mensis, -is (m.), month.

mentio, -onis (f.), mention.

mereor, meritus sum (2), earn, deserve, merit.

meridies, -ei (m.), noon.

meritum, -i (n.), reward, desert, good deed.

militia, -ae (f.), military service.

mimus, -i (m.), mime, farce.

ministro (1), hand out, distribute.

minitor (1), threaten.

mirificus, -a, -um (adj.), amazing.

miror (1), wonder at.

misereor, -seritus sum (2), pity, be sorry for.

miseri, -orum (m.), the poor, the unfortunate.

miseria, -ae (f.), wrtechedness, distress.

misericordia, -ae (f.), compassion, pity.

modestus, -a, -um (adj.), moderate, unassuming.

modicus, -a, -um (adj.), moderate, modest, ordinary.

modo (adv.), just now.

modus, -i (m.), measure; limit; manner, fashion.

moleste fero, ferre, take amiss, be upset, disgruntled.

molestia, -ae (f.), trouble, annoyance.

molestus, -a, -um (adj.), troublesome.

mollio (4), soften.

mollis, -e (adj.), soft, gentle.

mollities, -ei (f.), softness, gentleness.

moneo, monui, -itum (2), warn, advise.

monstrum, -i (n.), portent, wonder; monstrosity.

morbus, -i (m.), sickness, disease.

mos, moris (m.), custom, habit; traditional practice.

motus, -us (m.), motion, movement; riot, commotion.

muliercula, -ae (f.), dimin. form of *mulier*.

multiplicatus, -a, -um (adj.), many-folded, multiplied.

mundus, -a, -um (adj.), charming, polite, elegant.

munitus, -a, -um (adj.), fortified, secured.

munus, -eris (n.), office, function, duty; favour, service; gift; a public show.

mutuus, -a, -um (adj.), reciprocal, shared.

nactus, p. part. of *nanciscor.*
nanciscor, nactus sum (3), get, obtain; meet with.
nascor, natus sum (3), be born, come into being, arise.
navo operam (1), give help, aid.
ne (exclam. adv.), truly, certainly.
necessarius, -i (m.), close friend, near relation.
nefas (indecl. n.), that which is sinful or forbidden.
neglego, -lexi, lectum (3), disregard, overlook.
negotium, -ii (n.), business, affair.
nequedum (adv.), and not yet.
nequeo, -ivi, -itum (4), be unable.
nequiquam (adv.), to no avail, fruitlessly.
nexo (1), tie, bind together.
nimirum (adv.), doubtless, certainly.
nimis (adv.), too much.
nimium (adv.), too much.
nimius, -a, -um (adj.), excessive.
nitor, nisus sum (3), depend on; strive, strain.
nitrum, -i (n.), nitre, soda.
nobilis, -e (adj.), noble, of noble birth.
nominatim (adv.), by name, expressly.
numero (1), count, number, reckon.
nundinae, -arum (f.), market-day.
nuptiae, -arum (f.), marriage, wedding ceremony.

obduco, -duxi, -ductum (3), draw over, interpose; introduce.
obire diem, die, meet one's fate.
obitus, -us (m.), death.
oblectatio, -onis (f.), amusement, entertainment.

oblecto (1), amuse, divert.
oblitus, -a, -um (adj.), smeared over, defaced.
obliviscor, oblitus sum (3), forget, lose sight of.
obscurus, -a, -um (adj.), obscure, dark, concealed.
observantia, -ae (f.), attention, respect.
observo (1), respect, esteem.
obsto, -stiti, -stitum (1), oppose, hinder, obstruct.
obtempero (1), obey, conform with.
obtrectatio, -onis (f.), disparagement, detraction.
obtrecto (1), disparage, detract.
obviam ire, venire, go, come to meet.
obvius, -a, -um (adj.), in the way, meeting.
occido, -cidi, -cisum (3), fall; die; be ruined.
occultus, -a, -um (adj.), hidden.
occupatio, -onis (f.), business, occupation.
occupatus, -a, -um (adj.), busy, occupied.
occurro, -curri, -cursum (3), run to meet; come to mind.
offendo, -fendi, -fensum (3), (i) bump into, knock against; (ii) offend, displease.
offero, obtuli, oblatum (3), present, produce, offer.
officiosus, -a, -um (adj.), attentive, obliging, dutiful.
officium, -ii (n.), duty, obligation, service.
oleum, -i (n.), olive-oil, oil.
omnino (adv.), altogether, entirely.
onus, -eris (n.), load, burden; charge.
opera, -ae (f.), trouble, effort, exertion.

operae, -arum (f.), hired rowdies, gang.

operam dare, to work hard at, take pains.

operarius, -i (m.), hired labourer, workman.

opes, -um (f.), wealth, resources.

opinio, -onis (f.), belief, opinion, supposition.

oportet, -uit (impers. 2), it is proper, one ought, one must.

oppono, -posui, -positum (3), put before, oppose, object.

opportunus, -a, -um (adj.), opportune, favourable.

opprimo, -pressi, -pressum (3), put down, suppress, cow.

ops, opis (f.), might, influence, assistance.

optimates, -ium (m.), the aristocratic party.

opto (1), hope for; choose.

opulentus, -a, -um (adj.), rich, wealthy.

opus esse, there is need, it is necessary.

orbis, -is (m.), circle, ring.

orbis terrae, the world, the earth.

orbita, -ae (f.), wheel-mark, wheel-rut, track.

ordior, orsus sum (4), begin, start.

ordo, -inis (m.), line, row; set, class, rank.

oricula, -ae (f.), the lobe of the ear.

orno (1), equip, fit out; honour, praise, advance.

oro (1), beg, beseech, pray.

os, oris (n.), mouth; (meton.) face.

ostendo, -tendi, -tentum (3), show, display; hold out.

ostentum, -i (n.), prodigy, portent.

otiosus, -a, -um (adj.), free from duties, peaceful, restful, holiday.

otium, -ii (n.), rest, leisure, peacefulness.

paene (adv.), almost, nearly.

paenitet (impers. 3), it causes regret, remorse.

palam (adv.), openly, frankly.

par, paris (adj.), like, equal, worthy of.

parco, peperci, parsum (3), be sparing, moderate; spare, let off.

pareo, -ui, -itum (3), obey, yield to.

pario, peperi, partum (3), bring forth, give birth.

pars, partis (f.), part; side, party.

partes, partium (f.), party, faction.

particeps, -cipis (adj.), sharing, participating in.

partim (adv.), partly, in part.

parum (adv.), too little.

pascor, pastus sum (3), feed on, graze on.

patefacio, -feci, -factum (3), reveal, open up.

patientia, -ae (f.), patience, endurance.

peccatum, -i (n.), sin, misdeed.

pecco (1), commit a crime, fault.

peditatus, -us (m.), infantry.

pendo, pependi, -pensum (3), hang; weigh, consider; pay out.

penicillum, -i (n.), painter's brush or pencil.

percrebresco, -bui (3), become known, spread abroad.

perculsus, -a, -um (adj.), cast down, overwhelmed.

perditus, -a, -um (adj.), wretched, miserable; abandoned, wicked.

perdo, -didi, -ditum (3), destroy, ruin; squander.

peregrinor (1), travel abroad.

pereo, -ii, -itum (irreg.), perish, be lost or ruined.

perfidia, -ae (f.), treachery, deceit.

perforo (1), pierce through.

perfruor, -fructus sum (3), enjoy thoroughly.

perfungor, -functus sum (3), perform, discharge.

pergo, perrexi, -rectum (3), carry through, proceed with.

perhibeo, -hibui, -hibitum (2), bring forward; allege.

perhonorifice (adv.), with great deference.

perluctuosus, -a, -um (adj.), very grievous.

pernicies, -ei (f.), ruin, disaster.

persalsus, -a, -um (adj.), very witty.

persona, -ae (f.), character, personality.

perstringo, -strinxi, -strictum (3), graze; touch, lay hold of; wound; touch on.

persuadeo, -suasi, -suasum (2), convince, persuade (w. dat.).

pertempto (1), try, test.

pertexo, -texui, -textum (3), weave entirely; complete.

pertimesco, -timui (3), to be very much afraid.

pertineo, -tinui (2), reach, extend; relate, pertain to.

perturbo (1), disturb greatly, throw into confusion.

perurbanus, -a, -um (adj.), (over-) refined, civilized.

pervolo (1), fly through, fly away.

pestis, -is (f.), plague, disease.

petitio, -onis (f.), candidature.

petiturio (4), yearn to be a candidate.

peto, -ivi, -itum (3), seek, make for; seek election.

pietas, -atis (f.), dutiful affection, loyalty.

piger, -gra, -grum (adj.), lazy, slow, sluggish.

pingo, pinxi, pinctum (3), paint, decorate.

plane (adv.), entirely, thoroughly, plainly.

plausus, -us (m.), applause.

plebs, plebis (f.), the plebs; the Roman commons.

plecto (3), punish (with blows).

plerumque (adv.), mostly, generally.

ploratus, -us (m.), weeping, crying.

poema, -atis (n.), poem.

poena, -ae (f.), punishment; revenge.

politus, -a, -um (adj.), polished, refined.

pons, pontis (m.), bridge; a gangway leading to the voting point at an assembly.

posterus, -a, -um (adj.), subsequent, next.

postridie (adv.), next day, the day after.

postulo (1), demand, beg, claim.

potestas, -atis (f.), power; official authority; opportunity.

potior (4), get possession of, master.

potius (adv.), rather, preferably.

prae (prep.), before; in consequence of.

praeceps, -cipitis (adj.), headlong.

praecipio, -cepi, -ceptum (3), anticipate; warn, instruct, teach.

praecipitatus, -a, -um (adj.), sinking fast, rushing down.

praeclarus, -a, -um (adj.), famous, renowned.

praedico (1), declare, assure.

praeditus, -a, -um (adj.), endowed with.

praemitto, -misi, -missum (3), send ahead.

praemoneo, -monui, -monitum (2), warn, advise; foretell.

praepono, -posui, -positum (3), place before, set over.

praeproperus, -a, -um (adj.), over-hasty.

praerogativus, -a, -um (adj.), voting first.

praescribo, -scripsi, -scriptum (3), prescribe, ordain.

praesertim (adv.), especially, chiefly.

praesidium, -ii (n.), defence, protection.

praesto, -stiti, -stitum (1 irreg.), go bail for; perform, execute.

praesto esse, to be at hand, to back up.

praestolor (1), wait for.

praeter (prep.), apart from, in addition to.

praetereo, -ii, -itum (irreg.), escape the notice of.

praeteritus, -a, -um (adj.), past, gone by; neglected.

praetermitto, -misi, -missum (3), neglect, overlook, omit.

praeterquam (adv.), except, except that.

praevaricatio, -onis (f.), collusion.

prandeo, prandi, pransum (2), take breakfast, lunch.

prensatio, -onis (f.), canvassing.

prenso (1), canvass, solicit votes.

primarius, -a, -um (adj.), of the first rank.

princeps, -cipis (adj.), first; first in rank or order.

princeps, -cipis (m.), statesman, leading citizen.

pristinus, -a, -um (adj.), former, earlier, old.

privatus, -i (m.), a private citizen.

probo (1), prove, test; approve.

procuratio, -onis (f.), administration, executive commission.

prodicere diem, prosecute, bring to trial, indict.

produco, -duxi, -ductum (3), lead forth; prolong, hang out.

profectio, -onis (f.), departure.

profecto (adv.), truly, really.

profero, -tuli, -latum (3), bring to light, make known.

proficio, -feci, -fectum (3), make progress; be of use, assistance.

proficiscor, -fectus sum (3), depart, set out.

profiteor, -fessus sum (2), acknowledge, avow.

progredior, -gressus sum (3), advance, make progress.

progressus, -us (m.), a going forward, advance.

proicio, -ieci, -ectum (3), throw out, throw away, abandon, reject.

proinde ac (adv.), just as if.

prolixus, -a, -um (adj.), wide, broad; copious.

promissum, -i (n.), promise.

promitto, -misi, -missum (3), promise, assure.

promulgo (1), promulgate, publish.

propediem (adv.), very soon.

propensus, -a, -um (adj.), inclined to, disposed to.

propono, -posui, -positum (3), propose, propound; threaten, promise.

proprius, -a, -um (adj.), special, peculiar to; one's own.

prorogo (1), prorogue, extend, prolong.

prorsus (adv.), utterly, entirely.

prostratus, -a, -um (adj.), cast down, prostrate.

protinus (adv.), straightway; entirely.

provideo, -vidi, -visum (2), look forward to, take precautions.

proximus, -a, -um (adj.), next, nearest; **proxime** (prep.), next to, close to.

prudens, -entis (adj.), sensible, cautious.

prudentia, -ae (f.), good sense, caution.

pudeo, -ui, -itum (2), be ashamed.
pudet (impers.), it is a cause for shame.
pudor, -oris (m.), shame, modesty, decency.
putidus, -a, -um (adj.), rotten; offensive; tedious.

quadriga, -ae (f.), a four-horse chariot.
quaero, quaesivi, quaesitum (3), seek; inquire, ask.
quaeso, -ivi (3), beg, beseech; seek for.
quaestorius, -a, -um (adj.), of quaestor's rank, quaestorian.
quamdudum (adv.), how long, for as long as.
queo, quivi, quitum (irreg.), be able.
querela, -ae (f.), complaint.
queror, questus sum (3), complain.
quia (conj.), because.
quin (conjunct.), indeed, really.
quisnam, quidnam (interr. pron.), who then, what then?
quivis, quaevis, quidvis (pron.), whoever, whatever you will.
quomodonam (adv.), however then?
quondam (adv.), once, in the past.
quoniam (conj.), since, seeing that.
quorsus (adv.), in what direction, whither?
quotiens (adv.), as often as.

ratio, -onis (f.), reason, method, calculation, plan.
recedo, -cessi, -cessum (3), withdraw, retire.
recido, -cidi, -cisum (3), cut away, lop off.
recipio, -cepi, -ceptum (3), withdraw; recover.
recordatio, -onis (f.), recollection.

recordor (1), recollect.
recreo (1), refresh, renew.
recte (adv.), properly, correctly; safely.
reditus, -us (m.), return, going back.
reduco, -duxi, -ductum (3), bring back; restore from exile.
refero, -tuli, -latum (3), refer, bring back; submit, raise.
referre acceptum alicui, to put down to the credit of somebody.
refertus, -a, -um (adj.), crammed, stuffed.
refrigesco, -frixi (3), cool down, flag, grow cold.
reicio, reieci, reiectum (3), reject, repel.
relatio, -onis (f.), motion, proposal.
relaxo (1), ease, lighten, relax.
religio, -onis (f.), religious feeling, belief, observance.
reliquiae, -arum (f.), leavings, remains.
remaneo, -mansi, -mansum (2), remain, abide.
reminiscor (3), call to mind, recollect.
remotus, -a, -um (adj.), remote from.
renuntio (1), announce, proclaim.
repente (adv.), suddenly.
reperio, repperi, repertum (4), find, discover.
reprimo, -pressi, -pressum (3), check, restrain.
repulsa, -ae (f.), defeat, setback.
requiro, -quisivi, -quisitum (3), seek, miss, need.
res, rei (f.), thing, matter, affair, business.
res familiaris, possessions, private property.
reservo (1), reserve, retain, save.
resideo, -sedi, -sessum (2), sit down; abide, remain.

resipisco, -sipivi (3), recover one's senses.

resisto, -stiti (3), resist, oppose (w. dat.).

respondeo, -spondi, -sponsum (2), answer, reply.

restituo, -stitui, -stitutum (3), restore, put back.

restitutio, -onis (f.), restitution.

retego, -texi, -tectum (3), unweave; reveal.

reus, -i (m.), an accused person, defendant.

revertor, -versus sum (3), **reverto, -verti, -versum** (3), return, revert, come back.

revivisco, -vixi (3), come to life, revive.

rideo, risi, risum (2), laugh, jest; make fun of.

ridiculus, -a, -um (adj.), laughable, ridiculous.

rivalis, -is (m.), rival.

rogatio, -onis (f.), bill, proposal.

rogatus, -us (m.), a request, entreaty.

rogo (1), ask; propose (a bill).

rostra, rostrorum (n.), the speakers' platform in the Forum.

rumor, -oris (m.), common talk, hearsay, rumour.

ruo, rui, rutum (3), fall, sink, be ruined, collapse.

rusticus, -a, -um (adj.), rural; homely, simple.

salus, -utis (f.), health, well-being; deliverance.

salutatio, -onis (f.), greeting; formal call.

saluto (1), greet, pay one's respects to.

sane (adv.), really, certainly.

sane quam, pretty well, extremely.

satis facio, feci, factum (3), give satisfaction.

scaena, -ae (f.), stage, scene.

scaenicus, -a, -um (adj.), theatrical.

scelus, -eris (n.), crime, deed.

scilicet (adv.), naturally, of course.

secundus, -a, -um (adj.), favourable, successful.

seditiosus, -a, -um (adj.), seditious, turbulent.

seduco, -duxi, -ductum (3), lead, take aside.

sedulitas, -atis (f.), application, assiduity.

sella, -ae (f.), chair, seat.

sella curulis, curule chair, the official chair of a magistrate.

semisomnus, -a, -um (adj.), half-asleep.

senesco, senui (3), grow old.

sensus, -us (m.), feeling, sense.

sententia, -ae (f.), opinion, *esp.* one given in a debate.

sentio, sensi, sensum (4), feel, perceive, think.

serius (adv.), later, too late.

sermo, -onis (m.), talk, conversation.

sero (adv.), late, too late.

servio, -ivi, -itum (4), serve, be obedient to, adapt oneself to.

sescenti, -ae, -a (adj.), six hundred; innumerable.

severitas, -atis (f.), sternness, austerity.

severus, -a, -um (adj.), stern, strict.

sibilus, -i (m.), hissing, whistling.

signa, -orum (n.), (inscribed) plate, statuary.

significatio, -onis (f.), indication, sign, meaning.

significo (1), indicate, signify.

sillybus, -i (m.), title-strip of a book.

simplex, -icis (adj.), uncomplicated, natural, straightforward, single.

sincerus, -a, -um (adj.), pure, upright, honest.

singillatim (adv.), one by one.

singularis, -e (adj.), individual, singular.

sinus, -us (m.), lap; bay, gulf.

situs, -us (m.), place, site, situation.

societas, -atis (f.), association, partnership; friendship, alliance.

sodalitas, -atis (f.), club, brotherhood.

solacium, -ii (n.), consolation, solace.

soleo, solitus sum (2), be accustomed, used to.

solitudo, -inis (f.), solitude, loneliness.

sollicito (1), concern, agitate, upset.

sollicitudo, -inis (f.), worry, concern.

sollicitus, -a, -um, worried, upset.

solvo, solvi, solutum (3), loosen, untie; pay (a debt).

sonitus, -us (m.), sound, reverberation.

sordes, -is (f.), dirt, filth; *hence* mourning garments.

spectaculum, -i (n.), sight, show.

spectatio, -onis (f.), looking at, viewing.

splendor, -oris (m.), brilliance, distinction.

statuo, -ui, -utum (3), establish, resolve, decide.

status, -us (m.), status, position, condition.

stipendium, -ii (n.), tax, tribute; pay (of a soldier); military service.

stomachus, -i (m.), stomach; taste, liking; anger.

structio, -onis (f.), book-racks, shelving.

studeo, studui (2), be eager; side with, support (w. dat.).

studiosus, -a, -um (adj.), keen, eager; partisan.

studium, -ii (n.), keenness, energy; support.

stultus, -a, -um (adj.), stupid, silly.

suadeo, suasi, suasum (2), advise, recommend, persuade (w. dat.).

suavis, -e (adj.), pleasant, agreeable.

suavitas, -atis (f.), charm, agreeableness.

subiaceo, -iacui (2), be under, be subject to.

subinvito (1), invite tentatively, suggest.

subirascor, -irasci (3), be a little angry, vexed.

subitus, -a, -um (adj.), sudden, unexpected.

subiungo, -iunxi, -iunctum (3), join with, subjoin.

subrostranus, -i (m.), an idler around the *rostra*, lounger.

subsidium, -ii (n.), help, assistance.

subsido, -sedi (-sidi), -sessum (3), sit down, subside.

subtilis, -e (adj.), subtle, acute.

subturpiculus, -a, -um (adj.), a little bit shameful.

successio, -onis (f.), succeeding, succession.

suffero, sustuli, sublatum (3), carry, take away; endure, suffer.

suffragium, -ii (n.), vote.

summatim (adv.), summarily, in brief.

sumptus, -us (m.), expenditure, cost.

superficies, -ei (f.), structure, fabric (of a buidling).

superior, -oris (adj.), earlier, previous; higher.

suppedito (1), provide, supply.

supplicatio, -onis (f.), a solemn public thanksgiving.

surrigo, -rexi, -rectum (3), raise up, lift; get up.

surripio, -ripui, -reptum (3), steal, take away secretly; rescue.

suscenseo, -censui, -censum (2), be angry with.

suscipio, -cepi, -ceptum (3), undertake; support, maintain.

suspicor (1), suspect.

suspiro (1), sigh, sigh for.

sustento (1), support, sustain; delay, hold up.

sustineo, -tinui, -tentum (2), sustain; delay, hold up.

susurrator, -oris (m.), a whisperer, murmurer.

tabella, -ae (f.), picture; voting tablet, ballot.

tabellarius, -ii (m.), letter-carrier.

tabernaculum, -i (n.), tent.

tabesco, tabui (3), waste away, languish.

tabula, -ae (f.), painting, tablet.

tabulae, -arum (f.), accounts, records.

taedet, taeduit and **taesum est** (2), it is a matter for disgust or distaste.

tanto opere (adv.), so much, so greatly.

tantulus, -a, -um (adj.), so little, so small.

tarditas, -atis (f.), slowness, lateness.

tectum, -i (n.), roof.

tectus, -a, -um (adj.), covered, concealed.

temere (adv.), rashly, inadvisedly.

tempestas, -atis (f.), season; weather; bad weather, storm.

tenuis, -e (adj.), slight, slender, thin.

tenus (prep.), up to, as far as (w. abl.).

ter (adv.), three times.

testatus, -a, -um (adj.), attested, certified.

testificatio, -onis (f.), testifying, witnessing.

testimonium, -ii (n.), evidence, witness; proof.

togatus, -a, -um (adj.), wearing a toga; *hence* on civil as opposed to military business.

totiens (adv.), so often.

trado, -didi, -ditum (3), hand over, entrust.

transitus, -us (m.), crossing, passage, transition.

transverbero (1), pierce, transfix.

tribunicius, -a, -um (adj.), tribunician, of tribune's rank.

tribunus, -i (m.), tribune (tribal officer).

tribuo, -ui, -utum (3), allot, assign, attribute.

tribus, -us (f.), tribe, voting-division.

triduus, -a, -um (adj.), of three days space.

tueor, tuitus sum (2), look at; look after, protect, guard.

turpis, -e (adj.), shameful, disgraceful.

tute (pron.), intensive form of *tu*.

tuto (adv.), safely.

uber, -eris (adj.), rich, fruitful.

una (adv.), together.

urbanitas, -atis (f.), politeness, charm, refinement.

urbs, urbis (f.), city, *esp. the* city (of Rome).

urgeo, ursi (2), push; beset, bear hard on; press.

usitatus, -a, -um (adj.), customary, usual.

usus, -us (m.), use; social intercourse; enjoyment.

utique, at any rate, at least.

vadimonium, -ii (n.), bail, recognizance.

vado (3), go, walk.

valde (adj.), very, very much.

vale! goodbye!

valeant! goodbye! let them go!

valetudo, -inis (f.), health; ill-health.

vanus, -a, -um (adj.), empty, useless.

vapulo (1), be given a beating, drubbing.

varius, -a, -um (adj.), brightly coloured.

vehementer (adv.), vehemently, angrily.

vena, -ae (f.), vein.

venabulum, -i (n.), hunting-spear.

venatio, -onis (f.), hunting, hunt, chase.

vendito (1), offer for sale.

venenum, -i (n.), poison.

veneo, venire, venii, venum (irreg.), be up for sale, be sold.

ventito (1), come often, visit frequently.

versor (1), be engaged in.

versus (prep.), towards.

versus, -us (m.), verse.

verto, verti, versum (3), turn, turn round.

vestitum mutare, to go into mourning, put on mourning.

veto, vetui, vetitum (1), forbid, veto, prevent.

vexo (1), harass, molest, annoy.

viator, -oris (m.), traveller.

vicem (adv.), in place, instead.

vicinus, -a, -um (adj.), neighbouring.

vicus, -i (m.), village, hamlet; district.

vigeo (2), be vigorous, flourish.

vigilantia, -ae (f.), watchfulness.

vigilo (1), be awake, watchful.

vilitas, -atis (f.), cheapness, low price.

vinco, vici, victum (3), win, overcome; prove.

vindico (1), lay claim to; avenge, take vengeance on.

viscera, -um (n.), entrails.

viso, -si, -sum (3), visit.

vitiosus, -a, -um (adj.), vicious, corrupt, wicked.

voco (1), call, summon.

volumen, -inis (n.), papyrus-roll, book.

voluptas, -atis (f.), pleasure, delight; sensuousness.

vulgaris, -e (adj.), common, low-bred.

vulgo (adv.), generally, commonly.

vultus, -us, face, look; aspect.

INDEX OF PROPER NAMES

M'. Acilius Glabrio, 191.

Aelius Ligus (trib. 58), 104.

M. Aemilius Lepidus (cos. 46), 70.

M. Aemilius Scaurus, 151.

Aesopus, 136.

L. Afranius (cos. 60), 113, 119.

Ahenobarbus, *see* Domitius.

Alexandria, 57, 180.

T. Annius Milo, 21, 41, 105, 106, 119, 120, 122, 148, 151, 156, 157, 161.

Antioch, 168.

L. Antistius, 104.

M. Antistius Labeo, 32.

C. Antonius (cos. 63), 73, 75, 94, 193.

M. Antonius (cos. 44), 49, 65, 69–70, 172, 182, 200, 203.

Apamea, 164.

Apelles, 100.

C. Aquilius Gallus, 74.

Archilochus, 100.

Areopagus, 90.

Argiletum, 94.

Ariobarzanes, 168.

Aristarchus, 88.

Arpinum, 28, 183.

Arrius, 97.

Arsaces, 172.

Asconius, 151, 161.

Asia, 165.

Sex. Atilius Serranus, 113.

Atticus, *see* Pomponius.

T. Aufidius Palicanus, 74.

Augustus, *see* Iulius.

Aurelia, 145.

C. Aurelius Cotta (cos. 75), 145.

M. Aurelius Cotta (cos. 74), 145.

Bauli, 161.

Bellovaci, 160.

Bibulus, *see* Calpurnius.

Blandeno, 145.

Bona Dea, 86.

Britain, 152.

Brundisium, 13, 16, 110.

Buthrotum, 194.

C. Caecilius Cornutus, 94.

Q. Caecilius (uncle of Atticus), 75.

Q. Caecilius Metellus Creticus (cos. 69), 114.

Q. Caecilius Metellus Nepos (cos. 57), 83.

Q. Caecilius Metellus Pius Scipio Nasica (cos. 52), 78, 156.

M. Caelius Rufus, 40–1, 43, 49–50, 122, 157, 161.

Caesar, *see* Iulius.

M. Caesonius, 74.

L. Calpurnius Bestia, 126–7.

M. Calpurnius Bibulus (cos. 59), 9, 95, 99, 119, 123, 125, 167.

C. Calpurnius Piso (cos. 67), 74, 77.

C. Calpurnius Piso (qu. 58), 105, 131.

L. Calpurnius Piso (cos. 58), 14, 104, 107, 202.

Campania, 137.

Campanian Land, the, 25.

Campus Martius, 73.

L. Caninius Gallus (trib. 56), 138, 139, 163.

C. Caninius Rebilus (cos. 45), 63, 190.

A. Caninius Satyrus, 78–80.

Capena, porta, 112.

Cappadocia, 168.

Carinae, 128.

C. Cassius Longinus (conspirator), 168, 182, 196, 197.

L. Cassius Longinus, 75.

Catiline, *see* Sergius.

Cato, *see* Porcius.

Cato the Elder, 175, 202.
Catullus, x–xi, 41, 144, 147, 151.
Chrestus, 162.
Cicero, *see* Tullius.
Cilicia, 19, 41, 165.
Cincius, 73.
Circus Flaminius, 86.
C. Claudius Marcellus (cos. 50), 121, 179.
M. Claudius Marcellus (cos. 51), 121, 159.
App. Claudius Pulcher (cos. 54), 41, 44, 49, 79, 113, 147, 155, 165, 175.
Clodia, 41, 90, 122.
M. Clodius Aesopus, 183.
P. Clodius Pulcher, xvi, xxiii, 6, 9, 10, 12, 13, 21, 82, 86, 93, 96, 100, 107, 122–3, 125, 140, 148, 151.
Corinth, 186.
P. Cornelius Dolabella (cos. 44), 70, 131, 181, 183.
L. Cornelius Lentulus Crus (cos. 49), 104, 179.
Cn. Cornelius Lentulus Marcellinus (cos. 56), 118.
P. Cornelius Lentulus Spinther (cos. 57), 19, 41, 43, 108, 118.
P. Cornelius Scipio Aemilianus, 84, 124.
Faustus Cornelius Sulla, 132.
L. Cornelius Sulla (dictator), 130.
Q. Cornificius, 73, 75.
Cornutus, *see* Caecilius.
Crassipes, *see* Furius.
Crassus, *see* Licinius.
Ctesiphon, 172.
Cumae, 132, 137.
M'. Curius, 62.
M'. Curtius Peducaeus, 106.
M. Curtius Postumus, 147.
Cyrus (architect), 134.

Deiotarus, 193.
Cn. Domitius Ahenobarbus, 183.
L. Domitius Ahenobarbus (cos. 54), 49, 54, 79, 104, 147, 155, 160, 172, 173.
Cn. Domitius Calvinus (cos. 53), 127, 148, 155.
Dyrrachium, 16.

Egypt, 19, 116–17.
Ennius, 143.
Euripides, 149.

Q. Fabius Maximus (cos. 45), 190.
Q. Fabricius, 106.
T. Fadius, 106.
M. Favonius, 92, 115, 123.
Flaminia, via, 76.
Fufidius, 183.
M. Fufitius, 141.
Q. Fufius Calenus (cos. 47), 86, 92, 150, 182, 186.
Fulvia, 70, 194.
Furius Crassipes, 131.
C. Furnius, 179.

A. Gabinius (cos. 58), 19, 102, 104, 107, 132, 139.
Gallia Cisalpina, 76, 155.
— Cispadana, 76.
— Transpadana, 76, 159.
Gallic provinces, Caesar's, 167.
Gallicus, ager, 125.
Gutta, 156.

Hilarus, 94.
A. Hirtius (cos. 43), 194, 195, 202.
Horace: *Epistles*, 28; *Satires*, 32, 135, 183; *Ars Poet.*, 135, 136; *Odes*, 186.
Q. Hortensius Hortalus (cos. 69), 92, 118, 130, 151, 172.

Iulia, 78, 148, 154, 174.
C. Iulius Caesar, xiii, xvi, 6, 9, 10, 21, 31, 35, 37, 54, 55–6, 57, 63, 140, 145, 147, 155, 158, 159, 200.
C. Iulius Caesar Octavianus (Augustus), xix, 32, 65, 69–70, 77,

83, 114, 158, 194, 195, 199, 201, 203.
L. Iulius Caesar (cos. 64), 75, 202.
D. Iunius Brutus, 201, 203.
M. Iunius Brutus, 167, 196, 197, 200.
D. Iunius Silanus (cos. 62), 75.

T. Labienus, 63, 153.
C. Laelius, 84–5.
D. Laelius, 182.
Laodicea, 164.
Lentulus, *see* Cornelius.
Lepidus, *see* Aemilius.
Q. Lepta, 141.
Leucas, 177.
M. Licinius Crassus (cos. 70, 55), xiii, 9, 10, 21, 24–5, 74, 83, 88, 89, 100, 117, 119, 123, 124, 125.
P. Licinius Crassus (son of above), 78.
P. Licinius Crassus Iunianus (trib. 53), 156.
L. Licinius Lucullus (cos. 74), 77, 78, 86, 93.
M. Licinius Lucullus (cos. 73), 118.
C. Licinius Sacerdos, 75.
Livia, Empress, 150.
M. Livius Drusus Clodianus, 150, 176.
M. Lollius Palicanus, 74.
Lucca, 25.
L. Lucceius, 94.
C. Lucilius Hirrus (trib. 53), 148, 156.
Lucretius, 133, 188.
Lucrinus, lacus, 132.
Q. Lutatius Catulus (cos. 78), xxiv, 130.

Sp. Maecius Tarpa, 135.
C. Marcius Figulus (cos. 64), 75.
L. Marcius Philippus (cos. 56), 194, 202.
Mario, 177.
C. Marius, 28, 179.

M. Marius, 28, 135.
C. Matius, 66–7, 196, 199.
Medea, 143.
Megara, 186.
C. Memmius, 104, 155.
C. Messius (trib. 57), 114, 139.
Milo, *see* Annius.
L. Munatius Plancus (cos. 42), 161.
T. Munatius Plancus (trib. 52), 161.
Munda, 62–3, 153.
Musicus, 52.
Mutina, 195.

Cn. Naevius, 170.
Naples, 137.
Cn. Nerius, 125.
Nervii, 144, 154.
P. Nigidius Figulus, 104.
L. Ninnius Quadratus, 104.
L. Novius, 104.
Q. Numerius, 113.

Octavia, 121.
Octavius, Octavian, *see* Iulius.
Olbia, 128.
Osci, 137.

C. Papirius Carbo, 124.
Parthia(ns), 43, 167, 168.
Pelopidae, 189.
Phaethon, 107.
Pharsalus, 57, 127, 181.
Philippus, *see* Marcius.
Philotimus, 134.
Phrygia, 165.
Picenum, 125.
Pilia, 127.
Piraeus, 186.
Piso, *see* Calpurnius *or* Pupius.
Placentia, 145.
Cn. Plancius, 13–14.
P. Plautius Hypsaeus, 119, 156.
Pliny, the Elder, 134, 138.
Pliny, the Younger, 28, 31.
Pompeii, 135, 137.

Cn. Pompeius Magnus, vii, xvi, 4, 6, 9, 10, 19, 21, 24–5, 28, 40, 54–5, 74, 77, 78, 82–3, 86, 87, 105, 115, 123, 124, 133, 138, 140, 148, 151, 156, 159, 163, 202.

Sex. Pompeius (son of above), 119.

Q. Pompeius Rufus, 161.

Pomponia, viii, 127.

T. Pomponius Atticus, viii–ix, 3, 9, 10, 16, 24–5, 26, 77, 127, 131, 132, 134, 194.

Porcia, 167, 173.

C. Porcius Cato (trib. 56), 102, 121, 124, 125, 151.

M. Porcius Cato (Uticensis), 46, 49, 79, 87, 91, 98, 171.

Protogenes, 100, 137.

Ptolemy XII Auletes, 116–17, 118, 132.

M. Pupius Piso Frugi Calpurnianus (cos. 61), 85, 86, 93, 98.

Puteoli, 132.

Quintilian, xii.

C. Rabirius Postumus, 117.

Rhodes, 186, 200.

P. Rutilius Lupus (trib. 56), 119.

Sallust, 158.

Salus, 110.

Sardinia, 128.

Cn. Saturninus, 173.

Scipio Nasica, *see* Caecilius.

Scribonia, 119.

C. Scribonius Curio (cos. 76), 92, 123, 125.

C. Scribonius Curio (trib. 51), 91, 174, 176.

L. Scribonius Libo, 119.

Sebosus, 97.

Seleuceia, 171.

Ti. Sempronius Gracchus, 124.

Seneca, 28.

L. Sergius Catilina, vii, xiii–xiv, 3, 41, 73, 74, 81, 82, 91, 103, 138, 168.

Serranus Domesticus, 156.

Q. Servilius Caepio, 121.

P. Servilius Vatia Isauricus (cos. 79), 119.

P. Servilius Vatia Isauricus (cos. 48), 123.

P. Sestius, 25, 105, 125, 127.

Sicyon, 101.

Sophocles, 152.

Sosigenes, 205.

Spartacus, 89.

Spinther, *see* Cornelius.

Stabiae, 135.

P. Sulpicius Galba, 75.

Ser. Sulpicius Rufus (cos. 51), 59, 184, 202.

Synnada, 164.

Tacitus, 146, 185, 186, 202.

Tarsus, 166.

Terentia, 81, 97, 116, 134, 181.

Q. Terentius Culleo, 104.

M. Terentius Varro, 101.

Τεῦκρις, 84.

Thapsus, 78, 113.

Thermus, 75.

Thessalonica, 13.

Tiberius, Emperor, 127, 150, 158.

Tiro, *see* Tullius.

M. Titinius, 141.

C. Trebatius, 31–4, 200.

C. Trebonius (cos. 45), 69–70, 190, 201.

Tullia, xviii, 59, 81, 110, 131, 184.

M. Tullius, 126.

M. Tullius Cicero, early life, vii–viii; quaestor, x; as an orator, x–xii; aedile, xii; praetor, xii; consul, xiii–xiv, 1, 3, 4; coolness with Pompey, 4; and Clodius, 6, 9, 10, 12; exile, xvi–xvii, 13–14; return, 16; and Egypt, 19, 21; opposition and capitulation, xvii, 25; in retirement, xvii–xviii, 26–7; and

Caesar, xviii, 37–8, 56–7, 145; in Cilicia, 40–1, 43–4; and Cato, 46–9; augurship, 145; as a poet, 146; activity in 44–43 B.C., xviii–xix, 65, 69–70; death, xix; books about, xix–xx.

— Works: *Epistulae*, viii, xxvi–xxxi; *Philosophica*, xvii–xviii, 191; *Rhetorica*, xvii–xviii; *de re p.*, 85, 162; *de officiis*, 79; *pro Quinctio*, viii; *Verrines*, x, 83; *pro Roscio Amer.*, viii; *pro lege Manilia*, xii–xiii, 83; *pro Cornelio*, xii; *de lege agraria*, 83; *pro Caelio*, 122; *pro Plancio*, x; *pro Sestio*, 126; *post red. in sen.*, 112; *post red. ad Quir.*, 113; *de prov. cons.*, 129, 145; *Philippics*, xix, 70, 193, 201.

M. Tullius Cicero (son of above), 3, 81, 98, 154.

Q. Tullius Cicero, ix, 12, 13, 21, 35, 37–8, 79, 94, 108, 114, 128, 140, 144, 152, 181.

M. Tullius Tiro, 52–3, 177.

Turius, 75.

M. Valerius Messalla Niger (cos. 61), 87, 113.

M. Valerius Messalla Rufus (cos. 53), 148.

P. Varius, 78.

P. Vatinius, 25, 104, 139, 150–1.

Venus Victrix, 134.

C. Verres, 74.

Vespasian, Emperor, 151.

C. Vestorius, 196.

L. Vettius, 130.

C. Vibius Pansa (cos. 43), 194, 195, 202.

M. Vipsanius Agrippa, ix, 127.

Virgil, 157.

L. Volcacius Tullus (cos. 66), 119.

INDEX OF SUBJECTS

ablative, of attendant circs., 81, 96.
— of quality, 191.
abrogare, 121.
actio, 202.
ad = in relation to, 170.
adesse, 79, 120.
adoption, 75.
advocatus, 121.
agere, 78.
ain, 129.
album iudicum, 81, 86, 150.
ambulatio, 133.
anagnostes, 137.
Apollo, temple of, 86, 124.
aposiopesis, 193.
apparatus, 136.
archaisms, 158, 187–8.
argutus, 157.
assemblies, xxv–xxvi, 85, 91, 95, 111, 113, 120–1, 148, 190.
— centuriate, 76, 111, 190.
— tribal, 111, 120–1, 190.
asyndeton, 89, 110.
Atellanae fabulae, 137.
auctoritas, 110, 120.
auspices, 190.

beneficium, 79, 191.
boni, xxi, 85.
bribery, 148–9.

calendar, Roman, 204–5.
causa (alicuius) *velle*, 108, 117.
cedo, 184.
censor, 175.
chiasmus, 168.
Civil War, 174.
civitas libera, 181.
civitates, 165.
cliens, clientela, 103.
clubs, political, 126.

comitia, see 'assemblies'.
commodo, 177, 179.
compilatio, 162.
compositio, 162.
concordia ordinum, xxii.
conditions in *or. obl.*, 79.
congiarium, 162.
constare, 135.
consularis, 113, 202.
contio, contionare, 85, 99, 113, 121.
contionarius, 125.
corn-supply, 112.
courts, xxiii (*see also 'iudices'*).
— size of, 150.
cura, curator, 76.
cura annonae, 117, 128, 140.
cura ut, 77.
curia, 123.
cursus honorum, xxiii, 185.

dating formulas, 80.
day, Roman, 122.
dative, of disadvantage, 122, 161.
— ethic, 91, 97.
— of interest, 72, 118.
— predicative, 72, 143, 196.
decerno, decretum, 112.
decuriati, 126.
describo, 124.
desiderative verbs, 95.
dictator, 114, 148, 157.
diem dicere, 124.
dilectus, 179.
diminutives, 81, 85, 90, 133, 135, 139, 142, 186, 187.
disjunctive question, 89.
dolus malus, 77.
dum, in final clause, 164.

edictum, 99.
elections, see 'assemblies'.

electoral corruption, 148, 149.
ellipse, 123, 132, 161, 163, 165, 173, 192, 193, 195.
embaeneti..., 161.
enim, resumptive, 197.
Epicureanism, 133, 188.
epistolary tenses, 73, 85, 93, 106, 125, 134, 148, 156, 158, 161, 167, 176, 203.
equites, x, xxii, 150, 160.
esse, omission of, 90.
exclamations, grammatical expression of, 198.

fabulae Atellanae, 137.
familiam ducere, 142.
figere legem, 193.
frequentative verbs, 198, 199.
future perfect hortative, 133, 146.
future subjunctive, 199.

genitive, qualitative-descriptive, 136, 195, 199.
— of price or value, 87, 196.
— of matter involved, 158.
— objective, 174.
— partitive, 101, 136, 174.
germanus, 131.
gratia, 79, 128, 149, 151.
Greek, used by Cicero, 75, 192.
gymnasium, 80.

hendiadys, 105, 135, 143, 202.
Hermathena, 80.
honos, honores, 82, 185.
hortative future perfect, 133, 146.
horti, 131.
hours of Roman day, 122.
hyperbaton, 81.

iactura, 154.
imperator, 83.
imperium, 113, 121.
imperium maius, 114.

improbi, 85.
infamia, 197.
interrex, 155–6.
ita . . . ut, 72, 98, 104, 111, 120, 141, 178.
iudices, 81, 86, 150, 175 (see also 'courts').
ius Latii, 192–3.
iuventus, 90–1, 125.

Laconicum, 164.
Latin status, *Latinitas*, 76, 192–3.
legationes, 93, 120.
legatus, 114, 140.
legio IV, 203.
legio Martia, 203.
letter-carriers, 109, 164.
lex, 87, 115.
lex Domitia de sacerd., 172.
— *Fufia*, 150.
— *Iulia de aere alieno*, 197.
— *Iulia de repetundis*, 165.
— *Scantinia*, 176.
libertus, 104.
licitatio, 183.
locus, 88.
ludi, 134.
ludi Caesaris victoriae, 198–9.
— *Romani*, 112.
— *scaenici*, 137.

mancipium, 77.
meiosis, 107.
mimi, 135.
miseri, 85.
moderator rei pub., 85.
money, Roman, 207–9.
munus, 199.

ne, interjectory, 137, 189.
necessitudo, 84, 151.
nefas, 105.
nobilis, 82.
nomenclator, 111.
nomenclature, Roman, 82, 126.

novus homo, 82.
nundinae, 86.

officium, 77, 79, 116, 151.
optimates, xxi.
opus esse, 82.
ordo (= senate), 87.
ornare, ornatio, 121.
oxymoron, 89.

palinode, 129.
par+ablative, 196.
parenthetic relative clauses, 188.
Parilia, 134.
parties, political, xxiii.
patronus, 103.
per, 135.
per- (intensive), 97, 147.
perorare, 122.
persona, 187.
pietas, 116, 128.
plebiscitum, 87.
police, 106.
pomerium, 86, 179, 180.
ponere, 153.
pontes, 91.
pontifices, 115, 204.
popularis, xxi.
praefectus, 142.
praerogativus, 169.
praevaricatio, 82, 150.
present tense, vivid, 92.
principes, xxiii, 129.
privatus, 102, 119.
promulgatio, 87.
prorogare, 121.
publicani, 95, 98, 165.
puns, 135, 138, 160, 162, 195.

quaestor, 166.
Quirinalia, 123.
quisquam, in negative and interrogative clauses, 129.
quod, in limiting sense, 72, 118, 134.
— in noun clauses, 88.

ratio, 72, 139, 154, 182.
reicere, reiectio, 81.
relationem egredi, 202.
religious obstruction, 95.
res publica, 84.
respondere, 134.
reus, 124.
rogare, rogatio, 87, 125.
rostra, 91.

salutatio, 199.
sane quam, 159, 184.
scribal error, 176.
scribendo adesse, 188.
sella curulis, 133.
senate, numbers of, 92.
senatus consultum, 87, 113.
senatus frequens, 92, 114.
senatus, municipal, 137.
sententia, 112, 131, 149, 169, 202.
sescenti, 136, 194.
sestertius, 207.
Sibylline books, 117.
sillybi, 132.
slaves, slavery, 52, 104.
sodalitates, 126.
structio, 132.
sub- (minimizing prefix), 129, 130, 139, 201.
subjunctive, causal, 161, 177, 189, 191.
— conditional-concessive, 96.
— generic, 74, 107, 109, 114, 134, 135, 159, 161, 162, 173, 177, 188, 189, 191, 196.
— limiting, 72.
— potential, 77, 106.
— of alleged reason, 78, 84, 113, 124, 167.
— in *or. obl.*, 78.
supine, 176.
supplicatio, 154-5, 169.

taxes, 165.
tribe names, 126.

tribuni aerarii, 150.
— *militum*, 142.
— *plebis*, xxvi.
triumph, 86, 169, 171.

urbs, 111.
ut, explanatory, 178.

vadimonium, 147, 162.
vestitum mutare, 122.
veto, xxvi, 92, 157.
viatica, 131.
violence, 148.
voting procedure, 91 (*see also* 'assemblies').

PRINTED IN GREAT BRITAIN
AT THE UNIVERSITY PRESS, OXFORD
BY VIVIAN RIDLER
PRINTER TO THE UNIVERSITY